These volumes bring transper[...] contemporary era and expand its a[...] healing and growth. It is a pleasure [...] the seminal insights of transpersonal psychology into such areas as social action, diversity, and inequality, to connect the inner with the outer world, and to locate personal transformation in a context of social transformation, indeed as the most powerful form of social action. This is a much needed contribution to the field.

Brant Cortright, PhD
Author of *Psychotherapy and Spirit:
Theory and Practice in Transpersonal Psychotherapy*
Professor of Psychology, California Institute of Integral Studies

Drs. Kaklauskas, Clements, Hocoy, and Hoffman have pulled together an impressive display of talented Transpersonal Psychology writers who present the complexities of the theory and practice in a way that the reader can readily understand and grasp. The writings are applicable for numerous issues, conditions, and settings and will be a valuable resource that will enhance the teaching, learning, research, and practice in the field.

Nina W. Brown, EdD, LPC, NCC, FAGPA
Professor and Eminent Scholar

This collection literally has it all from scholarly reviews of the intellectual and cultural origins of transpersonal psychology through relevant research and moving personal experiences to contemporary cutting edge applications. It clearly demonstrates that transpersonal is alive and well as it passes from middle age to elderhood. Timely, yet timeless.

David Lukoff, PhD, Past Co-President Association for Transpersonal Psychology and the Institute for Spirituality and Psychology

This book takes the reader on a journey across time, cultures, and perspectives, arriving at a fully contemporary view of transpersonal psychology. A mindful look at impassioned living, this scholarly collection explores the crossroads of Human Science and Spirituality, and is a must read!

Donna Rockwell, PhD, President Elect, Society for Humanistic Psychology (American Psychological Association Division 32)

Shadows and Light is a stunning collection of essays that enables the reader/ seeker to take a deep dive into a richly imagined framework for transpersonal education. It is a timely and elegant offering of contemplative-based theories, research, and practices. I predict it will be heralded as a triumph in the field!

Gaea Logan, LPC-S, CGP
Executive Director, Founder, *International Center for Mental Health and Human Rights* - Social Responsibility Award Recipient, Group Foundation for Advancing Mental Health

This collection is filled with compassion and curiosity, hope and humility. By integrating contemporary research, multicultural and social justice perspectives, and the vitality of relationships with self, others, and the world, the essays and talks provide refreshing energy to psychological perspectives on growth, transformation, and finding one's place in this often challenging world.

Pat Denning, PhD, & Jeannie Little, LCSW
Founders, The Center for Harm Reduction Therapy

Shadows & Light:
Theory, Research, & Practice in Transpersonal Psychology

Volume 1: Principles & Practices

Francis J. Kaklauskas
Carla J. Clements
Dan Hocoy
Louis Hoffman
Editors

University Professors Press
Colorado Springs, CO

Book Copyright © 2016

Shadows & Light: Theory, Research, and Practice in Transpersonal Psychology (Volume 1: Principles and Practices)
By Francis J. Kaklauskas, Carla J. Clements, Dan Hocoy, and Louis Hoffman (Editors)

All rights reserved. No portion of this book may be reproduced by any process or technique without the express written consent of the publisher.

First Published in 2016, University Professors Press.

ISBN 10: 1-93968616-4
ISBN 13: 978-1-939686-16-9

University Professors Press
Colorado Springs, CO
www.universityprofessorspress.com

Front Photo by Charles Kershenblatt
Cover Design by Laura Ross

Dedication

To the faculty, students, alumni, and staff at Naropa University and Saybrook University who have carried the torch of transpersonal psychology into the 21st century.

Contents

Acknowledgments — i

Introduction — 1
    Francis J. Kaklauskas, Carla J. Clements, Dan Hocoy,
    & Louis Hoffman

Chapter 1: History, Development, and Contemporary Perspectives of Transpersonal Psychology — 9
    Carla J. Clements, Francis J. Kaklauskas, Dan Hocoy,
    & Louis Hoffman

Chapter 2: Transpersonal Psychology in the Age of ISIS: The Role of Culture, Social Action, and Personal Transformation — 31
    Dan Hocoy

Chapter 3: Toward a Transpersonal Structure of the Psyche — 45
    Carla J. Clements & Uri Talmor

Chapter 4: Empirical Foundations of Transpersonal Counseling and Psychotherapy — 71
    Francis J. Kaklauskas & Lindsey Randol

Chapter 5: Imaginal Mindfulness—Imaginal Intelligence: Musings on the Languages of Shadow and Light in Art, Meditation, and Clinical Practice — 101
    Michael A. Franklin

Chapter 6: Oracle of the Ultimate: Contemplative Practice and Mind/Body Assessment in Transpersonal Counseling — 123
    Ian Wickramasekera, II

Chapter 7: Transpersonal Dreams as Spiritually Transformative Experiences — 151
    Stanley Krippner

Chapter 8: Exploring the Lived Experience of Meditation Instructors   173
> *Xiaodan Zhuang, Daphne M. Fatter, & Peter Grossenbacher*

Chapter 9: Transpersonal Psychology in Education and Management/Leadership: The Creation of a New Evolutionary Paradigm   195
> *Pat Luce & Robert Schmitt*

Chapter 10: The Transpersonal Potential of Psychedelics   213
> *Charles Walter Angelo*

Chapter 11: Transpersonal Sexuality: A Paradigm Beyond the Normative   233
> *Satori S. Madrone & Debra L. Azorsky*

Chapter 12: A Thousand Invisible Threads: A Pedagogical Tool Weaving Together Transpersonal Psychology, Sustainability, and Ecopsychology   249
> *Deb Piranian*

Chapter 13: Awaking to Presence: The Potential of Ritual in Transpersonal Education   283
> *John Davis*

Chapter 14: Know Thyself: A Most Appropriate and Yet Most Resisted Ancient Directive for the 21st Century Human   295
> *Sandy Sela-Smith*

Index   315

About the Editors/Contributors   321

Acknowledgments

We would like to thank all the authors who gave their time, effort, expertise, and wisdom to this collection. We appreciate the encouragement of the staff and other faculty at Naropa University and Saybrook University in completing this collection. We also owe a great deal to the many creative, thoughtful, and passionate individuals and communities that forged many of the ideas and perspectives presented in these volumes, as well as to the many students and clients who helped inform this effort. We also would like to thank our families and friends for their continual support and patience throughout this process.

Introduction

Francis J. Kaklauskas
Carla J. Clements
Dan Hocoy
Louis Hoffman

Transpersonal psychology and the transpersonal movement have impacted the lives of countless individuals during its 50-year history. Interest in the core ideas of personal and community transformation, states of consciousness, and the integration of feelings, knowledge, and wisdom existed for a millennia prior to William James coining the term in the early 1900s (Taylor, 1996).

From personal perspectives, each of the editors remembers wondering from a very young age how the world works, our place in it, and the larger topics of God's will. We loved stories, myths, art, and music, and at the same time were curious little scientists. We were also deeply interested in relationships and connecting with others. We did not know the word transpersonal at that time, but had questions, passions, sensitivities, and longings that went beyond our limited world. Only as we grew older did we understand that many other people shared similar interests and appetites. Likewise, only as we engaged in our professional training did we become familiar with the field of transpersonal psychology. We all experienced the thrill and expansiveness of finding this field and the other people engaged in its study. We hope this collection will inspire the same childlike curiosity in its readers. While this volume is filled with academic ideas and references, it was also written with the desire that readers will find a personal connection with its messages and perhaps even be reminded of moments of awe.

The book developed from a collaboration of faculty from the transpersonal programs at Naropa University in Boulder, CO, and Saybrook University in Oakland, CA. The integration of Eastern, and particularly Buddhist, ideas are evident throughout this text, as Naropa's founder and Buddhist teacher Chöygam Trungpa Rinpoche regularly hosted conversations and collaboration between mental health clinicians, artists, scholars, and teachers of varied faith traditions (Midal, 2004) in the hope that when the East meets the West "the sparks will fly" (Bye, 2005). We have worked to ensure that the perspectives embodied in the book are inclusive of varied spiritual and religious traditions, including a range of valued wisdom traditions. Saybrook has been at the forefront of transpersonal education since its inception and has enabled many transpersonal scholars to share their work over the last several decades. Naropa's program has been educating transpersonal counselors, including art and wilderness therapists, for the last quarter of a century, and has integrated mindfulness and contemplative practices into all curricula. This collection draws on the knowledge and practice of faculty and visiting scholars from both schools.

Shadows & Light combines academic chapters, original research, reflection pieces, and public talks. We encouraged writers to explore practical, real-world applications of the transpersonal in addition to outlining theory and ideas. The collection is split into two volumes, with the first focused on a more traditional presentation of academic principles and practice, while the second volume allows for less formal contributions that elucidate the transpersonal in a more personal or concrete manner. When possible we allowed the authors to discuss their areas of interest in the voice they preferred. We are happy to have a combination of luminaries such as Stanley Krippner, Roger Walsh, John Davis, angel Kyodo williams, Judy Lief, and Charlie Tart as well as contemporary writers that include Ian Wickramasekera II and Jeanine Canty, along with newer voices, many of whom focused on either clinical practice or the teaching aspect of their work.

Introduction

The metaphor of shadows and light has countless evocative references from the ancient Bhagavad Gita and Plato's allegory of the cave to contemporary literature, psychology, and political theory. Many chapters explore the varied possible meanings of these words and the impact of the images they evoke. For the editors, the metaphor of shadows and light brings up personal memories and inspiration, which we share here.

For me (FK), the *Shadows and Light* title brings to mind the Rabindranath Tagore poem, *Fireflies*. When my son, Levi, was young, I would read poetry for children with him, including poems that Tagore wrote for his children. Tagore (1928) wrote *Fireflies* after the deaths of his two children and wife as he was facing his own potentially terminal illness. *Fireflies* came home to me in full embodiment one day as I watched my son play with toy trucks in our driveway. The scene and thoughts that Tagore captured in his poem seized me at that moment. Above my son's head in the distance was the fiery orange and red of the setting sun over the Continental Divide of the Colorado Rocky Mountains. The one-foot-tall metal trucks cast four-foot shadows. Between us and the ice glaciers in the distance, a storm was brewing. Lightning flashed purple and white, and charcoal clouds gathered. I felt terror as I told Levi we needed to go inside, and I thought of my parents and brother, long dead. I flashed on our family lineage of subjugation, both the Lithuanian Jewish and Irish Catholic sides, as well as all the privileges and gifts that had been provided to me up to this moment in my life.

What would my ancestors have thought of this wonderful, innocent child laughing as he loaded dirt from a miniature plastic backhoe into the rusty old metal dump truck his aunt—my sister—gave him? I got a deep sense of the temporal passing of all things, the awe and frightful fragility of existence, the magical flow of consciousness when impacted by nature and memories. In a moment, I wondered about the mysteries of many things much bigger and more essential than myself. When I held my son's hand as we walked up the back steps, I felt the warmth of his skin and smelled the dirt and sweat that covered his body.

I felt the love that is known, and all that is unknown or perhaps even unknowable. As we walked in, his mother, seeing the tears in my eyes, asked if I was all right. Likely I had never been better.

One night in March 1988 in Chaco Canyon, I (CC) sat alone on a hilltop and watched the full moon cross the sky until it darkened and the rain fell, and eventually a glimmer of dawn appeared. This was a formal ritual; I reclaimed the night and the darkness for my life, which I thought had been taken from me. At times it was so dark that I could not tell if I was still there, or who it was that was there. Seeing in the light of the moon and then in the unspeakable darkness, and seeing myself and the world as nothing more than shadows was a mystery I had not encountered before. One of the secrets revealed by the initiation was that the light and the dark are simply two sides of the same coin, with one always renewing the other, like breathing in and exhaling. This, I believe, is true of all duality. Why do we seem to think there is a choice? Better? More important? Right? Good?

One of the things I saw that night was my self—enacting an ancient initiation of women who have reclaimed pieces of themselves, much like Inanna (e.g., Campbell, 2008; Wolkenstein & Kramer, 1983). I did not encounter Ereshkigal that night. Instead I encountered music. All night long, I sang to myself and danced sometimes; and while I rocked "along," I wrote this song.

Shadowtime

The shadows are growing again
It's the way of the wheel on her spin,
That time of the day, when the sun fades away
And the light plays tricks on the wind.

The stillness leaves me feeling scared
In the darkness the unknown is bared,
So I hold my breath at the nearness of death
While its shadow slips by unaware.

Well, the shadows are yours and mine,
Merely tricks of the light with the mind.
So sing me a song, rock me along
While the wheel turns on toward the dawn.

Is life just a trick of the light?
Is a song just a rainbow at night?
Could we reach from this dream and grab a moonbeam
And split the sky like an eagle in flight?

The shadows have fallen again
I'm adrift with my soul on the wind,
So sing me a song and rock me along
'Til the wheel spins on toward the dawn.
In the darkness I reach for the dawn.

© Carla J. Clements, 1988

We're taught to privilege light over darkness. Darkness is commonly associated with negative or undesirable elements. But I (DH) consider this bias not unlike the Western bias against Judas Iscariot, the disciple of Jesus. It is simply an unexamined convention—reflective of our basic need for the assuring dichotomy of good and bad. Judas is the Betrayer, a quintessential archetype in the human story. But another narrative exists for Judas from the Gnostic gospels, a narrative in which Judas was divinely chosen to perform a great sacrifice for the grand purpose. Judas, the most trusted apostle of Christ, who would have died to prevent Jesus' capture, was instead secretly asked by Jesus to conspire with the authorities so that Jesus could be taken according to prophecy. Judas had to bear the burden of this intolerable task as well as the eternal scorn that followed.

Similarly, the thankless work of darkness is required for light to have its day. Without the shadows, the light has no identity, no purpose, and no meaning. What is Yin without Yang? Left without Right? Laurel without Hardy?

For me, the title *Shadows & Light* expresses a holistic understanding of the aspects of life we are taught to see as opposite and mutually exclusive. The metaphor of shadows and light aptly conveys the temporality and superficiality of human perception or judgment while pointing to the true underlying interdependence of existence and the unchanging oneness.

In relation to transpersonal psychology, I (LH) would consider myself an existential transpersonal psychologist. I have been long drawn toward transpersonal psychology while at the same time feeling hesitant. Consistent with an existential perspective, which is my primary psychological foundation, I deeply value the many shades of human experience—from sadness and grief to joy, wonderment, and awe. I have at times worried that some in the transpersonal movement have sought transcendence and privileged it to the embodied humanness that I greatly value. Shadows and light is a beautiful metaphor that captures the paradoxes at the root of being an existential transpersonalist. This metaphor addresses the sundry concerns that keep many who are drawn to transpersonal psychology concurrently cautious and hesitant.

Similar to Dan, I have a deep appreciation for the darkness. One of my favorite songs is Bruce Springsteen's (1978) "Darkness on the Edge of Town." One can find many levels of meaning in "darkness" in this song. At the edge of town, the city lights end, bringing a deeper darkness. This transition from the community of the town to the countryside or the wilderness can represent isolation or the unknown. This darkness is at the borderlands. Yet, darkness is a pervasive theme in Springsteen's music, often representing a place where people reflect on their own personal struggles and suffering. While there is something ominous, maybe even dangerous, in the darkness, there is also the possibility of redemption and finding something deeper within oneself. This is captured well in the concluding lines to the song "Darkness on the Edge of Town":

> Some folks are born into a good life
> Other folks get it anyway, anyhow

> Well me I lost my money and I lost my wife,
> Them things don't seem to matter much to me now
> Tonight I'll be on that hill 'cause I can't stop
> I'll be on that hill with everything I got,
> Lives on the line where dreams are found and lost
> I'll be there on time and I'll pay the cost
> For wanting things that can only be found
> In the darkness on the edge of town

It is in the darkness that one finds the light. In the darkness, too, it is possible to find aspects of oneself previously unknown—denied, repressed—or hidden aspects of ourselves that allow us to embrace a deeper wholeness.

Like Springsteen, I have always believed that there is something redeeming in the darkness. There are some lessons, too, that can only be found in the shadows. In the title *Shadows & Light*, I hear something redeeming for transpersonal psychology as well. Like Daniels (2005), I have worried at times that transpersonal psychology has avoided the shadows, which has also challenged its light. In this book, our hope is that we have been able to bring these together—that we have been able to appreciate the shadows as well as the light.

References

Bye, R. (2005). The founding vision of Naropa University: Let East meet West and the sparks will fly. In F. Midal (Ed.), *Recalling Chögyam Trungpa*. Boston, MA: Shambhala.

Campbell, J. (2008). *The Hero with a Thousand Faces*. Novato, CA: New World Library.

Clements, C.J. (1999). Shadowtime. *Creationship* [CD]. Englewood, CO: Raven Recording.

Daniels, M. (2005). *Shadow, self, spirit: Essays in transpersonal psychology*. Charlottesville, VA: Imprint Academic.

Midal, F. (2004). *Chögyam Trungpa: His life and vision*. Boston, NY: Shambhala Publications.

Springsteen, B. (1978). *Darkness on the edge of town* [CD]. New York, NY: Columbia Records.

Tagore, R. (1928). *Fireflies*. New York, NY: Collier.

Taylor, E. (1996). William James and transpersonal psychiatry. In B.W. Scotton, A.B. Chinen, & J.R. Battista (Eds.), *Textbook of transpersonal psychiatry and psychology* (pp. 21–28). New York, NY: Basic Books.

Wolkenstein, D. & Kramer, S.N. (1983). *Inanna: Queen of heaven and earth*. New York, NY: Harper Row.

Chapter 1
History, Development, and Contemporary Perspectives of Transpersonal Psychology

Carla J. Clements
Francis J. Kaklauskas
Dan Hocoy
Louis Hoffman

The incorporation and assimilation of transpersonal practices and ideas into the United States mainstream culture this past half century has been extraordinary. Fifty years ago, we could only imagine the widespread acceptance of practices in the United States such as yoga or meditation, the legalization and medicinal use of compounds such as marijuana, or the inclusion of alternative health methods into traditional medicine. It might be said that the transpersonal project, of which transpersonal psychology is a part, has been a passageway that has allowed quantum understandings to enter into mainstream human consciousness—at least in countries that can afford such luxuries—leading to a significant paradigm shift (Ferrer, 2002; Tarnas, 2006). As Hartelius, Rothe and Roy (2013) recently stated, the transpersonal project,

> is no simple undertaking, and no modest effort merely to add to psychology by including human spirituality. Rather, it is an ambitious effort to redefine ourselves as humans and the world as

we know it. It is a project that sets out to understand the cosmos in ways that are not constrained by either the sometimes-heavy hand of religious tradition or the objectifying eye of science. Instead, the transpersonal approach seeks a new vision, one in which both human science and human spirituality can be honored. (p. 3)

As often occurs with interdisciplinary dialogue, mixing science and spirituality has produced a profound change in our vision. It is as though we had just put on 3-D goggles, allowing a completely new view that both includes and transcends dualism. Like a high mountain vista, the scene it has revealed has been far more expansive than two vaguely related, but obviously disenfranchised, mountain peaks. Instead, what has been exposed is an entirely different frame for relating to reality—one that both necessitates and generates a transformation in cultural consciousness. This new vision has the potential to shift humanity away from the inevitability of environmental destruction and/or planet annihilation through war and violence, greed, and self-centeredness into more profound understandings of our deeper—and higher, and even wider—nature (Davis, 2011; Ferrer, 2002; Grof, 1985, 2000, 2008).

Our Intention and Invocation

For many hundreds of years, Western humanity's fundamental essence has been seen as individual and separate, and certainly this is one rather obvious view of reality. With an expanded transpersonal lens, however, the essence is revealed as the connectivity *between* individuals; and this connective tissue is a network of potentiality—from which a different reality is possible. When individuals are inextricably connected to each other and to all of nature and the world, then their responsibility to each "other" births new truths, and a transformed worldview emerges out of the shadows and into the light. The spark of potential ignited by the transpersonal project is still small and may not have yet reached its potential; however, without this early inspirational brushfire, there would be far less hope for the future. We hope that this book provides additional sparks to this spreading wildfire.

Following the pioneers of the transpersonal movement, once can see the transpersonal as a science-informed theory and practice whose interests have exceeded that of mainstream positivistic materialism. Naming, recognizing, and acknowledging the presence of an oceanic consciousness and connectivity between all things has changed the understanding of the world.

History and Development of Transpersonal Psychology

Historical Roots of Transpersonal Psychology

In many ways the areas of interest in transpersonal psychology are timeless. Eugene Taylor (1994) argues that the roots of transpersonal psychology can be found in various indigenous psychologies, including the "classical traditions of Asia" (p. 170) as well as the Judeo-Christian mystical traditions, shamanism, and other ancient influences (see also Taylor, 1999). In part this large scope has been a blessing of inclusivity; however, it also creates a challenge in identifying the boundaries of the transpersonal.

Even in the earliest years of Western psychological development, transpersonal themes were prevalent. Several researchers (Daniels, 2013; Ryan, 2008; Taylor, 1996) have argued that William James was the first transpersonal psychologist based on the content of material he chose to study, particularly his interest in psychic and religious experience. James' (1902/1929) focus on consciousness and his defense of the validity of spiritual experience remain central to contemporary transpersonal psychology. James was also the first to use the term transpersonal in a lecture as early as 1901–1902 (Taylor, 1996). He may have also been "the first American psychologist to establish relationships with or to influence a number of Asian meditation teachers," (Taylor, 1996, p. 21) including Swami Vivekananda, Anagarika Dharmapala, and D.T. Suzuki (p. 24). James was a well respected scientist and professor at Harvard when he established the first United States psychological laboratory and published *The Principles of Psychology* in 1890 (James,

1890/1918a, 1890/1918b). He demonstrated his positivistic scientific bent by treating consciousness as he would any other phenomena in the natural world, but later in his career he developed "radical empiricism" that gives authority to sensory experience, to the experiential, and to whatever might be found in subjective experience. He insisted that these phenomena could be tracked and studied, even "if conventional scientific opinion found them unthinkable" (Ryan, 2008, p. 27). Wilhelm Wundt and his collogues in Europe were also studying consciousness around this same time; however, they believed that such topics were beyond the scientific methodology of the time (Danziger, 1980).

James' interest in alternative and substance-induced states of consciousness, as well as in parapsychological and mediumistic phenomena, foreshadowed the transpersonal field's wide-ranging interest in topics outside the materialistic framework. James' experiments with nitrous oxide (Walsh & Vaughan, 1993) and his experimentation with peyote (Taylor, 1996) likely influenced his interest in non-ordinary states of consciousness. His long observation of Mrs. Piper (Ryan, 2008, p. 28), his founding of the American Society for Psychical Research (ASPR) in 1884 (Taylor, 1996, p. 23), and his own mystical experience led him to state: "Our normal waking consciousness, rational consciousness as we call it, is but one special type of consciousness, whilst all about it, parted from it by the filmiest of screens, there lie potential forms of consciousness entirely different" (1902/1929, p. 378). James was strongly interested in the work being done by several researchers on subliminal consciousness, and he considered the discovery of this aspect of consciousness as one the most important (Ryan, 2008, p. 228). Such interests earned him the disdain of the general scientific community over time, which was a common fate for many early, and even contemporary, transpersonal researchers.

While Freud is often chided by transpersonalists for his devaluations of spiritual experience, particularly his pre/trans confusion (Wilber, 1993) reducing mystical ecstasy to regressive, womblike, "oceanic" feelings, Epstein (1996) says that he "pioneered" the study of spirituality, was "deeply interested in the subject and made great contributions to it" (p. 29). Epstein credits Freud with three primary contributions to the transpersonal field including a) his descriptions of the sensation of mystical experience with oceanic oneness that continue to be used today, b) his exploration of voluntary attentional control, including hypnosis and evenly suspended attention, and c) conceptual strides in understanding pleasure seeking as a source of suffering, paralleling Buddhist teachings. Freud's investigations into the unconscious have been foundational to all successive perspectives on human functioning and his elucidations of childhood developmental processes have influenced all subsequent psychological theories. It would be hard to imagine a transpersonal psychology without the foundations built by Freud and so many of his contemporaries and followers.

Carl Gustav Jung, a Swiss psychiatrist, colleague of Freud, and founder of analytical psychology, similarly believed in the existence of a personal unconscious that influenced an individual's experiences and behavior. Diverging from Freud, Jung's conception of the unconscious also included a second, deeper, transpersonal level that he referred to as the *collective unconscious* (Jung, 1959). For Jung, the collective unconscious is shared among all human beings and contains *archetypes* or autonomous forms of universal patterns and images that take shape when they enter consciousness and manifest in the cultural expressions of the individual. According to Jung, the collective unconscious underpins the personal unconscious mind and influences individuals through its timeless human patterns and symbols. Psychotherapeutic applications of analytical psychology involve exploring the individual's relationship to the collective unconscious (Fordham, 1978). Jung was also an early progenitor of art therapy and suggested that artistic expression, especially of images recurring in an individual's dream life, can serve to bring insight, restore balance, and resolve personal conflicts (Malchiodi, 2006). Jung's transpersonal framework was greatly influenced by his study of Eastern philosophical and spiritual traditions, especially Taoism (Lachman, 2010). For these reasons, Jung is also frequently considered the founder of transpersonal psychology, and, like James, was discounted and pathologized by contemporaries.

Wilhelm Reich was another of Freud's early colleagues who broke away from the psychoanalytic community over differences of opinion, primarily pertaining to the understanding of sexuality and Freud's ideas regarding the death instinct (Boadella, 1973). Reich is the founder of somatic therapy and psychosomatically unified conceptions of human functioning and a pioneer of energy psychology and therapies. He practiced a science of humans not as minds but as bodies. In one of his earliest works, Reich (1949) demonstrated his theory of psychosomatic identity. Reich's vegetotherapy view purported that the body seeks its inherent healthy state but is blocked by armor created through early wounding and the restrictions of social and governmental forces (Lowen, 1975, p. 18). He believed he had discovered the most basic life force, which he called orgone energy. He developed an orgone accumulator to gather and focus its healing power (Boadella, 1973, p. 260; Pierrakos, 1973, p. 13). While many of Reich's areas of interest are of interest to transpersonal psychologists today, they were quite threatening to the status quo of the mid 20th century. In 1947, the U.S. Food and Drug Administration obtained an injunction against the interstate shipment of orgone accumulators, and Reich was charged with contempt in 1956 for having violated the injunction. He was sentenced to two years' imprisonment, and that summer more than six tons of his publications, specifically those mentioning orgone, were burned by order of the court. He died in prison of heart failure nine months into his imprisonment, days before he was due to apply for parole (Mann, 1973).

Roberto Assagioli (1965), an Italian psychiatrist and another contemporary of Freud's, founded the movement known as Psychosynthesis, which continues to be practiced today. He was inspired by Freud's theory of the personal unconscious and Jung's theories of the collective unconscious, but ultimately found Freud's views limiting, negative, and deterministic. Psychosynthesis became the first approach born of psychoanalysis that included the artistic, altruistic, and heroic potentials of the human being and foreshadowed Maslow's work by some 50 years (Vargiu, 1975, p. 6). Assagioli's egg diagram of the personality includes a Higher Self and a lower, middle and higher unconscious, in addition to the conscious self (Assagioli, 1965, p. 17). In an interview by Sam Keen (1974), Assagioli discussed the differences between psychoanalysis and Psychosynthesis:

> We (in psychosynthesis) pay far more attention to the higher unconscious and to the development of the transpersonal self. In one of his letters Freud said, "I am interested only in the basement of the human being." Psychosynthesis is interested in the whole building. We try to build an elevator which will allow a person access to every level of his personality. After all, a building with only a basement is very limited. We want to open up the terrace where you can sun-bathe or look at the stars. Our concern is the synthesis of all areas of the personality. That means Psychosynthesis is holistic, global and inclusive. It is not against psychoanalysis or even behavior modification but it insists that the needs for meaning, for higher values, for a spiritual life, are as real as biological or social needs. We deny that there are any isolated human problems. (p. 97)

Assagioli (1973) is also known for his descriptions of the will, wherein the aspects of the "fully developed human will are the strong will, the skillful will, the good will, and the Transpersonal Will" (p. 15). He described the will of the personal self as aligned with the Transpersonal Will when

> This relationship leads to a growing interplay between, and ultimately to the fusion of, the personal and transpersonal selves and in turn to their relationship with the ultimate reality, the Universal Self, which embodies and demonstrates the Universal, Transcendent Will. (p. 18)

In these early works we find the basic structures of the human being as they are seen in the transpersonal field, including the body, the mind, and the soul as well as the themes of consciousness, transcendence, inherent health, holism, spiritual nature, etc.

The second force of psychology is usually identified as behaviorism, built on the work of Edward Thorndike, John B. Watson, B.F. Skinner, and others who took the American psychology movement by storm in the middle part of the last century. In its focus on *behavior,* it ignored any inner experience, including religious or spiritual experiences (Walach, 2013). Additionally, phenomena such as mind and consciousness needed to "be removed from the discourse of the day because they could not be directly observed by scientists" (Watson, 1924/1958 as cited in Garcia-Romeu & Tart, 2013, p.127). This effectively eliminated transpersonal subjects from behavioral and positivistic scientific journals; however, many skilled scientists continued to study and write about the transpersonal even though they and their texts were "excommunicated" from the church of acceptable "truth." Both psychoanalysis and behaviorism influenced our cultural beliefs about ourselves by highlighting that we are not objective and rational beings with full access to our free will, but in fact are deeply influenced by our pasts, our interactions with our environment, and unseen parts of ourselves.

Concerned about the reductionist, pathologizing, and positivistic themes that dominated the field of psychology, Carl Rogers, Abraham Maslow, Rollo May, James F. T. Bugental, and others championed a third wave in psychology: humanistic psychology. At the outset, humanistic psychology began largely as a group of individuals who were discontent with the current state of psychology but did not agree on what served as the best alternative (Grogan, 2013). Although many discussions, articles, and even books already had been written, the formal development of humanistic psychology began at the Old Saybrook Conference in 1964. As the organization and structural elements of the movement were formalized, its influence was positioned to grow.

Also in 1964, James F. T. Bugental published a seminal article that identified five basic postulates of humanistic psychology, which state that individuals 1) supersede the sum of their parts, 2) have a human context, 3) are aware, 4) have a choice, and 5) are intentional beings. Later, these five postulates were adapted by Tom Greening and placed at the front of the *Journal of Humanistic Psychology* for many years during Greening's editorship.

Within humanistic psychology emerged the American existential movement, which today is typically identified as existential–humanistic psychology (Hoffman, Serlin, & Rubin, in press). The movement began with the publication of *Existence* by Rollo May and colleagues in 1958 (May, Angel, & Ellenberger, 1958). Considered a humanistic psychology, there remain some differences from much humanistic psychology, including greater emphasis on balancing human potential with the recognition of human limitation and giving greater consideration to the concept of evil, or the daimonic (Hoffman et al., in press). Common humanistic and existential values can be seen across contemporary therapeutic approaches, including the emphasis of the therapeutic relationship, therapist presence and authenticity, positive regard for the client, and therapist–client collaboration (Elkins, 2009; Grogan, 2013).

Formal Development

Transpersonal psychology emerged, in part, from the humanistic tradition, and included many of the same founders (Taylor, 1994). Today, some still consider humanistic psychology to be the proper placement of transpersonal psychology in the various forces. Maslow (1964), often considered a founder of both movements, advocated for a more healthful and positive view of being human. Inspired by Maslow, Sutich (1969) identified humanistic psychology as *the third force in psychology*, noting that it is "concerned with topics having little place in existing theories and systems: e.g., love, creativity, self, growth...self actualization, higher values,...psychological health" (p. 2). Shortly after the establishment of humanistic psychology, Maslow in 1967 predicted the emergence of a fourth force in psychology, identifying many of the influences and values that would become part of transpersonal psychology (Ruzek, 2007). Sutich (1969), who laid the foundation for transpersonal psychology with Maslow and others, viewed this as more of an orientation than a force. Yet, as transpersonal psychology developed, many began to advocate for it as the fourth force, particularly adding the dimensions of consciousness and spirituality to the understanding of what it means to be human (Ruzek, 2007).

Transpersonal psychology has formalized in many ways since Maslow's 1967 prediction, including the development of professional organizations, peer-reviewed journals, and training programs, including programs at Naropa University, Saybrook University, Sofia University (formerly the Institute of Transpersonal Psychology), John F. Kennedy University, and the California Institute for Integral Studies. Despite this significant development, Ruzek (2007) questions whether transpersonal psychology has successfully actualized becoming a force in psychology. Mainstream counseling and psychology, including the American Counseling Association and American Psychological Association, have done little to recognize transpersonal psychology and often have been antagonistic to accepting it. Thus, while transpersonal has been successful in structural, philosophical, and theoretical development, it has not of yet become influential enough to rightly be called the fourth force. However, we remain confident that transpersonal psychology speaks important themes and will continue to grow in influence over time.

Furthermore, although the term "transpersonal" may have failed to gain wide acceptance or usage in traditional academic and lay conversations since Maslow, Grof, and Sutich first inspired interest in establishing this new "branch of psychology" (Grof, 2008), transpersonal constructs and practices have gained wide recognition and assimilation into broad fields of academic study and within the general population. For example, the national and international interest in mindfulness awareness practices, as illustrated in Dialectical Behavior Therapy and Mindfulness-Based Stress Reduction, have taken root in various university settings, including Brown University, University of Washington, and University of California, Los Angeles (UCLA), and have become part of mainstream medical care. These are practices that have long been researched and recommended by transpersonal psychologists (Cortright, 1997; MacDonald, Walsh, & Shapiro, 2013; Scotton, Chinen, & Battista, 1996; Walsh & Vaughan, 1993), as well as the world's wisdom traditions that provided the transpersonal field its foundation.

The transpersonal movement centralized the importance of the spiritual and transcendent aspects of human nature and reclaimed humanity's spiritual essence, an idea that William James (1902/1929) had foreshadowed more than 50 years before. Early transpersonal founders believed that the humanistic tradition was primarily focused on the therapeutic process, underemphasized transcendent experiences and optimal functioning, and had an ethnocentric and cognicentric bias (Harner, 1990).

Transpersonal psychology was the first to see the value of acknowledging the findings of the psychological perspectives that had come before it by suggesting that the transpersonal "included and transcended" the other theoretical perspectives in the field (Wilber, 2000; Combs, 2013). Wilber's (2000) capacity to conceptually organize the dozens of psychological and related theories into categories of waves, streams, stages, and lines offered for the first time an opportunity for psychologists to expand by including the plural truths of many systems rather than trying to prove or argue for superiority between one or two or just a few. This was transformational for psychology as a whole and helped move the field into a higher level of integration and perspective. Nevertheless, the inclusion of the spiritual aspect was then, and remains, quite challenging for some traditional psychologies that continue to reject the transcendent aspect of human nature and human functioning and exclude it from the content of psychological study. We see this as a holdover from the Cartesian/Newtonian conclusion that spirit and science are incompatible both for political and empirical reasons. In the transpersonal world, this is a fundamental flaw.

The contemporary practice of positive psychology arguably has roots in humanistic and transpersonal traditions (Froh, 2004; Resnick, Warmoth, & Serlin, 2001); however, there also has been significant tension between these branches of psychology at times (Robbins, 2008, 2015). Meanwhile, Buddhism has studied consciousness for 2500 years; its path of study leads from *samsara*, or conditioned existence, to *nirvana* and "contains a comprehensive system for understanding the functioning of the mind and producing higher states of consciousness" (Scotton et al., 1996, p. 121); it teaches adherents to track and shift from "impure, unwholesome and unhealthy mental properties to pure, wholesome and healthy ones" (Goleman, 1996, p. 229).

Altered states of consciousness, induced through various compounds and practices, have been primary research areas in transpersonal psychology for decades (Bravo & Grob, 1996; Grof, 2000). Use of altered states in healing has been employed by shamans for at least 30,000 years and likely used by lay persons for millennia (Harner, 1990; McKenna, 1999). Consistent with this interest, current research with a wide variety of medicines constructed from psychedelic and other plant-based compounds are promising significant positive results for difficult-to-treat symptoms such as those in chronic, treatment-resistant posttraumatic stress disorder (PTSD; Bouso et al., 2008; d'Otalora, 2004; Doblin, 2002; Greer, & Tolbert, 1998; Mithofer, 2011; see also the Multidisciplinary Association for Psychedelic Studies website: MAPS).

The contemporary cultural zeitgeist is currently advertising ancient methods of growth and transformation with dizzying regularity. Usually these are not identified as ideas or practices that have been studied by transpersonal psychologists for the past 50 years, let alone that they have been maintained and passed down by our ancestors from around the world for millennia. It is important to recognize that transpersonal counselors and psychologists are not the first to discover these transformative practices, the transpersonal realities, and the wholeness of our human selves; however, they are rediscovering them from a vantage point that allows mental health professionals and scholars to better understand their value and utility.

While the transpersonal movement can be found in nearly every field of study (Hartelius et al., 2013), it started and was named as a branch in the field of psychology. However, many suggest that multicultural psychology, not transpersonal, is the fourth force (Pedersen, 1990, 1991; Ratts, & Pedersen, 2014; David, Okazaki, & Giroux, 2014). Certainly multiculturalism has had a more pervasive influence on the field of psychology, at least recently, than transpersonal psychology. Although transpersonal psychology has historically maintained values consistent with embracing a multicultural perspective, it has struggled to actualize these values. Recently, in some aspects of transpersonal psychology, this has begun to change. In particular, at Naropa University there have been significant efforts to increase the focus and impact of diversity awareness and skillfulness for counseling students. Every class is expected to offer diverse materials for students to read, diverse perspectives for discussion, and diverse examples and techniques for practice. While the intention has perhaps not yet been achieved, stating the goal of designing and presenting a diverse clinical perspective for creating a more just and equitable world is a strong and worthy commitment.

Despite its wide reach of interest and significant longevity, transpersonal psychology does have identity and definitional challenges (Hartelius et al., 2013). The depth and breadth of transpersonal topics and interests have made it difficult to capture them in a clear, succinct manner. Furthermore, there has not been unified agreement on what should be considered part of transpersonal psychology. Hartelius and colleagues (2013) have recently published a unified and inclusive definition of the transpersonal field based on its actual research and academic activity as:

> a transformative psychology of the whole person in intimate relationship with an interconnected and evolving world; it pays special attention to self-expansive states as well as to spiritual, mystical, and other exceptional human experiences that gain meaning in such a context. (p. 14)

This definition identifies three primary constructs 1) self-transcendence, 2) integrative, relational wholeness, and 3) transformation. This grounded and utilitarian definition should continue to help many articulate the transpersonal movement more clearly as we move forward. While this definition is not likely to end the definition debate on transpersonal psychology, we believe it is the best attempt at a unified definition of transpersonal psychology thus far. Furthermore, such a definition may help transpersonal psychology to better actualize its potential through providing a clear, unifying vision.

Capturing the Transpersonal Field

Early in its history, nearly everyone contributed a different definition of transpersonal psychology. Like the proverbial blind men and the elephant, contributors seemed to describe quite different constructs, which resulted in a field so broad that by containing everything it failed to describe anything useful. John Davis (2000), one of the field's early contributors, joked about this in a paper titled "We Keep Asking Ourselves, What is Transpersonal Psychology?" This seems to have been one of the reasons Wilber (2003) seceded from the field. The proposed focus of transpersonal psychology varied from a spiritual definition, noting that it was separate and broader than the psychology of religion (Fontana, 2003; Walsh & Vaughan, 1993); the highest states of human potential (Grof, 2008); ancient mystical knowledge and enlightenment (Caplan, 1999; Cortright, 1997); parapsychology (Tart, 1997, 2002); the study of consciousness itself (Wilber, 1977; Lancaster, 2004); the developmental process of higher states (Wilber, 1977); states of consciousness (Grof, 2000; Garcia-Romeu & Tart, 2013; Tart, 1972, 1975; Wickramasekera II, 2013), and soteriological agenda (Caplan, Hartelius, & Rardin, 2003; Daniels 2013; Hartelius & Ferrer, 2013).

When we ask our graduate students to define transpersonal psychology, their answer is usually a highly linguistic one, such as "beyond or through the personal." When asked to further clarify, they often struggle to articulate their ideas. Their answer often comes as a paraphrase of Cortright's (1997) "melding of the wisdom of the world's wisdom traditions with the learning of modern psychology" (p.8). Although their answers are technically correct, they are, like all definitions of the transpersonal so far, inevitably limited and restricted by a focus on a single aspect of what might be meant by this word—or field. The one-line elevator speech description of transpersonal remains open to discussion, debate, and disagreement.

Hartelius, Caplan, and Rardin (2007) reviewed 160 definitions of transpersonal psychology from the scholarly literature, identifying three major themes: a beyond–ego psychology, an integrative/holistic psychology, and a psychology of transformation. The transpersonal as a beyond-ego psychology includes study of human beings from a wider perspective, encompassing, but also beyond, the personal — functioning parts such as the id, ego, and superego; its ill pathologies; its quantifiable behavior; and its traditionally states of consciousness such as waking, sleeping, and dreaming. The transpersonal beyond-ego includes a broad look at the self and all its component parts and developmental stages, as well as its ability to enter into a variety of states of consciousness from the mundane to the spiritual. Many of these are valued for their healing potential, the meaning they bring to one's life, and the sense of awe and wonder they help one recover. As William James (1902/1929) stated, the boundaries of the self or ego are arbitrary limitations on a potentially limitless self; as individuals reclaim more of these states and see them as parts of themselves, they expand their understanding of their role and place on the Earth and increase the ethical and moral perspective of responsibility they have to the whole of it.

Daniels (2013) outlines three vectors of the transpersonal: ascending—"ultimate realization of absolute consciousness and union with spirit"; descending—"the depth psychological approach"; and extending—"moral and spiritual concern outwards...other people, and the larger political, economic, and ecological systems" (pp. 34–36). The ascending vector is most likely to be associated with transpersonal psychology as it emphasizes upward ego expansion such as transcendence and spiritual experiences, and follows the earliest writings in the transpersonal field (Wilber, 1977). The descending vector represents a diving into the depths of the psyche or the unconscious where primitive drives, mythic forces, and the collective unconscious can be accessed for greater personality integration and functioning, (Jung, 1964; Washburn, 1988). The extending vector seeks the transpersonal through participatory relationships with others and the world (Achterberg & Rothberg, 1998; Davis & Canty, 2013). It is moving beyond our own ego-centrism through the path of service to others and through greater connection with the communities of the world (Ferrer, 2002) and to the earth (Davis, 2011).

The personal self or ego is altered and grown by connecting and coming into relationship with the "other"—whether it is to a personal or non-dual universal force, to other people, including groups and communities, or to its environment such as with nature and the greater-than-human world. Hartelius et al. (2013) proposed calling this facet of transpersonal psychology "a psychology of self expansiveness" (p. 7). This capacity necessitates that the study of humans be equally expansive. Humans, as they are defined in the transpersonal field, are infinitely more complex than innate drives and defenses or organisms simply waiting to be programmed through rewards, punishments, or modeling. A human is also a consciousness in contact with *The Consciousness*. For Hartelius et al. (2013), human consciousness is "capable of expanding to include others, nature, or all of space and time, of embodying some larger aspect of the world" (p. 7). As such, the transpersonal has also ventured into study of the consciousness beyond the human ego as part of the "other" that is within and without, and that ultimately engulfs and enfolds all this world contains.

Hartelius et al. (2013) have also identified the transpersonal as a "whole person psychology" with a multi-disciplinary orientation (p. 8; see also Serlin, 2007). It is not merely integrative and holistic in defining the self as a whole being, but also emphasizes that the self becomes itself in relation to others—to the environment and to the context, as "the whole person in intimate relationship with an interconnected and evolving world" (Hartelius et al., 2013, p. 14). This expands the study of the human psyche beyond psychology and into an interconnected world of other disciplines of study, relationships, communities, cultures, nature, and universals such as time and space, sometimes called the transpersonal orientation (Boucouvalas, 1999) or transpersonal studies (Wilber, 1995). This interconnected view is found in many world traditions, including some Vedic/Buddhist and Native American (e.g. the concept of Mitakuye Oyasin, all are related) spiritualities. Such a wide perspective requires multiple methods of inquiry and research beyond the Western gold standard of quantifiable double-blind studies and positivistic research methods. It also requires significantly more respect for the "others" that inhabit this new world than the West has shown to date.

The third theme identified by Hartelius et al. (2013) is that the transpersonal is a psychology of "transformative process (and) is a journey in which there is not simply movement from one place to another, but in which the landscape, the destination, and the journeyer shift and change as part of that movement" (p. 10). With this in mind, the project of living becomes a co-created experience between the awakened person and the energies of life. Transformation itself becomes an energy or force that can be felt and channeled, like heat or gravity. Movement does not always result in improvement. As seen throughout the Industrial Age, faster does not necessarily mean better and production without ethics is a disaster. Growth has typically been seen as an increase in size or strength; however, unbridled growth is often deadly.

The transformational power to be harnessed through transpersonal study and practice is a more balanced and ethically intended journey. The questions have less likely answers and certainty. Reality is much less real from here; yet it is important to realize that what one does and how one does it matters. Transpersonal is an antidote to the certitude of nihilism and cynicism that is taking hold in many areas of our world. Transpersonal is in the world and in the small moments and experiences. While it can be found in prayer and meditation, it also can be found in a mother changing a baby's diaper, listening and learning about other peoples' experiences and their cultures, through environmental activism, and even the pursuits of contemporary physics. For that and many other reasons, we endorse the sharing of not solely theoretical concerns in transpersonal psychology but strongly endorse its real-world applications as well.

References

Achterberg, J., & Rothberg, D. (1998). Relationship as spiritual practice. In D. Rothberg & S. Kelly (Eds.), *Ken Wilber in dialogue: Conversations with leading transpersonal thinkers* (pp. 261–274). Wheaton IL: Quest Books.

Assagioli, R. (1965). *Psychosynthesis: A manual of principles and techniques.* New York NY: Penguin/Arkana.

Assagioli, R. (1973). *The act of will.* New York, NY: Penguin Books.

Boadella, D. (1973). *Wilhelm Reich: The evolution of his work.* Boston, MA: Vision Press.

Boucouvalas, M. (1999). Following the movement: From transpersonal psychology to a multi-disciplinary orientation. *Journal of Transpersonal Psychology, 31*(1), 27–39.

Bouso, J. C., Doblin, R., Farré, M., Alcazar, M.A., Gomez-Jarabo, G. (2008). MDMA-assisted psychotherapy using low doses in a small sample of women with chronic posttraumatic stress disorder. *Journal of Psychoactive Drugs, 40*(3) 225–236.

Bravo, G. & Grob, C. (1996). Psychedelics and transpersonal psychiatry. In B. W. Scotton, A. B. Chinen, & J. R. Battista, (Eds.), *Textbook of transpersonal psychiatry and psychology* (pp. 176–185). New York, NY: Basic Books.

Bugental, J. F. T. (1964). The third force in psychology. *Journal of Humanistic Psychology, 4*(1), 19–26.

Caplan, M. (1999). *Halfway up the mountain: The error of premature claims to enlightenment.* Prescott, AZ: Hohm Press.

Caplan, M., Hartelius, G., & Rardin, M. A. (2003). Contemporary viewpoints on transpersonal psychology. *Journal of Transpersonal Psychology, 35*(2), 143–162.

Combs, A. (2013). Transcend and include: Ken Wilber's contribution to transpersonal psychology. In H.L Friedman & G. Hartelius (Eds.), *The Wiley-Blackwell handbook of transpersonal psychology* (pp. 166–186). West Sussex, UK: John Wiley & Sons.

Cortright, B. (1997). *Psychotherapy and spirit: Theory and practice in transpersonal psychotherapy.* Albany, NY: State University of New York Press.

Daniels, M. (2013). Traditional roots, history and evolution of the transpersonal perspective. In H.L Friedman & G. Hartelius (Eds.), *The Wiley-Blackwell handbook of transpersonal psychology* (pp. 23–43). West Sussex, UK: John Wiley & Sons.

Danziger, K. (1980). The history of introspection reconsidered. *Journal of the History of the Behavioral Sciences, 16*(3), 241–262.

David, E. J. R., Okazaki, S., & Giroux, D. (2014). A set of guiding principles to advance multicultural psychology and its major concepts. In F.T.L. Leong, L. Comas-Diaz, G.C. Nagaayama-Hall, V.C. McLoyd, & J.E. Trimble (Eds.), *APA Handbook of Multicultural Psychology, 1,* 85–104.

Davis, J. (2000). We keep asking ourselves, what is transpersonal psychology. *Guidance & Counseling, 15*(3), 3–8.

Davis, J. (2011). Ecopsychology, transpersonal psychology, and nonduality. *International Journal of Transpersonal Studies, 30*(1–2), 89–100.

Davis, J. & Canty, J.M. (2013). Ecopsychology and transpersonal psychology. In H.L Friedman & G. Hartelius (Eds.), *The Wiley-Blackwell handbook of transpersonal psychology* (pp. 597–611). West Sussex, UK: John Wiley & Sons.

Doblin, R. (2002). A clinical plan for MDMA (Ecstasy) in the treatment of posttraumatic stress disorder (PTSD): Partnering with the FDA. *Journal of Psychoactive Drugs, 34*(2), 185–194.

d'Otalora, M. (2004). MDMA and LSD therapy in the treatment of posttraumatic stress disorder in a case of sexual abuse. Available from https://www.maps.org/research/mdma/moaccount.html

Elkins, D. N. (2009). *Humanistic psychology: A clinical manifesto*. Colorado Springs, CO: University of the Rockies Press.

Epstein, M. (1996). Freud's influence on transpersonal psychology. In B.W. Scotton, A.B. Chinen, & J.R. Battista (Eds.), *Textbook of transpersonal psychiatry and psychology* (pp. 29–38). New York, NY: Basic Books.

Ferrer, J. N. (2002). *Revisioning transpersonal theory: A participatory vision of human spirituality*. New York, NY: State University of New York Press.

Fontana, D. (2003). *Psychology, religion, and spirituality*. Leicester, UK: BPS Blackwell.

Fordham, M. (1959). *Jungian psychotherapy: A study in analytical psychology*. New York, NY: Wiley and Sons.

Froh, J. J. (2004). The history of positive psychology: Truth be told. *NYS Psychologist, 16*(3) 18–20.

Garcia-Romeu, A.P., & Tart, C.T. (2013). Altered States of Consciousness and Transpersonal Psychology. In H.L Friedman & G. Hartelius (Eds.), *The Wiley-Blackwell handbook of transpersonal Psychology* (pp. 121–140). West Sussex, UK: John Wiley & Sons.

Goleman, D. (1996). Meditation and consciousness: An Asian approach to mental health. In S. Boorstein (Ed.), *Transpersonal psychotherapy* (2nd ed., pp. 227–240). Albany, NY: State University of New York Press.

Greer, G.R., & Tolbert, R. (1998). A method of conducting therapeutic sessions with MDMA. *Journal of Psychoactive Drugs, 30*(4), 371–379.

Grof, S. (1985). *Beyond the brain: Birth, death, and transcendence in psychotherapy*. Albany, NY: State University of New York Press.

Grof, S. (1988). The adventure of self-discovery. Albany, NY: State University of New York Press.

Grof, S. (2000). *Psychology of the future: Lessons from modern consciousness research*. Albany, NY: State University of New York Press.

Grof, S. (2008). Brief history of transpersonal psychology. *International Journal of Transpersonal Studies, 27*, 46–54.

Grogan, J. (2013). *Encountering America: Humanistic psychology, sixties culture and shaping of the modern self*. New York, NY: Harper.

Harner, M. (1990). *The way of the shaman*. San Francisco, CA: Harper and Row.

Hartelius, G., Caplan, M., & Rardin, M. A. (2007). Transpersonal psychology: Defining the past, divining the future. *The Humanistic Psychologist, 25*(2), 135–160.

Hartelius, G. & Ferrer, J.N. (2013). Transpersonal philosophy: The participatory turn. In H.L Friedman & G. Hartelius (Eds.), *The Wiley-Blackwell handbook of transpersonal psychology* (pp. 187–202). West Sussex, UK: John Wiley & Sons.

Hartelius, G., Rothe, G., & Roy, J. (2013). A brand from the burning: Defining transpersonal psychology. In H.L Friedman & G. Hartelius (Eds.), *The Wiley-Blackwell handbook of transpersonal psychology,* (pp. 3–22). West Sussex, UK: John Wiley & Sons.

Hoffman, L., Serlin, I. D., & Rubin, S. (in press). History (Existential-humanistic therapy). In E. van Duerzen, K. Schneider, E. Craig, A. Langle, & D. Tatum (Eds.), *Wiley world handbook of existential therapy*. Hoboken, NJ: Wiley.

James, W. (1918a). The principles of psychology (Vol. 1). New York, NY: Dover. (Original work published 1890)

James, W. (1918b). The principles of psychology (Vol. 2). New York, NY: Dover. (Original work published 1890)

James, W. (1929). *The varieties of religious experience: A study in human nature.* New York, NY: The New American Library. (Original work published 1902)

Jung, C. (1959). *Archetypes and the collective unconscious.* Princeton, NJ: Princeton University Press.

Jung, C.G. (1964). *Man and his symbols*. New York, NY: Bantam Doubleday Dell.

Keen, S. (1974). The golden mean of Roberto Assagioli. *Psychology Today, 8,* 97–107.

Lachman, G. (2010). *Jung the mystic.* New York, NY: Tarcher/Penguin.

Lancaster, B. L. (2004). *Approaches to consciousness: The marriage of science and mysticism*. New York, NY: Palgrave Macmillan.

Lowen, A. (1975). *Bioenergetics*. New York, NY: Penguin.

MacDonald, D. A., Walsh, R., & Shapiro, S.L. (2013). Meditation: Empirical research and future directions. In H.L Friedman & G. Hartelius (Eds.), *The Wiley-Blackwell handbook of transpersonal psychology* (pp. 433–458). West Sussex, UK: John Wiley & Sons.

Malchiodi, C. A. (2006). *The art therapy sourcebook.* New York, NY: McGraw-Hill Professional Publishing.

Mann, W.E. (1973). *Orgone, Reich and eros: Wilhelm Reich's theory of life energy*. New York, NY: Simon and Schuster.

Maslow, A. H. (1964). *Religions, values and peak-experiences*. New York, NY: Penguin Compass.

May, R., Angel, E., & Ellenberger, H. F. (Eds.). (1958). *Existence*. Northvale, NJ: Jason Aronson.

McKenna, T. (1999). *Food of the gods: The search for the original tree of knowledge: A radical history of plants, drugs, and human evolution.* New York, NY: Random House.

Mithofer, M.C. (2011). The safety and efficacy of {+/-}3,4-methylenedioxymethamphetamine-assisted psychotherapy in subjects with chronic, treatment-resistant posttraumatic stress disorder: The first randomized controlled pilot study. *Journal of Psychopharmacology, 25*(4), 439–452.

Pederson, (1990). The multicultural perspective as a fourth force in counseling. *Journal of Mental Health Counseling, 12,* 93–95.

Pederson, (1991). Introduction to the special issue on multiculturalism as fourth force in counseling. *Journal of Counseling and Development, 70,* 4.

Pierrakos, J. (1973). Foreword. In W.E. Mann's *Orgone, Reich and eros: Wilhelm Reich's theory of life energy.* New York, NY: Simon and Schuster.

Ratts, M. J., & Pedersen, P. B. (2014). *Counseling for multiculturalism and social justice: Integration, theory, and application.* John Wiley & Sons.

Reich, W. (1949). *Character-Analysis* (3rd ed; Theodore P. Wolfe, Trans.). New York, NY: Orgone Institute Press.

Resnick, S., Warmoth, A., & Serlin, I. A. (2001). The humanistic psychology and positive psychology connection: Implications for psychotherapy. *Journal of Humanistic Psychology, 41,* 73-101.

Robbins, B. D. (2008). What is the good life? Positive psychology and the renaissance of humanistic psychology. *The Humanistic Psychologist, 36,* 96–112. doi: 10.1080/08873260802110988

Robbins, B. D. (2015). Building bridges between humanistic and positive psychology. In S. Joseph (Ed.), *Positive psychology in practice: Promoting human flourishing in work, health, education, and everyday life* (2nd ed., pp. 31–45). Hoboken, NJ: Wiley.

Rodrigues, V. & Friedman, H.L. (2013). Transpersonal psychotherapies. In H.L Friedman & G. Hartelius (Eds.), *The Wiley-Blackwell handbook of transpersonal psychology,* (pp. 580–596). West Sussex, UK: John Wiley & Sons.

Ruzek, N. (2007). Transpersonal psychology in context: Perspectives from its founders and historians of American psychology. *The Journal of Transpersonal Psychology, 39,* 153–174.

Ryan, M. B. (2008). The transpersonal William James. *The Journal of Transpersonal Psychology, 40*(1), 20–40.

Scotton, B.W., Chinen, A.B., & Battista, J.R. (Eds.) (1996). *Textbook of transpersonal psychiatry and psychology.* New York, NY: Basic Books.

Serlin, J. (2007.) Whole person healthcare (Vols. 1-3). Westport, CT: Praeger,

Sutich, A. J. (1969). Some considerations regarding transpersonal psychology. *The Journal of Transpersonal Psychology, 1*(1), 11.

Tarnas, R. (2006). *Cosmos and psyche: Intimations of a new world view.* New York, NY: Plume/Penguin.

Tart, C.T. (1972). *Altered states of consciousness.* Oxford, England: Doubleday.

Tart, C.T. (1975). *States of consciousness.* New York, NY: E.P. Dutton.

Tart, C.T. (Ed.). (1997). *Body, mind, spirit: Exploring the parapsychology of spirituality.* Charlottesville, VA: Hampton Roads Publishing Company Incorporated.

Tart, C.T. (2002). Parapsychology and transpersonal psychology: "Anomalies" to be explained away or spirit to manifest? *The Journal of Parapsychology, 66*(1): ProQuest Psychology Journals.

Taylor, E. (1994). Transpersonal psychology: Its several virtues. In F. Wertz (Ed.), *The humanistic movement: Recovering the person in psychology* (pp. 170–185). Lake Worth, FL: Gardner Press.

Taylor, E. (1996). William James and transpersonal psychiatry. In B.W. Scotton, A.B. Chinen, & J.R. Battista (Eds.), *Textbook of transpersonal psychiatry and psychology* (pp. 21–28). New York, NY: Basic Books.

Taylor, E. (1999). *Shadow culture: Psychology and spirituality in America*. Washington, DC: Counterpoint.

Vargiu, J. (Ed.). (1975). In memoriam: Roberto Assagioli (1888–1974). *Synthesis Volume 2: The realization of the self* (pp. 5–7). Redwood City, CA: Synthesis Press.

Walach, H. (2013) Criticisms of transpersonal psychology and beyond—The future of transpersonal psychology. In H.L Friedman & G. Hartelius (Eds.), *The Wiley-Blackwell handbook of transpersonal psychology* (pp. 62–87). West Sussex, UK: John Wiley & Sons.

Walsh, R. & Vaughan, F. (1993). *Paths beyond ego: The transpersonal vision*. New York, NY: Penguin Putnam.

Washburn, M. (1988). *The ego and the dynamic ground: A transpersonal theory of human development*. Albany, NY: State University of New York Press.

Watson, J.B. (1958). *Behaviorism*. Chicago, IL: Chicago of University Press. (Original work published 1924)

Wickramasekera II, I. (2013). Hypnosis and transpersonal psychology : Answering the call within. In H.L Friedman & G. Hartelius (Eds.), *The Wiley-Blackwell handbook of transpersonal psychology* (pp. 492–511). West Sussex, UK: John Wiley & Sons.

Wilber, K. (1977) *The Spectrum of consciousness*. Wheaton, IL: Theosophical Publishing House.

Wilber, K. (1993). The pre/trans fallacy. In R. Walsh & F. Vaughan (Eds.), *Paths beyond ego: The transpersonal vision*. New York, NY: Penguin Putnam.

Wilber, K. (1995) *Sex, ecology, spirituality: The spirit of evolution*. Boston, MA: Shambhala.

Wilber, K. (2000). *Integral psychology: Consciousness, spirit, psychology, therapy*. Boston, MA: Shambhala Publications.

Wilber, K. (2003). Waves, streams, states and self: An outline of integral psychology. *The Humanistic Psychologist, 31*, 22–49.

Chapter 2
Transpersonal Psychology in the Age of ISIS: The Role of Culture, Social Action, and Personal Transformation

Dan Hocoy

Differing personal experiences of the transpersonal, filtered through traditional spiritual traditions and combined with globalization, social media, and forced migrations, have raised intercultural conflicts to new levels and are of a nature unseen in human history. The role of transpersonal assumptions and religious differences can be seen in global military conflicts, cultural problems in the European integration of refugees, and ideological clashes between groups like ISIS and those that maintain the conventional idea of the nation-state. These conflicts take place on both personal and collective levels, as well as in local and international contexts. The recent conflicts raise the question of how we as humans can co-exist in a world with such spiritual diversity. At this point in our evolution, in which multicultural interactions are increasing because of technology, global economics and unprecedented migration, there is a need to address the fundamental issues related to conflicting spiritual worldviews. Transpersonal psychology has a unique role, and perhaps responsibility, in helping to create greater inter-religious understanding and dialogue, as well as a framework or model for spiritual co-existence. The transpersonal field is also being afforded an opportunity to be more relevant than it ever has historically.

It is interesting that transpersonal psychology was the first branch of psychology to make claims of being the fourth force (Tart, 1975) in the history of Western psychology. Although this new force was self-identified as recognizing the cultural bias in applications of psychology (e.g., Rosenzweig, 1992), it is evident from the leading textbooks in the field (e.g., Friedman & Hartelius, 2015; Scotton, Chinen, Battista, 2009; Boorstein, 1996, 1997) that this is more of an aspiration than a reality. Culture, if discussed in these and other transpersonal texts, is usually defined in terms of the cross-cultural (e.g., Eastern) roots of transpersonal approaches or the cultural context in which the transpersonal became prominent (Friedman & Hartelius, 2015) in the West. Although there are discrete articles that consider specific cultural aspects (e.g., Hastings et al., 2001), many of these exemplify what Friedman (2009) calls a *xenophilia* (p. 107) or a type of romanticism for Eastern spiritual traditions. Friedman argues that transpersonal psychology has privileged religions and spiritual perspectives considered exotic by Westerners; he cites various scholarly articles from the Western academy that point to Buddhism as the psychological spiritual tradition most illustrative of this romanticism. Myers (1985) declared any systematic consideration of the role of culture (i.e., a set of specific values, constructions, customs) in transpersonal studies to be "conspicuously absent" (p. 34). And Davis (2003), while considering transpersonal psychology to be inherently multicultural, found the field to be deficient and requiring development in certain aspects; for instance, in his comprehensive overview of transpersonal psychology, Davis could not find studies related to social class.

Yet, culture has become increasingly relevant in the context of the rapidly changing demographics of the United States and current projections of greater diversification by the U.S. Bureau of the Census (2015). The changing populations of the developed world stemming from migrations and differential growth, demand a greater consideration of the role of culture in the transpersonal for the ethical and relevant theorist, educator, and counselor (Birdsell, Kelley, & Sinding, 2001). Concomitant with this cultural diversity is a multiplicity of truths and individual realities that co-exist but may be contradictory, ultimately requiring a postmodern approach to capture.

The predominant assumption that seems to contribute to the lack of attention given to culture is the claim that the transpersonal takes place at such a deep spiritual level that superficial cultural underpinnings have no real impact or relevance. As an example, Louchakova and Lucas (2007) cogently assert that "transpersonal psychology's clinical theory remains the only kind of psychological theory hardly touched by the conceptualization of culture and gender, as if the universalistic nature of our lofty vocation places us beyond the scope of ego-related relativities such as gender or ethnicity" (p. 113). Although the subject material of transpersonal theories may be free of such relativities, the theories themselves are the products of individuals who are inevitably culturally situated. Western academic transpersonal theory derives from a specific historical context and set of values and constructions that are distinctly Euro-American in origin. As such, they implicitly favor and perpetuate a Western worldview in their articulation. The transpersonal canon is replete with instances of its preeminent theories being unconsciously culturally bound, that is, anchored in Western cultural biases. For instance, according to Goldenberg (1976), the concepts of Carl Jung, which have been foundational for transpersonal theory and psychotherapy, clearly have biases consistent with a traditional, Western patriarchal worldview. We see an example of this in Jung's explanation of his archetypal concepts of anima and animus, defined respectively as the unconscious feminine psychological qualities that a man possesses and the unconscious masculine psychological qualities that a woman possesses. Jung provides the following description:

> *A* woman's consciousness is characterized more by the connective quality of Eros than by the discrimination and cognition associated with Logos. In men, Eros, the function of relationship, is usually less developed than Logos. In women, on the other hand, Eros is an expression of their true nature, while their Logos is often only a regrettable accident. (Jung, 1953/1968, p. 14)

Jung (1948/1980) also equates primitive states of mind or unconscious processes with what he termed "primitive" (p. 176) people, for instance, viewing the psyches of people of African descent as less developed and inferior to those of Europeans (Dalal, 1988).

Rudolf Steiner, considered by some (e.g., McDermott, 2008) to be one of the preeminent transpersonal theorists of the 20th century, also espoused theories containing strong racist tenets. As the founder of Anthroposophy (spiritual science), Waldorf education, and biodynamic agriculture, Steiner has had considerable impact on Western consciousness and has left a significant, global educational and agricultural legacy. According to Steiner's (1906/1990) teachings on soul travel, the same soul could assume different "races" in different lives. What race it would incarnate depends on how one behaved in the previous life. Steiner claimed that "a soul can be incarnated in any race, but if this soul doesn't become evil, it doesn't need to be reincarnated in a descending race, it will reincarnate later in an ascending race" (p. 42). Steiner's (1910/1997) racial judgments are consistent with traditional European biases, with people of African descent described as childlike in their simplicity, Asians as a "lower class of people," Native Americans as a "degenerated human race," (p. 4) and Europeans by nature the most advanced and evolved. In his treatise on the mission of the Germanic people, Steiner claimed that "the most mature (human) characteristics are found in the European area. It is simply (a natural) law" (p. 4).

Apologists of Jung and Steiner have argued that because they were merely men of their time and their theories are naturally tinged with the gender and racial biases of their era, this should not take away from the validity of their theories (e.g., Stevens, 1990). But how does one tease out from their theories the valid, timeless, and universal aspects from those that are merely culturally conditioned and baseless. And how do these theories not negatively impact people's perceptions of and attitudes toward themselves or others? These are seminal theories for transpersonal studies and impact the work of researchers, instructors, and clinicians as well as the people they serve and influence. How can the hundreds of thousands of Waldorf students, teachers, and parents worldwide, of all different races and nationalities, not be influenced by the racist philosophies of Rudolf Steiner, Waldorf's founder? Can psychotherapists, trained in analytical (Jungian) psychology, truly bracket the racist and sexist tenets of Jung in their treatment of others? Or do these assumptions lurk in the shadow of these therapists, exacting an unconscious impact on their practice with individuals of all gender orientations and all cultures.

It is clear that these and other transpersonal theories lack a critical awareness of the cultural perspective from which they originate. Inherent within them are the constructions, assumptions, and values of a particular, typically Euro-American, culture. It is natural for these theories to contain the biases of the various societies from which they derive, but for a field that some consider inherently multicultural in perspective (e.g., Davis, 2003), the absence of scholarship in how to address the cultural biases inherent in the field's own theories is noticeable. When these culture-bound theories are taught or applied to clinical practice unconscious of their cultural underpinnings, they have the effect of being forces of enculturation, assimilation, or worse, Western imperialism (Hocoy, 2002). Transpersonal theories that are culture bound also tend to promote a cultural blindness about their applicability to individuals of different cultural backgrounds. Educators and therapists that are culture blind treat all clients and populations without consideration of their cultural origin and assume that a person's culture is irrelevant.

The assumption that there are no differences across cultures leads to potential misunderstanding and mistreatment. A culture-blind therapist treats all individuals without considering that the person's cultural characteristics may have a bearing on the therapist's assessment, interpretation, and intervention. Cultural blindness can lead a therapist to unethical practice if he or she is working outside of their area of cultural competence (e.g., Acton, 2001). The culture-blind therapist can engage in malpractice by unwittingly serving as an agent of assimilation, implicitly imposing Euro-American cultural norms on their clients. Clearly, these biases are not confined to transpersonal therapists and educators; however, as a field seeking to be as advanced, ethical and relevant as possible, transpersonal psychology could benefit from a systematic examination of the role of culture in its theory, research, and practice.

Clinical Vignette on Cultural Blindness

During my training as a clinical psychologist in 1997, I worked as an intern at the Nova Scotia Hospital in Canada. One day, our multidisciplinary team was tasked with assessing a nine-year old First Nations (i.e., Native American) girl who had been referred to us from social services. She had no living relatives as her parents had recently died in a car accident. She was referred to us because she claimed to still see and have conversations with her deceased parents. The Canadian psychiatrist on the team identified the behaviors as psychotic and probably the result of posttraumatic stress. She suggested we reassess the girl a few months later, which we did and found that she was still seeing and having conversations with her parents. At that point, the psychiatrist suggested that the girl be committed to a psychiatric institution as a ward of the Crown.

Because the girl had expressed no distress by these sightings and conversations, I suggested to the team that perhaps the behaviors they had identified as psychotic may actually be culturally appropriate and that we should ask the tribe of the girl's family if the behaviors that were exhibited by the girl were out of the ordinary for their culture. Through a connection of one team member, we spoke with the nearest Micmac tribe and were told that these behaviors were perfectly normal, and that the tribe believed deceased parents could present themselves to counsel and comfort their living children. Based on that information, we concluded that the girl was adjusting appropriately for her culture and that she did not require further psychiatric treatment. If we had assessed this girl without consideration of her cultural background, we might have made a misdiagnosis that would have resulted in unnecessary medication and institutionalization. It is easy to forget that our definitions of dysfunction and mental illness are culturally based and do not necessarily apply to individuals of other cultures. The potential for "monocultural universalism" (Fowers & Richardson, 1996, p. 609) requires a systematic and comprehensive approach to addressing ethnocentricity in transpersonal psychology. An understanding of the cultural underpinnings of Western academic transpersonal approaches is critical for the field to identify the limits of its applicability to individuals of different cultural backgrounds.

The Real "Fourth Force" of Psychology

Given the lack of a systematic examination of culture in transpersonal psychology, it may be fitting that many believe the mantle of the fourth force of psychology has been conferred to multicultural psychology (e.g., Pedersen, 1990, 1991) instead of transpersonal psychology. Bouchner (1999) defines multicultural psychology as the study of human experience and behavior as it takes place with individuals of different cultural backgrounds. The central assumption of multicultural psychology is that all aspects of human behavior are ultimately learned and expressed in a cultural context. Psychologists need to consider the cultural context in which the behavior is expressed if they intend to validly interpret and comprehensively understand an individual's behavior. As the global context and U.S. demographics reflect a great need for such systematic study, multicultural psychology has grown in prominence, impact, and significance and has established itself as the fourth major paradigm shift in the history of Western psychology. The impact of the multicultural perspective on counseling (Sue, Ivey, & Pedersen, 1996), for example, illustrates the significance this approach has had on psychology. Accordingly, the American Psychological Association (APA) now has nine divisions that focus on issues of diversity (Divisions 9, 17, 27, 35, 36, 44, 45, 48, and 51). In addition, in 2002, the APA issued its Ethical Principles of Psychologists and Code of Conduct containing a General Principle (E) that specifically recommends

> that psychologists: are aware of and respect cultural, individual, and role differences, including those based on age, gender, gender identity, race, ethnicity, culture, national origin, religion, sexual

orientation, disability, language, and socioeconomic status, and consider these factors when working with members of such groups. Psychologists try to eliminate the effect on their work of biases based on those factors, and they do not knowingly participate in or condone activities of others based upon such prejudices. (APA, 2002, p. 1063)

In addition, in 2003, the APA also issued its Guidelines on Multicultural Education, Training, Research, Practice, and Organizational Change for Psychologists, requiring that psychologists possess or acquire the requisite skills, knowledge, and values to competently work in a culturally diverse society. If the many significant changes in ethical principles and guidelines for practice by the nation's major association of professional psychology are any indication of the societal impact and importance of multicultural psychology to the larger field, it is difficult to argue that transpersonal psychology has had a similar revolutionary impact and is deserving of "fourth force" status. It seems ironic that one of the significant areas in which transpersonal psychology is lacking is the one that has surpassed it in societal influence.

Culture, Social Action, and Personal Transformation
Sue and Sue (2003) suggest that the neglect of culture by any branch of psychology has serious socio-political implications and, ultimately, is of ethical concern. The biases and preferences of any culture derive from the societal structures therein, which are developed from a particular set of power relations that privilege some individuals at the expense of others. A transpersonal discipline that is culture bound and culture blind will inescapably perpetuate a social order that maintains disparities in resources and status between communities as well as other inequities. A transpersonal field that is ever conscious of cultural and equity considerations, however, can mitigate against the hidden structures of injustice and marginalization. Transpersonal scholars can benefit from the revolutionary perspectives offered by multicultural psychology and ensure that the field does not unwittingly become complicit to oppressive societal arrangements and serve as a tool of social control.

The transpersonal discipline has a unique opportunity here to serve as a much needed source of liberation and justice in society. The field can adopt a multicultural perspective and examine its role in enculturation and the transmission of divisive ideologies and power relations.

There exists an emergent body of literature that explicitly identifies social justice and societal transformation as desirable outcomes of transpersonal studies. Rothberg and Coder (2013) identify a transpersonal social engagement that they define as a "form of inquiry and action connecting psychological, social, and spiritual dimensions" (p. 626). This scholarship asserts that creating wholeness in society should be both an explicit goal as well as the topic of study for the discipline. Hocoy (2005) makes a direct connection between social action and the transpersonal approach by illustrating the interdependence between personal and social transformation and between individual and collective wholeness; he regards the relationship between social circumstances and individual psychic developmental stages as reciprocal in which they co-create one another.

Hartelius, Caplan, and Rardin (2007) identify a psychology of transformation as one of three essential definitional aspects of transpersonal psychology. They argue that the development of both individuals and communities into "larger potentials"—including ethical thought and right action, service to humanity and compassionate social action—is a critical aspect of the discipline (p. 8). Similar to Hocoy, Coder (2011) emphasizes the interdependent relationship between the interior individuality and sociocultural conditions that promote individual and social transformation. She provides a model for the synergistic relationship between psycho-spiritual maturity and social activism, which she describes as "spiritually advanced social change" through "mystic activism" (p. 156). This emergent emphasis on socially engaged objectives in the discipline seems critical in this time of global political, and social instability.

Cultural differences in spirituality and transpersonal experiences are highlighted in the emergence of the Islamic State (ISIS) and the social difficulties arising from the integration of Middle Eastern and North African migrants into Europe and other Western nations, including the

United States, from which at least one 2016 presidential candidate wanted to bar Muslims from entering. It is also a time in which a professor at Wheaton College, an evangelical Christian institution, was fired for suggesting that Christians and Muslims worship the same god. The intolerance for another's spiritual experience and a different cultural narrative of the transpersonal has risen to a level unseen since the Crusades and Inquisition. Although cultural differences in relationship to the transpersonal have long been known, developments in the first two decades of the 21st century have heightened those differences. The emergence of ISIS seems to be the direct result of historical conflicts that have been cleaved along religious lines, and with new technologies and economic globalization, forces have mobilized around these spiritual differences. Migrations resulting from warfare and economic need have led to cultural conflicts that have religious differences at their core. The forced juxtaposition of different traditions in the experience of the transcendent has led to intolerance and the declaration of one's own tradition as the truth. In this context, a socially engaged transpersonal discipline can have a significant and lasting impact on inter-group relations. The knowledge, practice, and values of the transpersonal approach can be applied to serve community, national, and international needs for inter-group understanding and harmony.

Opportunities and Implications for Transpersonal Psychology

The transpersonal discipline is in a process of developmental evolution and can benefit directly from the insights of multicultural psychology, which because of its relevance and wide applicability seems to have supplanted transpersonal psychology from "fourth force" status. Transpersonal psychology has a unique opportunity in this age of Isis and increasing global religious conflict to apply its theory, research, and practice to make a salutary and lasting impact on world peace. The transpersonal discipline provides unique insight into the interdependence of interior and external realities and the reciprocal influence of individual and collective consciousness, as well as the belief that unconscious attitudes and societal circumstances co-create and reinforce each other. Transpersonal psychology can provide a unique contribution to addressing these real-world issues of today. Three implications for a transpersonal field informed by multicultural perspectives become most salient:

1. A comprehensive review is needed from a multicultural perspective of the validity and applicability of the theoretical constructs, assumptions, and values that undergird the transpersonal field, with an identification of specific modifications and qualifications based on cultural considerations.
2. The transpersonal field would benefit from the inclusion of social engagement and a transformation of the society of which it is a part as explicit disciplinary goals. Wholeness and higher states of being leading to personal and social transformation should be objectives for actualization in addition to being subjects of study for the field.
3. Transpersonal educators, theorists, and practitioners would benefit from: a) coming to terms with their own unconscious or shadow material and examining their own psyches for cultural biases, and b) actively addressing the social inequities in our society that contribute to the cultural biases in our individual psyches through personal transformation and a commitment to social action and advocacy.

References

Acton, D. (2001). The color blind therapist. *Art Therapy, 18,* 109-112.

American Psychological Association (2002). *Guidelines on Multiculural Education, Training, Research, Practice, and Organizational Change for Psychologists.* Washington, DC: American Psychological Association.

Birdsall N., Kelley A., and Sinding S. (2001). *Population matters: Demographic change, economic growth and poverty in the developing world.* Oxford, UK: Oxford University Press.

Bouchner, S. (1999). Cultural diversity within and between societies: Implications for multicultural social systems. In P. Pedersen (Ed.), *Multiculturalism as a fourth force* (pp. 19-36). Philadelphia, PA: Brunner/Mazel.

Coder, K. E. (2011). "Shaking the world awake": An interfaith multiple case study of spiritually advanced social change agents. *Dissertation International, 72* (11), 0669A (UMI #3468891).

Dalal, F. (1988). Jung: A racist. *British Journal of Psychotherapy, 4,* 263–279.

Davis, J. (2003). An overview of transpersonal psychology. *The Humanistic Psychologist, 31* (2–3), 6–21.

Boorstein, S. (1996). Transpersonal techniques and psychotherapy. In B. W. Scotton, A. B. Chinen, J. R. Battista, (Eds.), *Textbook of transpersonal psychiatry and psychology* (pp. 282–292). New York, NY: Basic Books.

Boorstein, S. (1997). *Clinical studies in transpersonal psychotherapy.* Albany, NY: State University of New York Press.

Fowers, B., & Richardson, F. (1996) Why is multiculturalism good? *American Psychologist, 51*(6), 609–621.

Friedman, H. (2009). Xenophilia as a cultural trap: Bridging the gap between transpersonal psychology and religious/spiritual traditions. *International Journal of Transpersonal Studies, 28,* 107–111.

Friedman, H., & Hartelius, G. (Eds.) (2015). *The Wiley-Blackwell handbook of transpersonal psychology.* West Sussex, UK: John Wiley & Sons..

Goldenberg, N. (1976). A feminist critique of Jung. *Signs, 2,* 443–339.

Hartelius, G., Caplan, M., & Rardin, M. A. (2007). Transpersonal psychology: Defining the past, divining the future. *The Humanistic Psychologist, 35*(2), 135–160.

Hastings, A., Balasubrahmanyam, P., Beaird, G., Ferguson, E., Kango, K., & Raley, S. (2001). Annotated bibliography of selected articles on ethnic minorities, cultural perspectives, and transpersonal psychology. *Journal of Transpersonal Psychology, 33*(2), 151–166.

Hocoy, D. (2002). Cross-cultural issues in art therapy. *Journal of the American Art Therapy Association, 19,* 141–145.

Hocoy, D. (2005). Art therapy and social action: A transpersonal framework. *Journal of the American Art Therapy Association, 22,* 7–16.

Jung, C.G. (1968). Psychology and alchemy. *Collected works of C.G. Jung* (Vol. 12). Princeton, NJ: Princeton University Press. (Original work published 1953)

Jung, C.G. (1980) The symbolic life: Miscellaneous writings. *Collected works of C.G. Jung* (Vol. 18). London: Routledge. (Original work published 1948)

Louchakova, O., & Lucas, M. (2007). Transpersonal self as a clinical category: Reflections on culture, gender, and phenomenology. *Journal of Transpersonal Psychology, 39,* 111–136.

McDermott, R. (2008). Reflections on the field. *Anthropology and Education, 39,* 117-126.

Myers, L. (1985). Transpersonal psychology: The role of the Afrocentric paradigm. *Journal of Black Psychology, 12,* 31–42.

Pederson, (1990). The multicultural perspective as a fourth force in counseling. *Journal of Mental Health Counseling, 12,* 93–95.

Pederson, (1991). Introduction to the special issue on multiculturalism as fourth force in counseling. *Journal of Counseling and Development, 70*, 4.

Rosenzweig, M. R. (1992). Psychological science around the world. *American Psychologist, 47*, 718–722.

Rothberg, D., & Coder, K. E. (2013). Widening circles: The emergence of transpersonal social engagement. In H. L. Friedman & G. Hartelius (Eds.), *The Wiley-Blackwell handbook of transpersonal psychology* (pp. 626–639). West Sussex, UK: John Wiley & Sons.

Scotton, B., Chinen, A., & Battista, J. (2009). *Textbook of transpersonal psychiatry and psychology*. New York, NY: Basic Books.

Steiner, R. (1990). *Vor dem tore der theosophie (Before the gates of theosophy)*. Stuttgart: Taschenbuch Publishers. (Original work published 1906)

Steiner, R. (1997). *An outline of esoteric science*. New York, NY: Anthroposophic Press. (Original work published 1910)

Stevens, A. (1990). *On Jung*. Princeton, NJ: Princeton University Press.

Sue, D.W., Ivey, A.E., & Pedersen, P.B. (1996). *A theory of multicultural counseling and therapy*. Pacific Grove, CA: Brooks/Cole.

Sue, D. W., & Sue, D. (2003). *Counseling the culturally diverse: Theory and practice* (4th ed.). New York, NY: J. Wiley.

Tart, C. T. (1975). *Transpersonal psychologies*. Oxford, UK: Harper & Row.

Chapter 3
Toward a Transpersonal Structure of the Psyche

Carla J. Clements
Uri Talmor

In this chapter, we offer a structural description of the human psyche based on a modified version of Wilber's Great Nest of Being (2000) that incorporates transpersonal elements as aspects of the personality; thus, it "transcends and includes" previous descriptions (p. 8). The proposed representation is intended to add to and integrate other descriptions of the structure of personality, as well as provide clinical relevance as a transpersonal model of psyche. We recognize that this model is presented as a universal model for being human that may not, in fact, represent many cultural perspectives, conceptualizations of what it is to be human, or how the spiritual is experienced. The model will likely need to be adjusted and reconsidered when working with people of non-U.S., Caucasian, English-speaking, Judeo-Christian cultures. We support clinical collaboration in the framing of client concerns to include each person's own worldview and spiritual realities. We also intend that it build on the tradition of Western psychological models of psyche and be useful in some circumstances for some clients as a model of some human experience.

Many psychological theorists have proposed analyses of the human psyche. The most well known perhaps are Freud's distinctions between the id, ego, and superego. These three aspects of personality might be said to represent different kinds of consciousness within the personal self, each holding the different needs and motivations that are expressed by that part of the personality (Mitchell, 1995). From the psychoanalytic perspective, *primary process* is the unconscious id or a libidinal driven, irrational, dream-like state unable to defer pleasure, while *secondary process* contains ego functions including rationality, reality checking, and impulse control. The superego represents what some have dubbed the conscience and holds moral and ethical values as well as other functions (Ellman, 2010). C.G. Jung and Assagioli developed theories of the personality that include transpersonal elements. Two archetypes within the collective unconscious, the Self and the mandala, were named by Jung (1967). The "Higher Self" (Assagioli, 1965), or what Whitmont (1969) and others have simply called the Self, has also been included in some models. Other writers and clinicians have also identified various parts of the human psyche that have generally been consistent with the structures identified in the Great Nest of Being including body, mind, soul, and spirit (Wilber, 2000).

In addition, a variety of exceptional states have been identified by researchers. For example, James (1958) named some of them in *The Varieties of Religious Experience*, Maslow (1964/1970) identified others in *Religions, Values, and Peak Experiences*, and Jung (1964) named yet others in *Man and His Symbols*. Previous structural explanations of psychic functioning have not typically attempted to account for what are often identified as altered states of consciousness, probably because they are states, not structures. The proposed transpersonal analysis is designed to bring more of our human self-capacities together, including providing an explanation of how transpersonal and exceptional states occur and describing a whole human being more completely.

Similar to Wilber's (1977/1993) conception of the spectrum of consciousness, this transpersonal integration of psyche is related to many fields of psychology as well as many mental health models and psychotherapeutic interventions in our ever-expanding field. The model also builds on Wilber's (2000) concept of *holon* that in this structural analysis is the word for each of the circles in the following figures. Unlike the Great Nest of Being model (2000), the holons do not represent a hierarchy of lower to higher levels of consciousness. Instead, as with

Freud's model (Mitchell, 1995), the proposed holons represent the layers or aspects of a personal self with differing kinds of consciousness holding various capacities, needs, and motivations. In addition, as in Assagioli's (1965) egg diagram model (which can be accessed at www.sythesiscenter.org/articles/0101.pdf), the different kinds of consciousness or parts of the personal self each have various degrees of capacity to relate to, balance with, and integrate other parts, which sometimes are in wounded or fragmented states.

In this chapter, each holon in the proposed transpersonal structure of psyche is described, as well as how the holons function in healthy and less healthy states. We discuss the parts and their capacities by summarizing the research of many clinicians and authors, including Freud (1989); Jung's (1997) Active Imagination; Perls' (1973) Gestalt Therapy; Assagioli's (1965) Psychosynthesis; Schwartz's (1995) Internal Family Systems; and our own clinical experience. Finally, this structure of psyche is related to the therapeutic process from an expanded, transpersonal perspective. Clinicians may use this transpersonal depiction to conceptualize client concerns when culturally appropriate and also to create effective and comprehensive plans for therapeutic intervention.

Constructing the Model

We begin with a simplified version of the Great Nest of Being model that includes four key holons: body, mind, soul, and spirit (Wilber, 2000, p. 6; see Figure 1). Traditionally, the Great Chain of Being was the term used to refer to a strict, religious hierarchical structure of all matter and life, believed to have been decreed by God. The chain starts from God and progresses downward to angels, demons (fallen/renegade angels), stars, moon, kings, princes, nobles, commoners, wild animals, domesticated animals, trees, other plants, precious stones, precious metals, and other minerals. This concept was promoted from Plato and Aristotle to Plotinus to Aurobindo and others and later reviewed by Smith (1976) in *Forgotten Truth: The Common Vision of the World's Religions*. Its central claim, which is known as the perennial philosophy, is that in virtually all of the world's wisdom traditions reality manifests in a hierarchy of levels or dimensions from the lowest to the highest, and all matter must develop and evolve through these levels. The lowest level is usually represented as the earth or body (or sometimes hell), rising to the human level and then to the heavenly level (or the levels of body, mind and spirit), The highest rung is the transcendent or spirit level, which is both the highest goal of development and the ground of all that is (Wilber, 1977).

Wilber (2000) described the levels in his modified version of the Chain of Being as a great "nested holarchy" that opens from the center, with each successive holon containing all those that came before (p.7). The center holon reflects the body/physical level of consciousness (studied by biologists) with the next holons the mind level (studied by psychologists) and the soul level (studied by theologians). The outer holon reflects the spirit level (the layer represented by mysticism) (p. 6). In this conception, human beings experience all of these levels, but spiritual evolution is conceived of as a progressive ascension through successive rungs or stages from inanimate matter to a future state of Divine Consciousness. Each stage or nest incorporates all of the preceding stages reflecting the "transcends and includes" concept (p. 8).

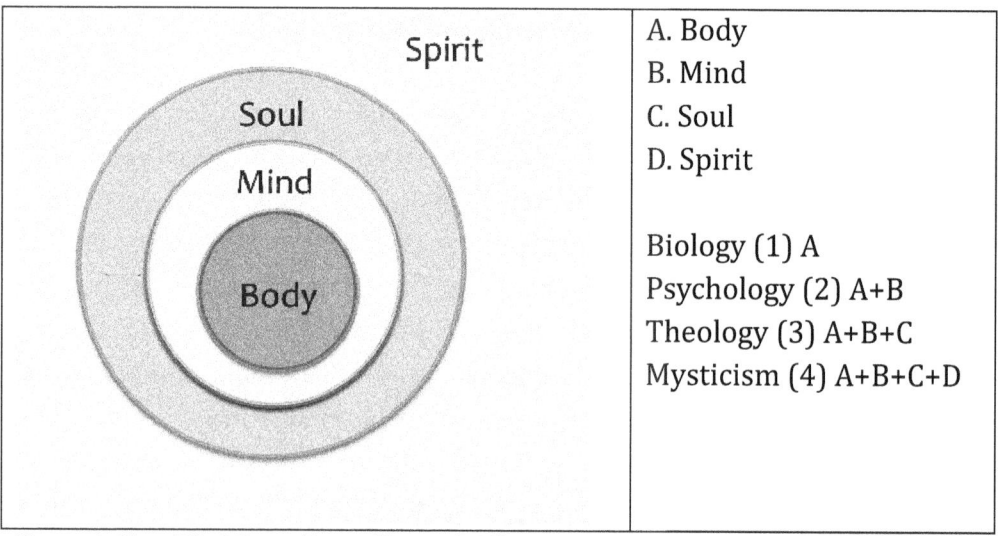

Spirit / Soul / Mind / Body (nested circles)	A. Body B. Mind C. Soul D. Spirit Biology (1) A Psychology (2) A+B Theology (3) A+B+C Mysticism (4) A+B+C+D

Figure 1: Simplified Great Nest of Being (Wilber, 2000, p.6)

3. Toward a Transpersonal Structure of the Psyche

The transpersonal structure we are proposing also consists of holons, named from innermost to outmost circles in the proposed transpersonal diagram: soul-spirit, emotional body, physical body, mental body, intellectual body, and Spirit-soul. Thus, we are dividing Wilber's (2000) body holon into the physical and emotional bodies, and we are dividing his mind holon into the mental and intellectual bodies. (See Figure 2.)

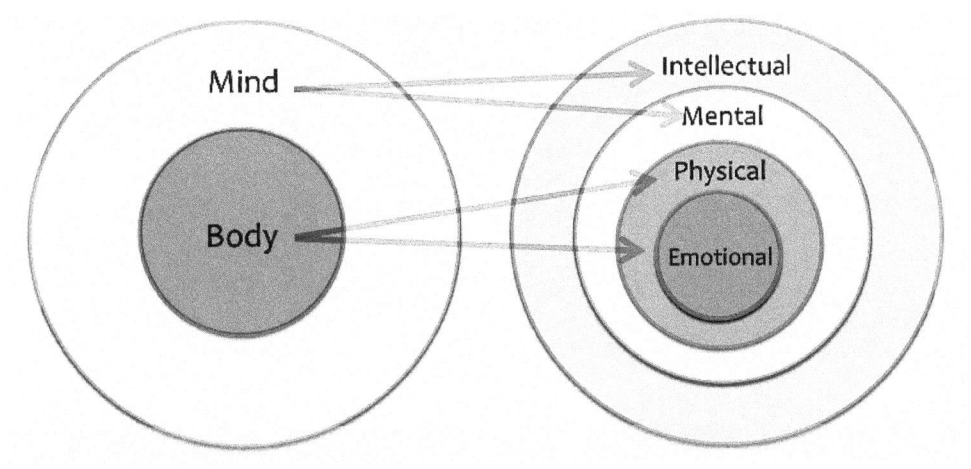

Figure 2: Differentiating the Body and Mind Holons from the Spectrum of Consciousness Model into the Emotional Body, Physical Body, Mental Body and Intellectual Body for the Transpersonal Model.

In the outermost layer and outside the personal levels of the holons, Spirit-soul replaces Wilber's "Spirit" and "Soul" holons. By using the terms soul-spirit and Spirit-soul to represent the innermost and outermost levels of transpersonal experience, respectively, a loop is represented for the personal self's ability to move from dual (soul-spirit) to non-dual (Spirit-soul) experiences and back again—or in theistic-relational frameworks, both away from (soul-spirit) and towards (Spirit-soul) God/Source/All-That-Is (see Figure 3). From now on, we use Source to mean all or any of these concepts. Connections between these two bodies account in part for some exceptional and transpersonal experiences.

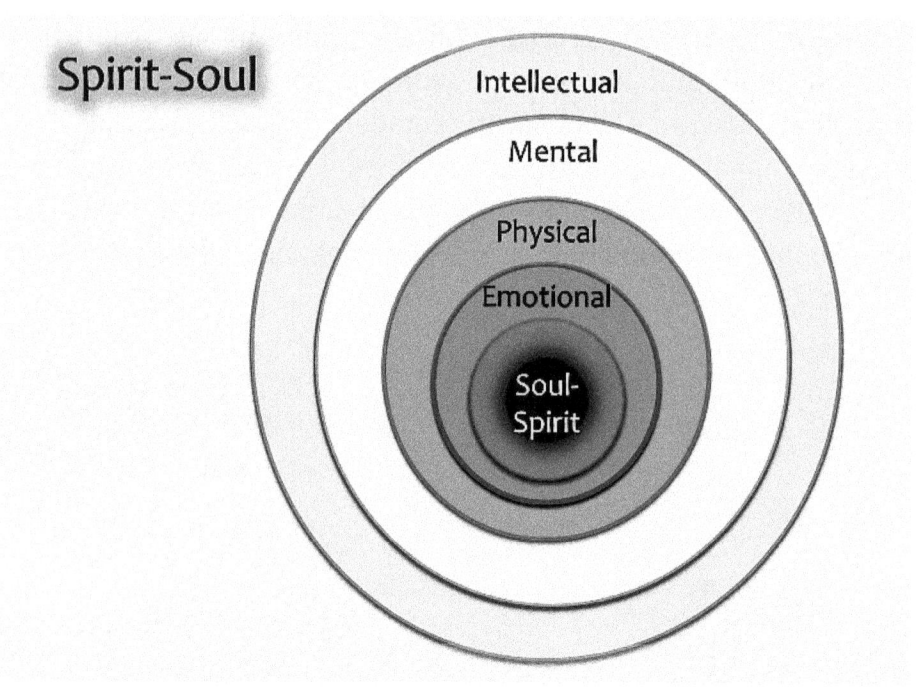

Figure 3: Proposed Transpersonal Structure of Psyche

As can be seen in various models of the psyche, such as the Individuated Self in Jung's work (Whitmont, 1969) or the Higher Self in Assagioli's (1965), many psychological models offer a vision of a healed or healthy version of self. In the proposed transpersonal model, we also use the term Higher Self to represent the state when the intellectual, mental, emotional, and physical bodies are functioning as an integrated whole. This Higher Self then becomes the vehicle through which one's soul-spirit emanates. This state reflects a stronger connection with the universal Spirit-soul and the softened boundaries of the personal self's parts that are evidenced in higher stages of spiritual development (see Figure 4) and during exceptional and transpersonal experiences (Maslow, 1964/1970; Wilber, 2001).

In psychosynthesis terminology, the process of integrating one's respective bodies is a process of "personal psychosynthesis" (Assagioli, 1965, p. 55). Once personality synthesis occurs, the psyche organically enters into the next four-stage "process of transmutation" or "spiritual psychosynthesis" in which one's personality wraps around, integrates and brings through a more transpersonal consciousness (pp. 56–57).

3. Toward a Transpersonal Structure of the Psyche 51

Assagioli notes that the process that Jung calls individuation is designed to achieve the same self-realized state as Assagioli's spiritual psychosynthesis that develops the Higher Self.

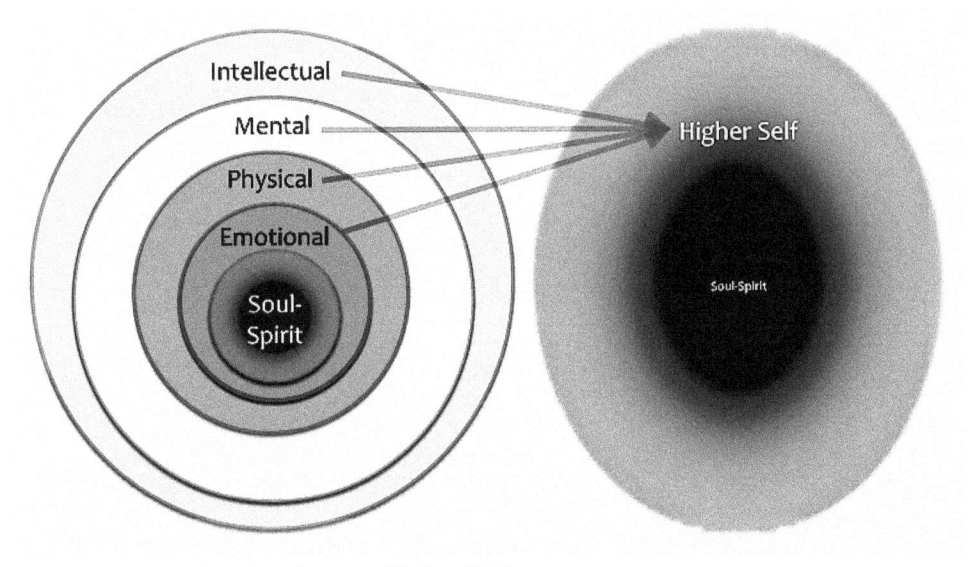

Figure 4: Personality Synthesis to Higher Self

Notice in the following charts that the transpersonal structure's differentiation of intellectual body, mental body, emotional body, and physical body accounts for the parts of self in the descriptions of psyche previously mentioned in other theoretical areas of psychology (see Table 1). Table 2 begins to differentiate the fields of psychology and the interventions that may be most therapeutically appropriate for the various bodies. Placements of some constructs into the chart are at times necessarily imprecise, especially the interventions, as many of these impact more than one body of self. We assigned them a place in the chart according to the part of self that the technique seems designed to impact first, recognizing that other self-bodies will also be affected as contact is made with the client. We will refer to these overlapping models and interventions in the holon descriptions below.

Transpersonal Structures	Freud's Structures	Jung's Structures	Assagioli's Structures	Wilber's Great Nest of Being (order changed)
Spirit-soul		Collective Unconscious	Collective Unconscious	Spirit
Higher Self		Individuated Self	Higher Self	
Intellectual Body	Super Ego	Persona		Mind
Mental Body (Ego or "I")	Ego	Ego	Conscious Self or "I"	
Physical Body (defensive structures)	Id	Shadow, Individual "unconscious complexes"	Lower and Middle Unconscious	Body
Emotional Body (unresolved feelings)				
(Core) Soul-Spirit		Self		Soul

Table 1. The Transpersonal Structures of Psyche Compared with Freud's, Jung's and Assagioli's.

Describing the Holons

The transpersonal structure of psyche presented here is not a cosmological or teleological representation; it is instead intended to be a model representing the personal self from a transpersonal perspective for use by psychotherapists and others working with clinical issues.

In this section of the chapter, all of the holons in the transpersonal structure of psyche will be described, beginning with the transpersonal holons, soul-spirit and Spirit-soul, which are qualitatively different from the self-body holons (emotional, physical, mental, and intellectual). Each body's states of consciousness and contributions to the formation of the whole person as a seemingly integrated consciousness are discussed, and a clinical example shows how each self-body holon reflects a client's concerns.

3. Toward a Transpersonal Structure of the Psyche

Transpersonal Psyche Aspect	Psychology Fields Emphasizing	Psychotherapeutic Model or Interventions (designed to impact)
Higher Self- (connection to Spirit-soul)	Humanistic and Transpersonal Psychologies	Soul Retrieval, Spiritual Psychosynthesis, Core Energetics, Diamond Heart approach, Constellation therapy
Intellectual Body	Narrative and Existential Psychologies	Narrative therapies, Logotherapy, Existential therapies
Mental Body (Ego or "I")	Cognitive Behavioral Psychologies	Cognitive Behavioral Therapy, Dialectical Behavioral Therapy, Acceptance and Commitment Therapy, Mindfulness therapies, Hypnosis, Guided Imagery, Loving What Is, Transactional Analysis
Physical Body	Behavioral Psychologies, Neurobiological-based approaches, Somatic Psychologies	Bioenergetics, Reichian therapies, Focusing, Somatic Experiencing (SE), Sensory-motor Integration, Hakomi, Brainspotting, EMDR, Neuromapping therapies, Wilderness therapies
Emotional Body	Psychoanalytic and Psychodynamic Psychologies, Person-Centered and Humanistic Psychologies, Gestalt	Psychoanalysis, Internal Family Systems (IFS), Voice Dialogue, Ego State Therapy, Object Relations, Gestalt, Inner-child work, Interpersonal Neurobiology
Soul-Spirit (Core)	Jungian Analytic Psychology, Psychosynthesis, Transpersonal Psychologies, Energy therapies	Psychosynthesis, Yoga therapies, Jungian Active Imagination and other symbolic therapies (dream analysis, sand play), Art therapies, Nature therapies, Energy therapies

Table 2. Fields of Psychology and Interventions Related to Each Transpersonal Structure

The Transpersonal Holons

There are two holons representing transpersonal aspects of experience in this transpersonal structure of psyche: the soul-spirit and the Spirit-soul. The soul-spirit holon represents the core of the person, a client's innermost center. In many Western spiritual traditions, this would simply be called the client's "soul." As described in Pierrakos' (1987)

Core Energy model, the spiritual energy of the person is the innermost core of the person's self (pp. 21–22). In a healthy person, the soul-spirit body is easily accessed and provides that person with a sense of strength, light, and connection with themselves and the world. Like an internal lighthouse, this part of the self directs the life energy toward its goals and life mission and is an ongoing source of guidance and strength. This internal personal soul-spirit body is intricately connected to the outer Spirit-soul energies and receives its sustenance from this Source-of-All-That-Is.

In healthy people, the body and mind boundaries are flexible and translucent enough to be permeated by the soul-spirit energy. In less healthy people, the soul-spirit holon is not visible or accessible to either the person themselves or to others in their world, even though it is always present. The soul-spirit holon does not become wounded or unhealthy, rather it is merely inaccessible, covered by wounds or destructive beliefs held by the other self-body parts or suppressed from conscious awareness. In these circumstances it is unable to guide, provide light, or strength (Pierrakos, 1987). This occurs when the person's intellectual and mental bodies are so trapped by consensus reality (Tart, 1987) and/or their physical and emotional bodies are so distorted by personal wounds that the soul-spirit is no longer available or accessible to—let alone, central to—that person's life. Restoring the soul-spirit holon is thus the primary therapeutic concern for a person whose life has become fundamentally unbalanced. Usually however, there are other more immediate and difficult issues that require resolution, so in therapy, it sometimes takes time and effort to clear away enough of the obfuscating layers of the other bodies to reestablish contact with the soul-spirit holon.

The Spirit-soul is the other transpersonal aspect of the model, permeating all of the area in and outside the personal self-body holons. We use this term to represent the spiritual consciousness that is continually available if we desire to and are able to access it because it is the fabric from which everything is woven (Assagioli, 1965; Pierrakos, 1987). This infinite holon represents the Source energies, the creative life force or consciousness surrounding us all the time as well as the

Source energy for every individual soul-spirit. It also represents the vast unconsciousness of being human in a largely inexplicable universe. The Collective Unconscious and archetypes also operate from this realm; however, not all of these are transpersonal elements even though they are collective and unconscious as Jung (1964) described.

The Spirit-soul is in the outer layer or *beyond the personal* layers of the psyche. It represents the Source of all that is—that indescribable, incomprehensible, ineffable consciousness beyond our personal selves. In this transpersonal structure, when there is coherence and integration with all parts of the self in connection and communication, the Higher Self emerges. When all the self-bodies are integrated and functioning together, contact with the Spirit-soul is continuous. This represents an experience of oneness, or non-duality, with our highest capacities.

When the soul-spirit is touched by a caring, loving presence (whether by another human being, nature, or by Source energies), it becomes reconnected with and reenergized by the external Spirit-soul. This encounter, regardless of how brief, may bring about profound change (e.g. Doblin, 1991). Touching the core occurs regularly for healthy people, which stimulates and enlivens it, making it more accessible and more relevant in the person's life. A single encounter with the Spirit-soul through a peak or mystical experience can transform even the most difficult of circumstances (Maslow, 1964/1970). Like a traumatic experience is able to be a sort of one-trial-learning and change one's life dramatically, often in an unhealthy way, a soul-spirit encounter that reconnects the personal soul with Spirit-soul or Source energies can also in one trial transform one's being, often in a healthy way.

The Self-Body Holons

The emotional body holon. The holon adjacent to the soul-spirit body in this model is the emotional body. In a healthy person, emotions are part of the overall intelligence of the being and flow of life. Without this natural ebb and flow, the overall health and well-being of the person is severely limited.

Everyday feelings in healthy people come and go with simple organismic validation, acceptance, and appropriate response, with only a momentary sense of pleasure or pain to remind the person of their ongoing relationship with life, needs, and experiences. Usually resolution occurs with an action or movement, an appropriate response, usually ending with a moment of relief and quiet before the next reaction emerges. Often there is no reaction even registered within the self-bodies in response to environmental cues and organismic stimulation. In health there is a sense of fluidity and ease within the self, a generally open and optimistic perspective, an ongoing ability to relate to and connect frequently with self, others, and the environment, as well as a seamless reaching out to meet one's needs or turning away from unwanted encounters (Clements, 2016).

When emotions are invalidated and/or repressed, they can become stuck and stifled, leading to out-of-proportion reactions to related future events. Strong emotional responses to unusually strong stimuli can be suppressed and lead to unresolved emotions for many years, as in chronic cases of PTSD (Levine, 1997). Unexpressed emotion may remain charged in one's nervous system and contribute to later physical disease and illness (Lowen, 1975; Maté, 2003). Emotions can also warn us that something is wrong within the alignment of our self-bodies.

Emotional blocks are often related to early and ongoing developmental wounds (Schwartz, 1995). When the person does not resolve emotional energy, emotional wounds and the unresolved feelings that are left over result in a burdened, repressed, and often "exiled" emotional body (p. 47). The emotional body can become a pressure cooker, doing its best not to allow emotions to leak out, but at times hijacking the person with extreme, built-up emotions collected over many situations in which the initial emotion was not resolved. When the emotional body becomes burdened with emotional wounds or exiled from one's consciousness, the person loses the ongoing relationship with their other self-bodies, soul-spirit body, other people, the environment, and access to Source energies.

When the defenses that are keeping emotions from being expressed are softened, deep emotional wounds may be fully expressed and resolved, allowing the soul-spirit core to be accessed more readily.

Emotional bodies access memories that have significant emotional charge; these are sometimes identified in the literature as implicit, eidetic, or event memories (e.g. Ogden, Minton, & Pain, 2006). Such memories are held at the experiential level and can reappear when triggered, as in flashbacks. These memories cannot be transferred to the semantic memory without providing a necessary linguistic description of the experience. As van der Kolk (1996) described them, "Traumatic memories are timeless and ego-alien" (p. 295). Once words are assigned, the memory is more likely to be retained in the language of the experience rather than in its felt or emotional sensations. This allows the memory to reside in the past where it belongs, rather than potentially triggering flashbacks in the present.

In therapeutic encounters, when a deep emotional block is released and the client is able to fully be with and express the emotional wound, therapeutic contact with the client can be made that is profoundly healing (e.g. Herman, 1997). The immediate softening of the blockage in the emotional body allows the soul-spirit to reconnect, perhaps for the first in a very long time, with self and other. This can also allow a reconnection with the Spirit-soul, with other people, and with the environment. This expansive transpersonal experience may be personally significant, and its effects may be relatively long lasting (Doblin, 1991). Sometimes when a client finally breaks through such a block, the sensation of liberation and the burst of the life force that results can lead to a permanent change in direction and focus. Often an experience of emotional freedom can start the movement back toward health and vitality, even if the catalyst for the shift is not readily apparent (Assagioli, 1965; Pierrakos, 1987).

When working with any of these bodies clinically, there are a number of ways they can be accessed and integrated. With Breuer and later Freud's free association (Breuer & Freud, 2000), both Breuer and Freud observed this as their patients shifted in and out of various parts. Moreno (1975) and many others (e.g. Assagioli, 1965) pointed out that all human beings have parts (or bodies of selves as identified here); infrequently they are disidentifed with the conscious self or "I" to the degree that they are considered problematic. Jung (1997) developed a process called *active imagination*, where one focuses within the psyche to create inner dialogues. Conversations between different parts of selves are also used in Assagioli's (1965) Psychosynthesis, Gendlin's (1978) Focusing, Stone and Stone's (1998) Voice Dialogue, and Schwartz's (1995) Internal Family Systems and by others to bring an unconscious or subconscious part to the surface that needs to be integrated into the holistic framework of self. Perls popularized a form of parts work using the empty-chair dialogue in Gestalt therapy (Woldt & Toman, 2005).

In Freud's (1989), Jung's (Whitmont, 1969), and Assagioli's (1965) structural descriptions, the emotional body is represented by the id, shadow unconscious, and lower unconscious, respectively. In Internal Family Systems (IFS), a wounded part that has split off from the emotional body is called an exile (Schwartz, 1995, p. 47). An exile is a repressed, undigested feeling or experience that is perceived as too overwhelming to bear or which has no available solution. In core energetics, these are called "primal negative feelings" (Pierrakos, 1987, p. 22). In bioenergetics, this part is simply called the "emotional layer" (Lowen, 1975, p. 119). In Gestalt therapy as constructed by Perls (1973), the emotional body represents the organismic needs and is often part of the underdog (Beisser, 1970).

Successful interventions for the emotional body are resources that focus on supporting people in safely accessing unresolved emotions and memories, expressing or experiencing them fully, bringing them to closure, and assimilating whatever wisdom, meaning, and maturity has been earned from these experiences. As Hoffman, Vallejos, Cleare-Hoffman, and Rubin (2015) point out, "Emotion is central to all approaches to psychotherapy. A primary reason most individuals enter therapy is to deal with emotional struggles" (p.14). While all therapies seek to resolve the concerns of the emotional body, different therapies access them from different layers of the self-bodies.

Emotional body example. Our clinical example is an adult who has significant anxiety, is highly self-critical, and engages in food restriction and cutting. In this example, the person's anxiety is held in the emotional body. A treatment goal is for the client to stop avoiding the anxiety and actually feel it fully, so we support our client to slow down and focus on the anxiety. The client may realize that the anxiety has been in their body for a long time. We ask how long, and the client says it has been there since they were five years old. A few moments staying connected to this anxiety conjures up a memory of their parents divorcing. The client realizes the part of self that was deeply wounded through the divorce has been exiled for decades within their psyche, but the emotional anxiety and stress continue to haunt them to the present day.

The physical body holon. In the transpersonal structure, the physical body holon is not just the actual physical body; it is also part of one's consciousness. It has as distinctive a temperament as any of the other holons. The physical self-body holon in this model represents the consciousness of the body as well as the defensive structures created by painful encounters (Lowen, 1975). The physical body has its own memory system, sometimes called cellular, implicit, kinesthetic, or procedural memory. The reality that bodies continue to hold unresolved life experiences has been a topic of much discussion and research these past three decades, as can be seen in the abundant resources produced by the somatic field (e.g. Caldwell, 1997; Herman, 1997; Levine, 1997; Ogden, Minton, & Pain, 2006; Rothschild, 2000; van der Kolk, 2014).

In addition to its other tasks, the physical body in its natural, regulated state has a core need to integrate or express emotions as well as a need to move and respond to environmental cues. The physical body is evidence of our life's encounter on Earth. A healthy body is free to move and express itself in meeting needs and expressing core creative and life-promoting functions (Lowen, 1975). It is agile, flexible, and free of structures that limit its experience or its ability to meet its needs. In a healthy person, the body and emotions are responsive, flexible, and resilient (Clements, 2016). Psychosomatic unity is a fundamental tenet in the holistic, transpersonal perspective of human body-mind (Hartelius, Rothe, & Roy, 2013).

Reich's (1933/1949) concept of characterological defensive structures provides a description of unhealthy or imbalanced physical body holons. In Reich's model the physical body contracts to defend against the experience and expression of difficult or painful emotional experiences. If this becomes a chronic reaction to emotional pain, it is reflected in chronically contracted musculature, which Reich called "body armor" (e.g. Lowen, 1975, p.13). Reich demonstrated that emotional wounds were contained and retained in the physical body and also that they can be treated with somatic therapeutic interventions such as bioienergetics (Lowen, 1975). Essentially, the energetic charge of the contraction must be released in order for healing to occur. When the contraction is resolved, the natural flow of the body returns, as does appropriate adaptation and responsiveness to the dynamic flow of stimuli (Levine, 1997). Both the emotional and physical self-bodies then return to their more natural state of fluid adaptability, which allows regular and sustained access to the core soul-spirit's balanced emotional guidance as well as to the other self-bodies, the environment, and the Spirit-soul.

Other primarily psychotherapeutic models, such as Internal Family Systems, (Schwartz, 1995) and Gestalt therapy (Perls, 1973), also use interventions designed to release emotional material as a means to free both emotions and the physical body. In Internal Family Systems, the physical parts of self are called "firefighters" (Schwartz, 1995, pp. 50–52). Firefighters will do whatever is necessary to regulate overwhelming emotions. This can be with in-the-moment fight-flight-freeze responses from our sympathetic nervous systems, through dorsal vagal hijacking (Porges, 2011) when threatening events occur, or with addictive behaviors that work to regulate both acute and chronic states of disregulation (Maté, 2010).

Gestalt uses empty-chair and other interventions designed to access the person's psyche from the present moment, which invites the parts that are suffering or contracted to express themselves (Perls, 1973). Somatic therapies have focused on accessing the physical body as a strategy to release what is negatively affecting the person through, on, or with the body as the primary point of access.

For Freud (1989), Jung (Jacobi, 1973), and Assagioli (1965), this holon would be part of the id, shadow unconscious, and lower unconscious, respectively, in their unintegrated states, along with the emotional body holon. Gestalt (Beisser, 1970) also does not differentiate between the two, with the physical body holon (or emotional body) usually playing the underdog role when integrating via empty-chair dialogues.

Physical body example. As a pre-teenager, our client learned to cope with his incessant stress and anxiety by restricting food. We ask him to focus on the desire to restrict food in his current experience, and he realizes these behaviors started at age 11. Our client mentally envisions himself as an 11-year-old who learned and then practiced restriction, and he can now see how this part split off. A few years later, the client discovered subtle self-harm behaviors, which eventually developed into cutting. The cutting part is 14 years old when the client visualizes it. As this client gets to know these parts better, the client comes to appreciate the parts' intentions to support emotional regulation. The client can sense in his adult body how his anxiety would have been much worse without these behaviors, and he can begin to soften his judgments about these accommodations made in what were for him as a child impossible circumstances.

The mental body holon. In the transpersonal structure of the psyche, the mental self-body holon is a person's ego self. It is accessed through language and reveals what is contained in the person's semantic memory. A healthy ego is necessary for the full functioning of the healthy person. Most people develop the ego—sense of self, identity and functioning—as they move through the developmental processes of infancy and childhood and emerge with a good enough sense of ego strength as an adult to live their lives successfully and be productive members of their families and society (e.g. Kernberg, 1995).

When people are functional, their ego or self-identity is like a completed concatenation of smaller circular narratives describing their lives. Someone who has a well-enough formed ego can respond to a question about themselves with an integrated narrative or story that is relevant. This short response could be expanded indefinitely, as the story is enlarged to include various other related stories. Imagine this ego holon as a circle of circular stories, each little circle connected like links in a chain in the larger ego circle representing the semantic memories and stories that hold us together and remind us of who we are. This is the self-body part that we go to sleep with and wake up with each morning; it is our known self.

A healthy ego does not require great effort or study to maintain. It is a natural outgrowth of adequate, satisfactory adjustment to one's own experience. When it functions well, it is a source of pleasure with which to engage the environment in a multitude of ways. In health the ego is adaptive, fluid, and creatively responds to the needs and goals of the self. It has a direct channel to the soul-spirit core and reaches for regular sustenance with the Spirit-soul, with its environment, and with others. The mental body simply wants to feel safe and balanced, and if the emotional and physical bodies are balanced, it is free to provide a witnessing container that harmoniously navigates one's life (e.g. Assagioli, 1965).

An unhealthy ego has crimps in the links of chain, or holes and gaps between links. The story of one's life is not a seamless structure of connected memories and moments; instead it is jumbled, chaotic and confused. Reactions to new stimuli are out of proportion to events as a new response tries to squeeze through old, overgrown, untended life places. Links become connected in the wrong places, creating paths from the chain that are hard to retrace. The person's life story often doesn't make sense when it is told. The emotion that should be logically connected to the story is often illogically misplaced. Defensive structures occlude understanding and insight. Connection with others is blunted and strained (Lowen, 1975; Schwartz, 1995).

Often a therapeutic connection rebuilds the shattered ego, mainly because the therapeutic connection offers a broader surrogate container for the emotional body to process its emotions, and for the physical body to process its stress. As a parent would tend to the everyday needs and well-being of a child and provide necessary resources for the child to function adequately in the world, the therapist teaches the mental-body ego to manage its experience and its environment, mainly by encouraging the mental body to have more acceptance toward emotional and physical stress sensations and to describe its experience and build the stories of its life. Connection and communication with another person helps to rebuild the links, restructure the overall sense of the life story, and reconnect emotion with its inspiration. As a person begins to name, reorganize, and understand their own experience, previous experiences can take their rightful place in the past, rather than being part of a jumbled present. Siegel and Hartzell (2013) describe this process as making the implicit (emotional and physical body memories), explicit (mental body memories) (p. 23).

For Freud (1989) and Jung (Whitmont, 1969, p. 232), the mental body is represented by the term ego, and for Assagioli (1965) it is referred to as the field of consciousness or "I" (p. 18). In Gestalt, the mental body is part of what shows up as the "top dog" (Beisser, 1970), and in IFS it shows up as one or more "managers" (Schwartz, 1995, pp. 48–50).

Mental body example. For our example client, as for many clients, the salient aspect of the mental body that is in the foreground of consciousness is an inner critic, or judge, with perfectionist tendencies. The judge has a lot of power in most people and so it is often the first part to show up in therapy. As counselors, our overarching goal is to help the client relate differently with the parts of themselves that they have split off or have made into their shadow. In the emotional body example above, as is often the case, this client's inner critic actually exacerbated the client's anxiety, even though he was trying to obfuscate the underlying anxiety from a five-year-old's memory. On a conscious level, all the inner critic knows is that it needs to *do better*. The client was encouraged to acknowledge his need for gaining acceptance from others, to feel good enough, and to recognize that his five-year-old part fundamentally needed to feel safe, loved, and accepted. When the client began to understand this, he was able to soften and support this young, vulnerable part.

The intellectual body holon. The intellectual body in the proposed transpersonal model represents the part of the self-structures that include the higher cognitive functions, such as our ability for metacognition, learning advanced mathematics, or theorizing about our lives. In a healthy person, the intellectual body is open and curious. Learning is joyful and continuous when in a balanced state.

When the other bodies are imbalanced, this ripples through to create an imbalanced intellectual body. If extreme emotions are not processed in the emotional body, the physical body tries to self-soothe with addictive behaviors, and the mental body then tries to control and/or suppress the overwhelming emotions, sensations, and judgments. Meanwhile, the intellectual body creates explanations and structures in an attempt to justify and minimize the internal chaos, often in the hope that no one else will notice and recognize that it is not as organized and functional as it should be. Compare this intellectual body burdened by dogma to an intellectual body integrated with balanced mental, emotional, and physical bodies. The latter intellectual body is free to stay curious and open instead of creating stories and worldviews to help explain and manage inner turmoil.

Unfortunately, the beliefs and decisions intellectual bodies create form perceptual filters that make people more likely to behave in ways that increase the turmoil that the intellectual and mental bodies try to avoid. Functionally, the intellectual body usually operates in the background, much like an operating system. The mental body acts as the psyche's manager, and the intellect acts as the psyche's CEO or board of directors—guiding and directing behind the scenes in the form of core beliefs and ideas that perhaps may not be useful at any given moment but are applicable in other situations. It has been well demonstrated that rigid beliefs, ideas, and dogma have tremendous power to affect our functioning and well-being, both positively and negatively (Lipton, 2015), and when the intellectual body is poorly integrated, it can be a powerful destructive force.

The intellect is also responsible for trying to force the self into a mold of what the person should be. This part would be known as the superego in Freud's model (1989), persona in Jung's (Whitmont, 1969, pp. 156–159), and the false self in Gestalt (Perls, 1973). It holds the known ethics, values structure, and moral sense and tries to force the unruly self to behave the way it believes it should. If the intellectual body is unbalanced or misdirected, ideas and patterns often end up controlling the functioning of a person, rather than the core energy serving as the juice or responses being appropriate to the event that stimulated them. Behaviors incongruent with a person's intentions may then erupt from the person's unconscious, such as from the body's defensive structures, the emotional self-body, or even the core self-spirit (Pierrakos, 1987). When developmental accommodations themselves come to be restrictive and retard growth, the core soul-spirit may step in to help by providing a symptom that needs attention. As with the emotional body, it is often helpful to assign each of the various self-bodies a part of the inner dialogue to try to show the parts what each is saying and how they are struggling with one another. The resulting committee meeting—or group therapy session—of internal parts can often demonstrate to a client how busy he is wrestling with his life instead of actually living. As with the mental body, cognitive therapy interventions may be used to challenge the faulty ideas and schemas, and mindfulness can help to reveal the patterns and silence the voices, at least for a little while.

In the transpersonal perspective, symptoms are not viewed as problems to be only biochemically addressed or eliminated. Rather, they are often viewed as evidence that the core soul-spirit or other parts are trying to communicate with the self, trying to get its attention to make needed changes in the accommodations the self has made in adjusting to life's challenges (Vaughan, 1979). Symptoms are not always evidence of incompetence on the part of the self. Instead, it is often the case that the self has made many successful accommodations to the circumstances of one's life, and those accommodations have only become problematic after the circumstances that inspired them have ended.

Internal Family Systems (Schwartz, 1995) does not distinguish this body, so in that model the manager parts cover both mental and intellectual. Gestalt also includes the intellectual body along with mental body parts in its representation of the "top-dog" (Beisser, 1970).

Intellectual body example. In our client in the emotional body example, the mental body part of self was a perfectionistic inner critic acting like a manager in the psyche. The intellectual body part was functioning as the board of directors. For this client, the intellectual body explained that it was his fault his parents got divorced, and if only he had been a better child, the family would have stayed together. The intellectual body needs to understand why things happen, and from a limited five-year-old's perspective, it is common to over-identify and believe one is the responsible factor. One reason may be to attain more perceived control over the situation (e.g. Herman, 1997). Anxiety is a natural response to losing control over one's environment, and our client reclaimed some control by taking responsibility for his parents' divorce. From a core belief level of taking responsibility for one's parents' divorce, it is easy to see how other self-bodies would then push toward perfectionism in order to avoid being at fault for future parental or other life conflicts and disappointments. This in turn created unbearable anxiety, which inspired the need for the ego to manage the out-of-control feelings.

As the client observed this part, he was able to link the anxiety to the experience of his parents' divorcing and see the core belief that was established during the divorce. It could then be reevaluated from an adult perspective. There are dozens of cognitive-behavioral-type inquires to expose thinking errors or cognitive distortions. One example is Katie's process called The Work (Katie & Mitchell, 2002). Here the counselor gently questions the part of the self who believes it is the cause of the parents' divorce: "Is that true?" "Can you absolutely know that's true?" "How do you react when you believe that story?" "Who would you be without that story?" After these questions are fleshed out, The Work recommends looking for an opposite story that may be just as, or more, true. In this clinical example, the client was able to say, "Perhaps, I was a good enough five-year-old, and my parents' divorce was due to many factors, not just me."

Conclusion

We have presented a transpersonal structure of the psyche for conceptualizing mental and emotional concerns that might be presented for clinical treatment. It includes previously identified structures of the personality and integrates transpersonal parts with other self-body parts to provide a more complete model of a human being. Charts and descriptions summarize a large body of psychological literature and suggest interventions that would be applied for specific client concerns. Both healthy and unhealthy states exist for each of the holons representing parts of the whole self. This information can be used to begin to conceptualize the practice and theory of transpersonal psychotherapy for some clients.

References

Assagioli, R. (1965). *Psychosynthesis: A collection of basic writings*. New York, NY: Viking Press.

Beisser, A. (1970). The paradoxical theory of change. In J. Fagan & I. L. Shepherd (Eds.), *Gestalt therapy now: Theory, techniques, applications* (pp. 77–80). Palo Alto, CA: Science and Behavior Books.

Berne, E. (1961). *Transactional analysis in psychotherapy*. New York, NY: Grove Press.

Bradshaw, J. (1990). *Home coming: Reclaiming and championing your inner child*. New York, NY: Bantam Books.

Brennan, B., & Smith, J. (1988). *Hands of light: A guide to healing through the human energy field: A new paradigm for the human being in health, relationship, and disease*. New York, NY: Bantam Books.

Breuer, J., & Freud, S. (2000). *Studies on hysteria* (J. Strachey, Trans.). New York, NY: Basic Books. (Original work published 1895)

Caldwell, C. (Ed.). (1997). *Getting in touch: The guide to new body-centered therapies*. Wheaton, IL: Quest Books.

Clements, C.J. (2016). Toward a transpersonal model of psychological illness, health, and transformation. *The Journal of Transpersonal Psychology, 48*, (1,) 1–31.

Doblin, R. (1991). Pahnke's "Good Friday experiment:" A long-term follow-up and methodological critique. *The Journal of Transpersonal Psychology, 23*(1), 1–28.

Ellman, S. J. (2010). *When theories touch: A historical and theoretical integration of psychoanalytic thought*. London: Karnac Books.

Emmerson, G. (2003). *Ego state therapy*. Bethel, CT: Crown House.

Freud, S. (1989). *The ego and the id* (J. Strachey, Trans.). New York, NY: Norton.

Gendlin, E. (1978). *Focusing*. New York, NY: Bantam.

Hanh, T. N. (2010). *Reconciliation*. Berkley, CA: Parallel Press.

Hartelius, G., Rothe, G., & Roy, P. J. (2013). A brand from the burning. In H. Friedman and G. Hartelius (Eds.), *The Wiley-Blackwell handbook of transpersonal psychology* (pp. 3–23). West Sussex, UK: John Wiley & Sons.

Herman, J. L. (1997). *Trauma and recovery*. New York, NY: Basic Books.

Hoffman, L., Vallejos, L., Cleare-Hoffman, H. P., & Rubin, S. (2015). Emotion, relationship, and meaning as core existential practice: Evidence-based foundations. *Journal of Contemporary Psychotherapy, 45*(1), 11–20.

Jacobi, J. (1973). *The psychology of C. G. Jung.* London and New Haven, CT: Yale University Press.

James, W. (1958). *The varieties of religious experience.* Cambridge, MA: Harvard University Press.

Jung, C.G. (1964). *Man and his symbols.* New York, NY: Dell.

Jung, C.G. (1967). Symbols of transformation (R.F.C. Hull, Trans.). In *The collected works of C.G. Jung* (Vol. 5, 2nd ed.). Princeton, NJ: Princeton University Press.

Jung, C. G. (1997). *Jung on active imagination* (J. Chodorow, Ed.). Princeton, NJ: Princeton University Press.

Katie, B., & Mitchell, S. (2002) *Loving what is: Four questions that can change your life.* New York, NY: Harmony Books.

Kernberg, O. F. (1995). *Object relations theory and clinical psychoanalysis.* New York, NY: Jason Aronson.

Laing, R. D. (1959). *The divided self.* Baltimore, MD: Penguin Books.

Levine, P. A. (1997). *Waking the tiger: Healing trauma: The innate capacity to transform overwhelming experiences.* Berkeley, CA: North Atlantic Books.

Lipton, B. H. (2015). *The biology of belief* (10th Anniversary ed.) : *Unleashing the power of consciousness.* Carlsbad, CA: Matter & Miracles. Hay House, Inc.

Lowen, A. (1975). *Bioenergetics.* New York, NY: Coward, McCann & Geoghegan.

Maslow, A.H. (1970). *Religions, values, and peak-experiences.* New York, NY: Penguin/Viking. (Original work published 1964)

Maté, G., (2003). *When the body says no: Exploring the stress-disease connection.* Hoboken, NJ: John Wiley and Sons.

Maté, G. (2010). *In the realm of hungry ghosts: Close encounters with addiction.* Berkeley, CA: North Atlantic Books.

Miscisin, M., Adams, J., & Haines, J. (2001). *Showing our true colors: A fun, easy guide for understanding and appreciating yourself and others.* Riverside, CA: True Colors.

Mitchell, S. A. (1995). *Hope and dread in psychoanalysis.* New York, NY: Basic Books.

Moreno, J. L. (1975). *Psychodrama, action therapy and principles of practice* (Vol. 3). Beacon, NY: Beacon House.

Ogden, P., Minton, K., & Pain, C. (2006). *Trauma and the body: A sensorimotor approach to psychotherapy* (Norton series on interpersonal neurobiology). New York, NY: W.W. Norton.

Pace, P. (2012). *Lifespan integration: Connecting ego states through time.* Snoqualmie, WA: Lifespan Integration.

Patanjali (2002). *The yoga sutras of Patanjali* (A. Shearer, Trans.). New York, NY: Bell Tower/Crown. (Original work published 1982)

Perls, F. (1973). *The Gestalt approach & eye witness to therapy*. Palo Alto, CA: Science & Behavior Books.
Pierrakos, J. C. (1987). *Core energetics: Developing the capacity to love and heal.* Mendocino, CA: LifeRhythm Publications.
Porges, S. W. (2011). *The polyvagal theory: Neurophysiological foundations of emotions, attachment, communication, and self-regulation (*Norton Series on interpersonal neurobiology*).* New York, NY: W.W. Norton.
Reich, W. (1949). *Character analysis* (3rd enlarged ed.*).* New York, NY: Orgone Institute Press. (Original work published 1933)
Roman, S. (1997). *Soul love. Awakening your heart centers.* Tiburon CA: H. J. Kramer.
Rothschild, B. (2000). *The body remembers: The psychophysiology of trauma and trauma treatment.* New York, NY: W.W. Norton.
Schwartz, R. (1995). *Internal family systems therapy*. New York, NY: Guilford Press.
Siegel, D. J., & Hartzell, M. (2013). *Parenting from the inside out: How a deeper self-understanding can help you raise children who thrive.* New York, NY: J.P. Tarcher/Putnam.
Smith, H. (1976). *Forgotten truth: The common vision of the world's religions.* New York, NY: Harper Collins.
Stone, H. & Stone S. (1998). *Embracing ourselves: The voice dialogue manual.* Novato, CA: New World Library.
Tart, C.T. (1987). *Waking up: Overcoming the obstacles to human potential.* New York, NY: Random House.
van der Kolk, B. A. (1996). Trauma and memory. In B.A. van der Kolk, A.C. McFarlane, & L. Weisaeth (Eds.), *Traumatic stress: The effects of overwhelming experience on mind, body and society* (pp. 279–302). New York, NY: Guilford.
van der Kolk, B. A. (2014). *The body keeps the score: Brain, mind and body in the healing of trauma.* New York, NY: Viking.
Vaughan, F. (1979). Transpersonal psychotherapy: Context, content and process. *The Journal of Transpersonal Psychology, 11*(2), 101.
Wallin, D. (2007). *Attachment in psychotherapy.* New York, NY: Guilford.
Whitfield, C. H. (1987). *Healing the child within: Discovery and recovery for adult children of dysfunctional families.* Deerfield Beach, FL: Health Communications.
Whitmont, E. C. (1969). *The symbolic quest: Basic concepts of analytical psychology.* Princeton, NJ: Princeton University Press.
Wilber, K. (1993). *The spectrum of consciousness.* Wheaton, IL: Theosophical Publishing House. (Original work published 1977)
Wilber, K. (2000). *Integral psychology: Consciousness, spirit, psychology, therapy.* Boston, MA: Shambhala Publications.
Wilber, K. (2001). *No boundary.* Boston, MA: Shambhala Publications.

Woldt, A., & Toman, S. (2005). *Gestalt therapy: History, theory, and practice.* Thousand Oaks, CA: Sage Publications.

Chapter 4
Empirical Foundations of Transpersonal Counseling and Psychotherapy

Francis J. Kaklauskas
Lindsey Randol

No philosophy can ever be anything but a summary sketch, a picture of the world in abridgment, a foreshortened bird's-eye view of the perspective of events... All follow one analogy or another; everyone is nevertheless prone to claim that his conclusions are the only logical ones, that they are necessities of universal reason, they being all the while, at bottom, accidents more or less of personal vision which had far better be avowed as such. (James, 1909, p. 7)

Transpersonal psychotherapy may be conceived as an open-ended endeavor to facilitate human growth and expand awareness beyond the limits implied by most traditional Western models of mental health. However, in the process of enlarging one's felt sense of identity to include transpersonal dimensions of being, the therapist may employ traditional therapeutic techniques. (Vaughan, 1979, p. 101)

When people find out that we work at Naropa University, they often ask about meditation and the positive effects that they have heard about in the popular media. We like this question, as there are many well-designed studies that show promising results in the areas of increased perceptual sensitivity, the ability to learn new information, improved social functioning and, more generally, enhanced physiological and psychological well-being (Davis & Hayes, 2011; MacDonald, Walsh, & Shapiro, 2015). These studies utilize a variety of methods including subjective self-reports, behavioral observations, performance-based pre/post-test designs, brain imaging techniques, and other methods. Many of these studies use random assignments, matched pairs, and other well-established research approaches. While the studies on meditation are not exempt from concerning confounds such as sample size, participants' lifestyle choices, placebo effects, researcher expectancy bias, and varied definitional and operational constructs (Awasthi, 2013), the general results indicate that meditation is good for you (Hart, Ivtzan, & Hart, 2013). Though meditators have qualitatively reported their own positive results for thousands of years, having modern science quantitatively reinforce these personal accounts has proven crucial to meditation gaining wider acceptance for its ability to support and enhance physical and mental health.

When people discover that we teach in the transpersonal counseling program, the follow-up questions are often, "What is transpersonal counseling and does it work?" These are not easy questions with simple or straightforward answers. In fact, these questions are frequently asked by many of the graduate students who are already studying in our program. This points to the importance of revisiting and clarifying questions pertaining to the effectiveness of transpersonal counseling and therapy. In this chapter, we will discuss misperceptions, operational and definitional challenges, limitations of contemporary research findings, and corroborating evidence for the transpersonal approach to counseling.

Transpersonal Psychotherapy and Counseling

Transpersonal counseling and therapy continue to have a definitional crisis (Daniels, 2015; MacDonald & Friedman, 2015). As seen in the varied chapters of this book, one unified definition has not been agreed upon, even among like-minded colleagues. Part of the challenge arises from the inclusive orientation and integrative worldview of our field. Transpersonal counselors attempt to amalgamate various psychological approaches that were established over the last 100 years, with the additional awareness of spiritual practices that have developed over millennia within various cultures and spiritual traditions. Transpersonal counselors frequently have interests in a broad range of disciplines (i.e., contemporary physics, anthropology, neuroscience, and the humanities), value multiple data streams and pluralistic ways of knowing, and seek to remain open and contemporary in their thinking and therapeutic approach. Even within the same overarching transpersonal orientation, each individual counselor often has unique areas of interest and focus. While this diversity can create challenges, it also generates creative interplay and continuous growth. Transpersonal counseling may be best understood as a dynamic, unfolding process that will never be static or discrete from the changing world in which it operates.

Concerns
Transpersonal counseling sometimes gets associated with the New Age movement. In fact, the two are not disconnected, but, as a result, a common misunderstanding is that transpersonal counseling is filled with beliefs and practices that have not and do not attempt to be scientifically tested and rationally analyzed. For the lay public, transpersonal counseling may bring up images of esoteric practices like Tarot card readings, substance-induced altered states of consciousness, and wilderness vision quests. For others, transpersonal counseling is more closely aligned with the theoretical human developmental models of Abraham Maslow (1968) or Ken Wilber (1975). Academics may locate transpersonal counseling as a branch of the humanistic and existential traditions or within the framework of pastoral or spiritual counseling. Clinically, transpersonal counseling can draw upon experiential Gestalt explorations in the here-and-now, mindfulness-based approaches, and Jungian analysis filled with symbols, archetypes, and mythic meanings, as well as more contemporary approaches such as cognitive behavioral techniques and systems theories, depending on the needs of the clients.

All of these varied ideas and practices are part of the transpersonal tradition, and it is in this multiplicity that the definitional and operational challenges of the field originate.

Some believe that transpersonal counseling is an approach that focuses solely on the personal growth of the worried well. However, with an emphasis on states of consciousness, life meaning and purpose, spirituality, mindfulness, connectedness, and altruism, transpersonal psychotherapy has been shown to be helpful for a diversity of clients across diagnostic spectrums (Kaminker & Lukoff, 2015). Critics of the transpersonal approach sometimes discount it as a modality that relies too heavily on ethereal theory, anecdotal evidence, and clinician intuition. It has also been noted that transpersonal counseling and therapy can be too dependent on spiritual practices without enough integration or consideration of pragmatic, empirically supported traditional approaches.

A significant concern is the practice of transpersonally oriented individuals appropriating other cultural and spiritual traditions without sufficient expertise, cultural permission, and/or understanding, often for commercial gain and to the detriment of those they serve (Daniels & McNutt, 1997). While this practice unfortunately occurs too frequently, some transpersonal therapists spend decades training toward the goal of properly drawing upon the wisdom of various world perspectives to move the field forward. We endorse thorough collaboration, training, and consideration in such areas.

Additionally, despite its vision of inclusivity, transpersonal psychology continues to fall short of fully embracing multiculturalism (see Hocoy chapter in this volume; Hoffman as well as Gregory & Kellaway chapters in *Shadows & Light*, Vol. 2). These are legitimate concerns that must be actively addressed to maximize the potential of transpersonal psychotherapy. However, if practiced with scholarship, supervision, ethical diligence, cross-cultural awareness and inclusivity, and thoughtful integration with other areas of the field, contemporary transpersonal psychotherapy and counseling, similar to humanistic psychology (Hoffman, Vallejos, Cleare-Hoffman, & Rubin, 2014) and contemporary psychodynamic traditions (Shedler, 2010, 2015), can be considered evidence-based and empirically supported practices.

Evidence-Based Practice
As charted by the American Psychological Association (APA) Presidential Task Force on Evidence-Based Practice in Psychology (2006), effective psychotherapy draws upon: (1) research, (2) clinical expertise or competency, and (3) patient characteristics, culture, and preferences. Contemporary evidence-based practice goes beyond implementing a specific modality for a particular diagnosis, but rather stresses the integration of applicable research, the development of proficiency in techniques and approaches, and the clear focus on each individual client's unique concerns and needs.

Transpersonal psychology draws upon research from varied sources including specific studies related to transpersonal psychology, relevant evidence from other theoretical models, and trans-theoretical research in psychotherapy effectiveness. Similar to other professional psychotherapy training approaches, transpersonal counselors and therapists study traditional, contemporary, and transpersonal models of assessment and practice (Friedman & MacDonald, 2002). While being additive, the transpersonal approach has its unique diagnostic and non-pathology-based taxonomies originating with Maslow (1968; 1973), Grof and Grof (1989), Grof (2015), and Wilber (1975), as well as technical recommendations and guidelines from Walsh and Vaughan (1993), Cortright (1997), and Rodrigues and Friedman (2015), among others. Consequently, transpersonal counselors employ a range of interventions in internships, practica, post-graduate fellowships, and organizational employment settings. The emphasis on pluralistically informed case conceptualization allows for transpersonal counselors to work within and incorporate a range of theoretical frameworks, with an emphasis on environmental and multicultural considerations (Pappas & Friedman, 2004).

Therapist competency and skills development is a lifelong pursuit (Parson & Zhang, 2014; Sperry, 2010). The transpersonal therapist aims not only to become adept at effectively challenging thought distortions and applying behavioral systems, but also seeks to develop personally and spiritually, to expand and understand their own presence, and acquire increasing empathy, relational skills, and understanding of diverse human experiences, values, and beliefs (Daniels, 2005).

Transpersonal psychotherapy is uniquely positioned to work with patient characteristics, culture, and client preferences. While Western psychology's emphasis has been on adaptation to cultural norms and controlling negative symptoms and behaviors, transpersonal psychotherapy seeks to help clients live a positive life (Cleare-Hoffman, Hoffman, & Wilson, 2013). This can include reducing symptoms, but it also means appreciating the potential of each client in the context of individual differences. Transpersonal psychology was born from a desire to rebel against pathology-driven orientations and nomothetic approaches. Hence, transpersonal therapy values the unique person in their environment, expands upon Western psychological knowledge and diverse wisdom traditions, and uses a collaborative and client-driven approach to therapy (Daniels, 2015; Grof, 2015).

Yalom (2002) suggests that psychotherapy is ideally reinvented with each client, and this may certainly be true with the more ideographic approaches such as the transpersonal. Accordingly, each transpersonal clinician, within their own style, is likely to offer a somewhat new and unique therapy with each individual client, given the specifics of the presenting situation and the client's personal history, cultural influences, and short- and long-term goals.

Transpersonal Contributions to the Counseling & Therapy Process
The transpersonal movement and transpersonal counseling may be best understood as a view, a perspective, or even a spirit toward our work. As Daniels (2015) points out, the transpersonal approach reaches across three vectors. Its descending vector is akin to traditional psychotherapy, particularly the depth approaches. The ascending vector is often associated with spiritual states, practices, and aspirations. Finally, the extending vector reaches into contact with others and the world. Kaklauskas (2016) emphasized that this extending vector can include intimate relationships as well as larger engagement in society, such as in the realm of social justice work. The successful navigation of our

therapeutic relationships, including navigating the therapeutic alliance with awareness, empathy, limits, presence, and collaboration, is a transpersonal pursuit. Extending into social movements and working collaboratively with others can also be a transpersonal endeavor, as altruism can arise from our cosmology and spiritual ethics (Friedman, 2015). A common misunderstanding is that transpersonal counseling and therapy are only interested in the ascending vector, but rather it is the balanced inclusion of multiple sides of our client's ontology that best encapsulates the transpersonal approach. As Vaughan (1979) stated, the transpersonal therapist works with "the balanced integration of psychical, emotional, mental, spiritual aspects" (p. 102). Through the history of transpersonal psychology, the goals have been to work with people's present needs while simultaneously holding a larger view of their full potential (Maslow, 1968, 1973; Rodrigues & Friedman, 2015).

In this overview of the transpersonal contribution, we return to Frances Vaughan's (1979) classic article, *Transpersonal Psychotherapy: Context, Content, and Process*. Vaughan highlights and summarizes the enduring major themes of transpersonal counseling including the openness of the therapist, the therapist's self-knowledge, open-ended perspectives regarding what is possible, disidentification with the ego, and a wider view than the client's current situation and symptoms. She emphasizes the centrality of consciousness in our work as transpersonal counselors as both a topic to be explored and a process of change. This focus on consciousness has been sustained throughout the varieties of transpersonal approaches (Friedman, 2015; Garcia-Romeu & Tart, 2015; Wickramasekera, 2015).

Transpersonal psychology does not retract from other schools of thought; rather, it welcomes integration and new approaches. As transpersonal counselors and therapists, we follow whatever works in service of and assistance to our clients, while making sure that our interventions are grounded in an ethical framework, clinical experience, theoretical rationale, and empirical support. The transpersonal approach values client-led interactions and traces clients' consciousness and their fluctuating patterns of thinking, affects, and behaviors. Like most contemporary schools of counseling and therapy, these are the essential objects of our explorations and understandings. More specifically, we may also follow our clients' ability to self-reflect, as well as their capacities for self-mastery, creative problem solving, connectedness to self and others, and levels of defensiveness versus openness. Through empathic tracking, reflecting back, and asking open-ended and clarifying questions, we help clients learn to follow their own processes, recognize their own patterns, and open up to new possibilities and experiences. We hold a space for the power of repetition, while supporting our clients' abilities to come to deeper understandings of their processes and create new ones.

Vaughan (1979) highlights the necessity for therapists not only to deeply understand their clients, but also to examine their own states of consciousness by doing their own psychological work. Therapists who have gone to therapy have been shown to have an increased self-awareness, as well as an expanded ability to use skills effectively, relate authentically, and use the self for the benefit of clients (Bike, Norcross, & Schatz, 2009; Kumari, 2011). Therapists who have attended their own therapy report feeling more attuned to their clients and show increased empathy, patience, tolerance, and understanding of transference and countertransference issues (Bike et al., 2009). Related research has indicated that clients also benefit when their therapists have a mindfulness awareness practice (Davis & Hayes, 2011). Additional studies suggest that the combination of these two elements has produced better clinical outcomes than either psychotherapy or mindfulness practices alone (Davis & Hayes, 2011).

Another element Vaughan (1979) emphasized is that both clients and therapists learn to tolerate ambiguity. When therapists sit with clients, they often listen to many inner voices, in the free-floating attention that Freud described and others endorsed (Epstein, 1984). Upon hearing about a client's family struggles, our awareness may shift across a spectrum of understandings from attachment issues, childhood trauma, addictive processes, the dance of intimacy, a constriction in the movement toward expansive awareness, or the inevitable difficulties of long-term relationships, all within one session. With such a multiplicity of ways to understand the issues that clients bring, both clients and therapists are encouraged to accept the inevitability of their own unique subjectivities. Transpersonal psychology, like multicultural and constructivist approaches, understands that each person experiences situations relative to their particular location, history, semantics, culture, and context (Comas-Diaz, 2012). In response to this irreducible complexity, "knowing not knowing is the best path" (Townsend & Kaklauskas, 2008, p. 61). Asking a client how he or she understands a situation, and potentially offering additional perspectives, allows for clients to increase their tolerance for ambiguity and frustration, as well as their self-reflective abilities and other self-processes (Kohut, 1971, 1977; Blanck & Blanck, 1974, 1979). If the therapist is able to stay curious, the client can learn to become more curious about their processes, disidentify with each passing state of consciousness, and move toward a more unified self-experience (Kohut, 1974, 1979). This type of psychotherapeutic technique is seen across modalities from modern analytic ideas of objectifying the ego (Spotnitz, 2004) through Sullivan's (1953) recognizing parataxic distortions, to Ellis' (1962) ideas of challenging thought distortions. In these ways, transpersonal counseling builds on and integrates into the wider tradition of psychology and psychotherapy theory and practice.

Vaughan (1979) discussed the importance of clients developing a healthy sense of self-responsibility. She suggested that individuals can take responsibility for their own lives by moving beyond historical patterning, in contrast to some of the overly deterministic views seen in other schools of thought such as behaviorism. Self-responsibility is a tricky topic, and one that is easily misunderstood. Assuming self-responsibility does not mean that one can create the life they want irrespective of context, as seen in some of the popular self-help movements or New Age philosophies. For example, a client whose parents were survivors of the Holocaust may not be able to completely transform and transmute intergenerational grief and trauma (Yehuda, Hallig, & Grossman, 2001). In a similar way, a person who finds themselves entrenched in systems of oppression will not be able to transcend experiences of discrimination through transpersonal counseling. However, transpersonal counseling takes the approach that individuals can recognize the challenges they face and explore new ways of responding to and working with trauma, tyranny, and oppression.

Reverend angel Kyodo williams (2000) reports that the recognition of the depth of racism against African Americans and her own feelings of tremendous anger, grief, and hopelessness were part of her path toward internal awareness and external action. Internally she found ways to work with her thinking and reactions that allowed for greater freedom in her responses to racism and helped her strategize the best ways to effect change. Based upon her experience, Williams reports that taking the time to turn inward helps her to reengage with others with more awareness and attunement, think about the issues more clearly, and become more effective in her responses.

In transpersonal counseling, like many other schools of clinical work, healing and growth are understood to take place beyond techniques and exercises. Instead, the transformation is seen to take place within the process of the therapeutic relationship (Mearns & Cooper, 2005), shifting identities (Rodrigues & Friedman, 2015), novel experiences (Schore, 2012), and new ways of thinking, feeling, and behaving (Cozolino, 2016). While transpersonal approaches include guidelines and technical strategies, it is the larger view of human potential and development, client–therapist collaboration, empathy, and the intentional stance of not knowing, informed by years of clinical experience and supervision, that makes it distinctive.

The Current State of Research in Transpersonal Counseling & Therapy

One criticism of transpersonal, humanistic, existential, and psychodynamic psychotherapies is the limited database of randomized, controlled, double-blind studies supporting these approaches (Anderson & Braud, 1998). Similar to these other highly relational ideographic psychotherapy models (RIPs), the challenges of operationalizing the transpersonal counseling approach into a program of repeatable interventions are extensive (Hoffman et al., 2015; MacDonald & Friedman, 2015). One challenge is that the foundation of transpersonal counseling rests beyond the discrete mechanistic paradigm underlying randomized control trials (RCTs). As such, transpersonal counseling has not fully integrated into the contemporary medical model of positivistic research.

Relational psychotherapeutic approaches have focused primarily on theory building, clinical work, qualitative analysis, and technical application of related findings rather than adapting themselves to the current research zeitgeist (Greene, 2012). Like the entire field of psychology, transpersonal counseling must continue to move beyond a collection of assorted observations and ideas to develop a comprehensively structured architecture through which to understand and positively address human suffering and growth (Millon, 2003). For psychotherapy to be a science and an ethical practice, it is essential that it have an empirical basis and rationale. While many RIP clients and clinicians may have larger or different goals than the ones able to be captured in pathology-oriented symptom measures, the failure to evaluate the therapeutic changes that are occurring in counseling does a disservice to clients and therapists. For example, recent findings suggest that the majority of clinicians overestimate their therapeutic effectiveness (Walfish, McAlister, O'Donnell, & Lambert, 2012). This should encourage therapists to question their subjective assessment practices and the limitations of their self-evaluations (Finlay & Gough, 2003). Relying solely on the perceptions of clients and clinicians, or on pathology-based symptom measures, neglects the importance of investigating multiple streams of data and ways of knowing as encouraged in transpersonal theory. While supervision, consultation, and clinical experience are crucial starting points, a broader and more integrative approach to research and clinical assessment is considered best practice from a transpersonal perspective.

Difficulties with Randomized Controlled Studies in Psychotherapy

Many psychotherapy research theorists have offered critical perspectives on the contemporary adoration of the "gold standard" of double-blind, randomized controlled studies (Greene, 2012). From a transpersonal perspective, the RCT method is seen as limited both in its approach, as well as in the type of data that is collected and analyzed (Hartelius &

Ferrer, 2015). The RCT approach is useful and appropriate for treatments designed to primarily decrease specific symptoms and return individuals to better day-to-day, culturally adaptive functioning. However, this positivist perspective assumes a particular ontology of living—one that may push people in the direction of cultural adaption and fewer symptoms, but perhaps also less aliveness and uniqueness.

Others have criticized RCT studies for their lack of crucial etiological and contextual information such as gender, class, ethnicity, and issues related to sexuality and spiritual interest, among other important factors. For example, McWilliams (2011) has challenged the focus of symptom reduction in research concerning patients diagnosed with depression. She argues that most studies do not consider the possibility that depression may derive from what psychoanalysts would describe as a blend of anaclitic, introjective, social, and biological factors. The current *Diagnostic and Statistical Manual of Mental Disorders*, Fith Edition (DSM-5; American Psychiatric Association, 2013) conceptualizations neglect the possibility that depression may also be understood as a process within a context of societal expectations and oppressions, challenging life events, and loss of meaning and connectedness. Consequently, McWilliams advocates for research methods that consider situational, historical, and developmental factors and do not solely rely on biological explanations to describe idiosyncratic patient presentations.

Generally speaking, the majority of clinical research infrequently measures the internal human constructs of purpose, spiritual connectedness, and altruistic impulses or the external factors of privilege or oppression, societal status, and power, in addition to other critical environmental influences (Roth & Fonagy, 2013). While transpersonal counseling does not ignore the important goal of symptom reduction, it also values other priorities such as increased self-awareness, openness to a full range of human experiences, and the possibility to explore and strive for deeper meanings, connectedness, purpose, and spiritual growth (Steger, Frazier, Oishi, & Kaler, 2006; Sutich, 1973; Vaughan, 1979). The transpersonal view also emphasizes the construct of the self in the environment, so contextual factors such as religious or spiritual upbringing and current cultural practices, as well as social challenges like poverty and prejudice, need to be addressed in our research metrics. From a transpersonal perspective, these aspects of our humanness are essential to understanding both health and illness.

In keeping with its focus on symptom reduction, most psychotherapy research is only able to measure a static articulation of goals. However, clients often come to psychotherapy based on feelings of vague distress, not seeking specific treatment for an identified diagnosis. Usually, client goals change over time as the therapeutic relationship develops and the client gains self-awareness into both the issues that hold them back and the areas in which they wish to grow (Elkins, 2009; 2015). Broad themes such as being a better parent can become more specific goals such as working on communication, not raising one's voice, self-care, and the consistent setting of expectations and the holding of boundaries. Conversely, specific issues can also become broader, such as the example of an individual deciding to come out to their family about their bisexuality. This could lead to discussions about fostering and nurturing intimate relationships that can sustain honesty, addressing the opinions and biases of others, and balancing physical, emotional, and spiritual needs and desires. Again, these types of important human issues are not captured in specific DSM-5 diagnostic criteria but are common themes in psychotherapy and counseling.

From a transpersonal standpoint, the biases underlying RCT research are seen to obscure diverse cultural and spiritual traditions that value emotional variance, periods of personal struggle, and processes of introspection and meaning making, as well as the wisdom of those who experience the world in unique ways. Despite some support for cultural adaptations that are seen to better serve diverse populations, many remain critical that psychotherapy research is not capturing the complexity and uniqueness of varied cultures and the individuals being studied (Huey, Tilley, Jones, & Smith, 2014). Indeed, many of the people seeking a transpersonal approach to counseling may not trend with the generalizable norms indicated by RCT findings. Such individuals' beliefs, lifestyle choices, social interests, and communities may diverge significantly from the individuals represented in RCT studies (Clay,

2011). These individuals could show too much complexity, comorbid symptoms, potentially strong spiritual orientations, or what could be seen as unrepresentative thinking for inclusion in RCT research (Shean, 2014). Also, such individuals may not respond positively to the overly technical and manual-driven "empirically validated" approaches.

Recently, RCTs have come under increased critique following initial discoveries of non-reproducibility of some RCT findings (Hoffman et al., 2015; Elkins, 2015; Wampold, 2009). Additionally, results from a meta-analysis of cognitive behavioral therapies indicated that this evidenced-based treatment is having less impact than it did in previous decades (Johnsen & Friborg, 2015). Other concerns regarding the current findings of clinical research include the practice of publishing studies that only show clear positive outcomes, the tendency of relying on F-scores versus probability data in reporting findings, and the preference of quantitative data over other methods (Cain, Keenan & Rubin, 2015; Hartelius & Ferrer, 2015; Lindheim, Kolko, & Cheng, 2012). The actual generalizability to and effectiveness of these studies in real-world application lack sufficient longitudinal data (Cain et al., 2015; Greene, 2012).

Tracking the Collaborative Process of Change

One fruitful new approach in counseling research is the increasing popularity of practice-based models (Thyer, 2013). Practice-based research utilizes a variety of assessment methods to track the effectiveness of therapy in real time and over time. In most situations, these assessments take the form of objective measures such as Outcome Questionaire-2 (Lambert, Kahler, Harmon, Burlingame, & Shimokawa, 2011) and the Symptom Checklist-90 (Derogatis, 1994). Transpersonal counselors may choose to follow these practice-based assessment protocols with some adaptation. Instead of using exclusively symptom-oriented objective measures, they may include other measures more aligned with transpersonal goals such as the Spiritual Transcendence Scale (Piedmont, 1999), the Short Index of Self-Actualization (Jones & Crandall, 1986), the Meaning in Life Questionnaire (Steger et al., 2006), and the Personal Growth Initiative Scale (Robitschek, 1998), among others. These assessments can provide new perspectives on our work and offer useful vantage points through which to evaluate therapy.

Another important dynamic emerging in psychotherapy research is the inclusion of process-based measures, such as therapeutic alliance, as seen in the Therapeutic Alliance Inventory (Munder, Wilmers, Leonhart, Linster, & Barth, 2010). Transpersonal counselors are encouraged to incorporate these types of inventories to check if therapy is progressing toward the agreed-upon goals. While much of evidence-based practice relies on objective measures, Lambert (2013b) along with Castonguay and colleagues (2013) suggest the use of collaborative individualized goals that can be constructed and measured through both quantitative and qualitative methods. Through supervision and consultation, qualitative findings can be reviewed and tested by other raters for rigor and reliability (Morrow, 2005). In this fashion, transpersonal counselors can continue to become increasingly empirically oriented to better meet clients' needs within the larger framework of the transpersonal view.

In some ways, the contemporary over-reliance on a positivistic, static, third-person approach to research may be outdated and not reflective of the current intellectual trends found in other sciences and philosophies such as constructivist, dynamic, and pluralistic views and research methodologies (Cooper & McLeod, 2011; Crotty, 1998; Lowenthal & Snell, 2003). In order to bridge these gaps, the psychological research movement is increasingly shifting toward mixed-method approaches, including the use of correlational and qualitative models, process-outcomes studies and multivariate analysis, with an added awareness of ideographic variables and practice-based outcomes (Anderson & Braud, 2011; Greene, 2012). Transpersonal research must stay current with the shifting state of knowledge in order to contribute to this emergent scientific inquiry and continue to offer best practice to clients.

Case Illustration

Transpersonal psychology is interested in encompassing larger domains of the human experience, beyond the limitations of pathology-based models. While it can be challenging or even sometimes impossible for individuals to move toward more meaning and connectedness if certain symptomatic patterns are not changed, as counselors, taking a broader view can be helpful. I (FK) think of a client I worked with for many years who suffered with a severe obsessive-compulsive disorder, substance abuse, and limited financial resources. He was a physically small male who moved to the United States from Mexico when he was a child and did not feel he could comfortably conform to the somewhat stereotypically male presentation of many of his peers. He was a devoted practicing Catholic who desired a committed intimate relationship and a life built on service to others. Despite the clarity of his aspirations and spiritual dedication, this client had tremendous difficulties functioning in his daily life. He was compelled to wash his hair in multiples of four before leaving the house each day. On days when he did not have negative thoughts while washing his hair, he could leave for work on time. On other days, 4 hair washings could become 16, or 64, or even 256. When he was not able to stop his compulsion, he would quickly fall into overwhelming states of self-loathing. Sometimes during these periods he would excessively use alcohol and masturbation to distract himself temporarily, but this would often be followed by endless prayers for God to kill him. At times when his symptoms were prevalent, it became difficult for him to sustain employment because he would miss work and avoid calling his employer, and his face and scalp would be raw from washing and detergents.

    In his early twenties, this client was accepted into an intensive residential treatment for obsessive-compulsive disorder (OCD), but he left after one week because he did not feel understood. He reported wanting to talk about his relationship with God and his desired path of service to others, but felt that these sides of himself were not welcomed at the treatment center. He reported leaving after he felt mocked by a staff member who allegedly said that maybe God could help him stop washing his hair, and perhaps with his desire to serve others he should be a beautician. It is hard to know the accuracy of these reports, but it was clear to me that this client desired to be seen for his spirituality rather than his symptoms and that he resented being mocked for his somewhat effeminate presentation and his spiritual beliefs.

After he left the treatment program, this client began working with me through public funding. In our first session he talked almost exclusively about his spirituality. He said he felt comfortable that I was familiar with Christianity and was named after one of his favorite saints. Through our work together, this client said that he felt that I (FK) was interested in a fuller picture of who he was as a person, and not solely focused on minimizing his OCD symptomology. In fact, he initially came to treatment assuming that his OCD symptoms would never improve and wanted to discuss career options that could accommodate his challenges. Given what I had heard from his previous experiences, I allowed for him to lead our sessions. After about six months of weekly meetings in which he progressively discussed his frustration with his symptoms, he eventually asked me to help him try to address his OCD in a direct manner. Together, we reviewed evidence-based treatment approaches, typical etiology and pathogenesis, and decided to split our sessions between topics of his choice and a more structured and evidence-based protocol for his symptom reduction. He generally did well completing homework assignments aimed at tackling his thinking and behavior, and sometimes successfully managed the exposure exercises. Progress was small and certain according to his reports, but after another six months he had a dramatic relapse into his old behaviors and alcoholism.

He asked for my help in getting more intensive treatment and, after many attempts, he was accepted into a low-fee intensive outpatient treatment program. He was able to work with a biracial female therapist with expertise in OCD. He was clear that as much as he valued me and my attempts as a white, cisgender male to talk about race and oppression issues with him, there was a certain way in which working with his new therapist allowed him to talk more easily and honestly about the impact of his experiences of race and oppression.

Through the three-month program, he also continued to work conjointly with me. The combination of transpersonal, social justice, and cognitive behavioral approaches as well as medications reduced his symptoms and dramatically increased his functionality. The intensive treatment program modified the traditional behavioral approach to OCD treatment and supported his experimentation with what he felt worked best for him. As an example, instead of using replacement thoughts written in English, he found that speaking to himself in Spanglish was more effective as it captured the complexity of his identity. He would use the rosary and prayer as replacement and alternative behaviors to combat hair-washing impulses. He moved beyond his internalized and systemically reinforced negative view of himself as being his OCD diagnosis to a larger sense of a multicultural, spiritual self in which his OCD symptoms were only one aspect of his self-understanding. I continued to work with him for another six months after he completed the program, and his symptoms were dramatically reduced. When we completed, he had sustained employment working at an animal rescue shelter, began dating, and became more active in his church's outreach program. This is one example of some of the capacity and flexibility of the transpersonal approach.

Central Counseling Research Themes Supporting the Transpersonal Approach

In general, psychotherapy and counseling research shows high rates of success across varied approaches and metrics (Barber, Muran, Keefe, & McCarthy, 2013; Lambert, 2013a; 2013b). As described throughout this chapter, transpersonal counseling aligns with therapeutic stances and practices that have been shown to be effective across theoretical perspectives. Saul Rosenzweig (1936) initially proposed the common factors model to explain how psychotherapeutic successes are seen across theoretically divergent approaches. For Rosenzweig, the therapeutic relationship and active engagement in the process seemed to account more for positive changes than a specific theory or approach. Jerome Frank (1961) reviewed the research of his era and drew upon qualitative studies that looked at the nuances of psychotherapeutic change, as well as quantitative outcome measures. He articulated four major themes in psychological change: the therapeutic relationship, the active participation of client and therapist, client expectancy, and a rational, conceptual scheme of the change process.

Multiple individuals carried this work forward, including Lisa Grencavage and John Norcross (1990), who updated Frank's list and identified 89 potential common factors across therapy approaches. They summarized the five overarching factors as the therapeutic relationship, therapist qualities, client characteristics, treatment structure, and change processes. In terms of change processes, Lambert (2013a) highlights that current research has yet to adequately understand the leaps of positive changes some clients will often make in therapy after a period of stagnation. These changes do not appear to be the result of the accumulation of a manualized approach but potentially arise from corrective emotional experience within the therapy.

Through analyzing existing research, Lambert (1992) attempted to measure the contributions of each of the factors of successful therapy. He estimated that common factors such as the therapeutic bond, empathic listening, and collaboration accounted for 30% of treatment outcome. He proposed that client expectancy, placebo effects, and understanding the therapy process, as well as the therapist's technical interventions, each accounted for 15% of the change process. Lambert suggested that the largest factor was the combination of extra-therapeutic factors, which accounted for 40%. These extra-therapeutic factors can be broken down into two subcategories. The first category is client qualities, which includes openness and psychological mindedness. In Lambert's schema, these qualities determine why many clients show marked improvement after about 15 to 20 sessions, while other clients need closer to 50 to have similar benefits (Lambert, 2013a). The second category is social support. This category highlights the need for an empirical transpersonal approach to psychotherapy that supports clients to build connections and support outside of the sessions; this may include incorporating social justice approaches (Ali, Liu, Mahmood, & Arguello, 2008), as well as integrating clients' cultural traditions such as rituals, myths, and identities (Canda & Smith, 2013).

Expanding from the common factors research of Grencavage and Norcross (1990), Tracy and colleagues (2003) analyzed therapist views of emotional experiences versus the technical and educational aspects of therapy. They suggested that the three major factors of successful therapy could be understood as the therapeutic alliance or emotional bonding, the information shared and meanings created between therapist and client, and finally, a structure that enables the client to understand the change process.

Imel and Wampold (2008) estimated that common factors account for between 30 and 70% of positive outcome in psychotherapy, and highlight the impact of the following factors that are consistent with transpersonal approaches. These factors include goal consensus and collaboration (11.5%), empathy (9%), therapeutic alliance (7.5%), positive regard (6.3%), congruence and genuineness (5.7%), and other therapist factors (5%). Surprisingly, treatment methods were shown to have only about 1% outcome variance. A more recent review strikingly echoes Vaughan's (1979) conceptualization, finding the most important common factors to be collaboration, empathy, therapeutic alliance, positive regard, congruence, and therapist factors (Laska, Gurman, & Wampold, 2014).

All of these highly regarded reviews align closely with the transpersonal ethos and approach. Transpersonal counseling is not dependent on a series of techniques but focuses on presence, connection, collaboration, accurate attunement, and an expansive view of the possibility of change and growth. It relies on the common factors and the relational approach that has repeatedly shown effectiveness (Elkins, 2015; Hoffman, Vallejos, Cleare-Hoffman, & Rubin 2015; Laska et al., 2014).

In some instances, additional techniques appear to be important for some specific changes and challenges, such as the behavioral-based exposure intervention discussed in the OCD case example above. However, in general, the common factors of treatment appear vital even when utilizing techniques such as exposure and response inhibition. Despite strong and consistent support for the common factors of psychotherapy and counseling, the focus of research has consistently turned toward techniques and theoretical orientation as the primary agents of change. As such, models with clear operationalized protocol, such as CBT, are able to produce substantial evidence that has deeply influenced the manner of mental health care implementation.

Nevertheless, many cognitive behavioral treatments are beginning to include the common factors in their trainings (Hoffmann & Barlow, 2014). Shedler's (2010, 2015) reviews comparing cognitive behavioral and psychodynamic therapy are relevant to transpersonal counseling in that a focus on the therapeutic relationship and experiencing feelings within therapy sessions appear to be more influential for positive outcome than strictly adhering to cognitive protocols. Castonguay and Hill's (2012) research demonstrates that helping clients develop the ability to self-reflect and gain insight are the essential elements for lasting change, regardless of theoretical orientation. The goals in these reviews are similar to transpersonal goals in that they rise above the strict symptom reduction paradigm and embrace counseling as a process aimed toward developing more awareness, aliveness, and integration.

The call for research methods that reach beyond the limitations of nomothetic theory and technique-driven, randomized controlled trials has increasingly been endorsed throughout the field (Hoffman et al., 2015; Greene, 2012). While transpersonal therapists should critically read and understand the findings of contemporary analysis such as meta-analytic, power, and mixed-method studies, room exists for other ways of learning and understanding. Accordingly, the American Psychological Association's Task Force on Evidence Based Practice (2006) greatly expanded its classification of appropriate research evidence to include designs such as clinical observation, single case studies, quasi-experimental designs, and ethnographic research. Utilizing one's clinical experience, areas of expertise, supervision, and consultation are also included as part of this larger vision of the evidence-based orientation. The APA reports that clinicians are considered to be evidence based if their case conceptualization focuses on the contextual complexity of individuals in their environment, sensitivity to cultural differences, unique client presentations, and individual client preferences. The APA Task Force summarizes that an evidence-based therapy needs to have research support (broadly defined), a rationally articulated theoretical approach, and consider individual differences. In all of these ways, transpersonal counseling finds itself well within the lines of the APA definition of an evidence-based approach.

Future Directions
While counseling and therapy, like all health-related endeavors, continue to become more specialized in research and training, the clinical work itself is often much more expansive. Although some psychotherapy research methodologies are being broadened, many researchers and journal publishers still hold tightly to prioritizing the randomized control trials that seek internal validity over other research approaches that may actually be more generalizable to clinical complexity. As Greene (2012) suggests, there is a gap between psychotherapy researchers and clinicians that has widened significantly over the last few decades. Researchers present their finding in journals that are read mainly by other researchers, and their studies often do not reach across the divide to communicate in a manner that typical clinicians can utilize. Clinicians also bear responsibility for not expending the energy and time to critically read and understand both the strengths and limitations of contemporary research findings.

Some researchers are moving toward more real-life, clinically based research, and with the advent of technology many clinicians could more easily add these research methods into their practices (Boswell & Castonguay, 2007; Lau, Ogrodniczuk, Joyce, & Sochting, 2010). Becoming adept and accomplished as both a researcher and clinician is very rare, as each focus can take decades of training to become proficient. However, building networks that include both researchers and clinicians for discussion and collaboration would be a significant start as both groups have much to offer the other. Graduate schools are essential for fostering lasting collaborative understanding and endeavors between researchers and clinicians, as well as exposing new professionals to the strengths and limitations of various research methodologies and their applications to clinical practice.

Transpersonal researchers and clinicians need to move outside of their own arenas and interact and collaborate with others with different orientations (Anderson & Braud, 2011). Without such active engagement with others different from ourselves, transpersonal counseling will continue to be misunderstood and misrepresented. The current trend in textbooks demonstrates that few even mention transpersonal counseling in their hundreds of pages. If transpersonal psychology and counseling are mentioned, the field is often given only cursory attention, such as a sentence in a review of Abraham Maslow's many contributions (e.g., Maslow, 1968, 1973). Sadly, colleagues of ours have reported not listing transpersonal psychology as an interest in conference presentation applications for fear of being misunderstood, pigeon-holed, and potentially biased against. Because of these conditions, the transpersonal approach may be becoming increasingly marginalized. Despite its direct influence on many contemporary psychological trends, transpersonal seems to be increasingly removed from the academic lexicon. Transpersonal psychotherapy has the breadth and inclusiveness to continue to be of service to individuals, to the field of psychotherapy, and potentially to reach beyond the realm of therapy and counseling. Reclaiming the transpersonal approach along with its empirical basis is essential.

References

Ali, S. B., Liu, W. M., Mahmood, A., & Arguello, J. (2008). Social justice and applied psychology: Practical ideas for training the next generation of psychologists. *Journal for Social Action in Counseling and Psychology, 2,* 1–3.

American Psychiatric Association. (2013). *Diagnostic and statistical manual of mental disorders* (5th ed.). Washington, DC: author.

American Psychological Association Presidential Task on Evidence Based-Practice in Psychology. (2006). Evidence-based practice in psychology. *American Psychologist, 61,* 271–285.

Anderson, R., & Braud, W. (1998). *Transpersonal research methods for the social sciences: Honoring human experience.* Thousand Oaks, CA: Sage.

Anderson, R., & Braud, W. (2011). *Transforming self and others through research: Transpersonal research methods for the human sciences and the humanities.* Albany, NY: State University of New York Press.

Awasthi, B. (2013). Issues and perspectives in meditation research: In search for a definition. *Frontiers in Psychology, 3.* doi: 10.3389/fpsyg.2012.00613

Barber, J., Muran, C., Keefe, J., & McCarthy, K. (2013). Psychodynamic approaches. In M. J. Lambert (Ed.), *Bergin & Garfield's handbook of psychotherapy and behavior change* (6th ed., pp. 443–491). New York, NY: Wiley.

Bike, D. H., Norcross, J. C., & Schatz, D. M. (2009). Processes and outcomes of psychotherapists' personal therapy: Replication and extension twenty years later. *Psychotherapy, 46*(1), 119–31.

Blanck, G., & Blanck, R. (1974). *Ego psychology: Theory and practice.* New York, NY: Colombia University Press.

Blanck, G., & Blanck, R. (1979). *Ego psychology II: Psychoanalytic developmental pathology.* New York, NY: Colombia University Press.

Boswell, J. F., & Castonguay, L. G. (2007). Psychotherapy training: Suggestions for core ingredients and future research. *Psychotherapy: Theory, Research, Practice, Training, 44*(4), 378–383.

Cain, D. J., Keenan, K., & Rubin, S. (Eds.). (2015). *Humanistic psychotherapies: Handbook of research and practice* (2nd ed.). Washington, DC: American Psychological Association.

Canda, E. R., & Smith, E. D. (2013). *Transpersonal perspectives on spirituality in social work.* New York, NY: Routledge.

Castonguay, L.G., & Hill, C. E. (2012). Corrective experiences in psychotherapy: An introduction. In L. G. Castonguay & C. E. Hill (Eds.), *Transformation in psychotherapy: Corrective experiences across cognitive behavioral, humanistic, and psychodynamic approaches* (pp. 3–9). Washington, DC: American Psychological Association.

Castonguay, L., Barkham, M., Lutz, W., & McAleavey, A. (2013). Practice oriented research: Approaches and applications. In M. J. Lambert (Ed.), *Bergin & Garfield's handbook of psychotherapy and behavior change* (6th ed., pp. 85–133). New York, NY: Wiley.

Clay, R. A. (2011). Mixing it up: Can adding case studies to randomized trial data help bridge the research/practice gap? *Monitor on Psychology, 42*(6), 36.

Cleare-Hoffman, H. P., Hoffman, L., & Wilson, S. S. (2013, August). Existential therapy, culture, and therapist factors in evidence based practice. In K. Keenan (Chair), Evidence in support of existential-humanistic psychotherapy: Revitalizing the third force. Symposium presented at the 121st Annual Convention of the American Psychological Association, Honolulu, HI.

Comas-Díaz, L. (2012). *Multicultural care: A clinician's guide to cultural competence.* Washington DC: American Psychological Association.

Cooper, M., & McLeod, J. (2011). *Pluralistic counseling and psychotherapy.* London: Sage.

Cortright, B. (1997). *Psychotherapy and spirit: Theory and practice in transpersonal psychotherapy.* Albany, NY: State University of New York. Press.

Cozolino, L. (2016). *Why therapy works: Using our minds to change our brains.* New York, NY: W. W. Norton & Company.

Crotty, M. (1998). *The foundations of social research: Meaning and perspective in the research process.* London: Sage.

Daniels, M. (2005). *Shadow, self, spirit: Essays in transpersonal psychology.* Exeter, UK: Imprint Academic.

Daniels, M. (2015). Traditional roots, history, and evolution of the transpersonal perspective. In H.L. Friedman & G. Hartelius (Eds.), *The Wiley-Blackwell handbook of transpersonal psychology* (2nd ed., pp. 23–43). West Sussex, UK: John Wiley & Sons.

Daniels, M., & McNutt, B. (1997). Questioning the role of transpersonal psychology. *Transpersonal Psychology Review, 1*(4), 4–9.

Davis, D. M., & Hayes, J. A. (2011). What are the benefits of mindfulness? A practice review of psychotherapy-related research. *Psychotherapy, 48*(2), 198–208.

Derogatis, L. R. (1994). *Symptom Checklist 90–R: Administration, scoring, and procedures manual* (3rd ed.). Minneapolis, MN: National Computer Systems.

Epstein, M. (1984). On the neglect of evenly suspended attention. *Journal of Transpersonal Psychology, 16,* 193–205.

Elkins, D. N. (2009). *Humanistic psychology: A clinical manifesto: A critique of clinical psychology and the need for progressive alternatives.* Colorado Springs, CO: University of the Rockies Press.

Elkins, D. N. (2015). *The human elements of psychotherapy: A nonmedical model of emotional healing.* Washington, DC: American Psychological Association.

Ellis, A. (1962). *Reason and emotion in psychotherapy.* New York, NY: Lyle Stuart.

Finlay, L., & Gough, B. (Eds.). (2003). *Reflexivity: A practical guide for researchers in health and social sciences.* Oxford: Blackwell Publishing.

Frank, J.D. (1961). *Persuasion and healing: A comparative study of psychotherapy.* Baltimore, MD: Johns Hopkins Press.

Friedman, H. L. (2015). Transpersonal self-expansiveness as a scientific construct. In H.L. Friedman & G. Hartelius (Eds.), *The Wiley-Blackwell handbook of transpersonal psychology* (2nd ed., pp. 203–222). West Sussex, UK: John Wiley & Sons.

Friedman, H., & MacDonald, D. A. (2002). Using transpersonal tests in humanistic psychological assessment. *The Humanistic Psychologist, 30*(3), 223–236.

Garcia-Romeu, A. P., & Tart, C. T. (2015). Altered states of consciousness and transpersonal psychology. In H.L. Friedman & G. Hartelius (Eds.), *The Wiley-Blackwell handbook of transpersonal psychology* (2nd ed., pp. 121–140). West Sussex, UK: John Wiley & Sons.

Greene, L. R. (2012). Group therapist as social scientist, with special reference to the psychodynamically oriented psychotherapist. *American*

Psychologist, 67(6), 477–489.

Grencavage, L. M., & Norcross, J. C. (1990). Where are the commonalities among the therapeutic common factors? *Professional Psychology: Research and Practice, 21*(5), 372–378.

Grof, S. (2015). Revision and re-enchantment of psychology: Legacy from half a century of consciousness research. In H.L. Friedman & G. Hartelius (Eds.), *The Wiley-Blackwell handbook of transpersonal Psychology* (2nd ed., pp. 23–43). West Sussex, UK: John Wiley & Sons.

Grof, S., & Grof, C. (Eds.) (1989). *Spiritual emergency: When personal transformation becomes a crisis.* Los Angeles, CA: Tarcher.

Hart, R., Ivtzan, I., & Hart, D. (2013). Mind the gap in mindfulness research: A comparative account of the leading schools of thought. *American Psychological Association Review of General Psychology, 17*(4), 453–466.

Hartelius, G., & Ferrer, J. N. (2015). Transpersonal philosophy: The participatory turn. In H.L. Friedman & G. Hartelius (Eds.), *The Wiley-Blackwell handbook of transpersonal psychology* (2nd ed., pp. 433–458). West Sussex, UK: John Wiley & Sons.

Hoffman, L., Vallejos, L., Cleare-Hoffman, H. P., & Rubin, S. (2015). Emotion, relationship, and meaning as core existential practice: Evidence-based foundations. *Journal of Contemporary Psychotherapy, 45,* 11–20.

Hofmann, S. G., & Barlow, D. H. (2014). Evidence-based psychological interventions and the common factors approach: The beginnings of a rapprochement? *Psychotherapy: Theory, Research, Practice, Training, 51*(4), 510–513.

Huey Jr., S. J., Tilley, J. L., Jones, E. O., & Smith, C. A. (2014). The contribution of cultural competence to evidence-based care for ethnically diverse populations. *Annual Review of Clinical Psychology, 10,* 305–338.

Imel, Z. E., & Wampold, B. E. (2008). The importance of treatment and the science of common factors in psychotherapy. In S. D. Brown & R. W. Lent (Eds.), *Handbook of counseling psychology* (4th ed., pp. 249–262). Hoboken, NJ: John Wiley & Sons.

James, W. (2008). *A Pluralistic Universe.* Rockville, MD: Arc Manor. (Original work published 1909)

Johnsen, T. J., & Friborg, O. (2015). The effects of cognitive behavioral therapy as an anti-depressive treatment is falling: A meta-analysis. *Psychological Bulletin, 141*(4), 747.

Jones, A., & Crandall, R. (1986). Validation of a short index of self-actualization. *Personality and Social Psychology Bulletin, 12,* 63–73.

Kaklauskas, F. J. (2016). Solitude. In K. Travis, W. Stone, F. J., Kaklauskas, & C. Landreneau (Eds.), *Courage to explore – The life cycle of a career: Three group therapists speak on solitude.* Oakland, CA: Hungry Minds Recordings.

Kaminker, J., & Lukoff, D. (2015). Transpersonal perspectives on mental health and mental illness. In H.L. Friedman & G. Hartelius (Eds.), *The Wiley-*

Blackwell handbook of transpersonal psychology (2nd ed., pp. 419–432). West Sussex, UK: John Wiley & Sons.

Kohut, H. (1971). *Analysis of the self.* New York, NY: International Universities Press.

Kohut, H. (1977). *The restoration of the self.* New York, NY: International Universities Press.

Kumari, N. (2011). Personal therapy as a mandatory requirement for counseling psychologists in training: A qualitative study of the impact of therapy on trainees' personal and professional development. *Counselling Psychology Quarterly, 24*(3), 211–232.

Lambert, M. J. (2013a). Outcome in psychotherapy: The past and important advances. *Psychotherapy, 50*(1), 42–51.

Lambert, M. J. (2013b). The efficacy and effectiveness of psychotherapy. In M. J. Lambert (Ed.), *Bergin & Garfield's handbook of psychotherapy and behavior change* (6th ed., pp. 169–218). New York, NY: Wiley.

Lambert, M. J., Kahler, M., Harmon, C., Burlingame, G. M., & Shimokawa, K. (2011). *Administration and scoring manual for the outcome questionnaire-*45.2. Salt Lake City, UT: OQ Measures.

Lambert, M. J. (1992). Psychotherapy outcome research: Implications for integrative and eclectic therapists. In J.C. Norcross & M.R. Goldfried (eds.) *Handbook of Psychotherapy Integration* (pp. 94-129). New York: Basic Books.

Laska, K. M., Gurman, A. S., & Wampold, B. E. (2014). Expanding the lens of evidence-based practice in psychotherapy: A common factors perspective. *Psychotherapy, 51*(4), 467–481.

Lau, M., Ogrodniczuk, J., Joyce, A. S., & Sochting, I. (2010). Bridging the practitioner-scientist gap in group psychotherapy research. *International Journal of Group Psychotherapy, 60,* 177–196.

Lindheim, O., Kolko, D. J., & Cheng, Y. (2012). Predicting psychotherapy benefit: A probabilistic and individualized approach. *Behavior Therapy 43*(2), 381–392.

Loewenthal, D., & Snell, R. (2003). *Postmodernism for psychotherapists: A critical reader.* London: Psychology Press.

MacDonald, D. A., & Friedman, H. L. (2015). Quantitative assessment of transpersonal and spiritual constructs. In H. L. Friedman & G. Hartelius (Eds.), *The Wiley-Blackwell handbook of transpersonal psychology* (2nd ed., pp. 281–299). West Sussex, UK: John Wiley & Sons.

MacDonald, D. A., Walsh, R. & Shapiro, S.L. (2015). Meditation: Empirical research and future directions. In H.L Friedman & G. Hartelius (Eds.), *The Wiley-Blackwell handbook of transpersonal psychology* (2nd ed., pp. 433–458). West Sussex, UK: John Wiley & Sons.

Maslow, A. H. (1968). *Towards a psychology of being* (2nd ed.). Princeton, NJ: Van Nostrand. (Original work published 1962)

Maslow, A. H. (1973). *The farther reaches of human nature.* Harmondsworth, Middlesex, UK: Penguin.

McWilliams, N. (2011). *Psychoanalytic diagnosis: Understanding personality structure in the clinical process* (2nd ed.). New York, NY: Guilford Press.

Mearns, D., & Cooper, M. (2005). *Working at relational depth in counseling and psychotherapy.* London: Sage.

Millon, T. (2003). It's time to rework the blueprints: Building a science for clinical psychology. *American Psychologist, 58,* 949–961.

Morrow, S. L. (2005). Quality and trustworthiness in qualitative research in counseling psychology. *Journal of Counseling Psychology, 52*(2), 250–260.

Munder, T., Wilmers, F., Leonhart, R., Linster, H. W., & Barth, J. (2010). Working alliance inventory-short revised (WAI-SR): Psychometric properties in outpatients and inpatients. *Clinical Psychology & Psychotherapy, 17*(3), 231–239.

Pappas, J., & Friedman, H. (2004). Scientific transpersonal psychology and cultural diversity: Focus on measurement in research and clinical practice. In W. Smythe & A. Baydala (Eds.), *Studies of how the mind publicly enfolds into being: Mellen studies in psychology* (Vol. 9, pp. 303–345). Lewiston, NY: Edwin Mellen Press.

Parson, R. D., & Zhang, N. (2014). *Becoming a skilled counselor.* Los Angeles, CA: Sage.

Piedmont, R. L. (1999). Does spirituality represent the sixth factor of personality? Spiritual transcendence and the five-factor model. *Journal of Personality, 67,* 985–1013.

Robitschek, C. (1998). Personal growth initiative: The construct and its measure. *Measurement and Evaluation in Counselling and Development, 30,* 183–198.

Rodrigues, V., & Friedman, H. L. (2015). Transpersonal psychotherapies. In H. L. Friedman & G. Hartelius (Eds.), *The Wiley-Blackwell handbook of transpersonal psychology* (2nd ed., pp. 580–594). West Sussex, UK: John Wiley & Sons.

Rosenzweig, S. (1936, July). Some implicit common factors in diverse methods of psychotherapy. *American Journal of Orthopsychiatry, 6*(3), 412–415.

Roth, A., & Fonagy, P. (2013). *What works for whom? A critical review of psychotherapy research.* New York, NY: Guilford.

Schore, A. (2012). *The science of the art of psychotherapy.* New York, NY: Norton.

Shean, G. (2014). Limitations of randomized control designs in psychotherapy research. *Advances in Psychiatry, 2014,* 1–5, Article ID 561452.

Shedler, J. (2010). The efficacy of psychodynamic psychotherapy. *American Psychologist, 65,* 98–109.

Shedler, J. (2015). Where is the evidence for "evidence-based" therapy? *The Journal of Psychological Therapies in Primary Care, 4,* 47–59.

Sperry, L. (2010). *Core competencies in counseling and psychotherapy: Becoming a highly competent and effective therapist.* New York, NY: Routledge.

Spotnitz, H. (2004). *Modern psychoanalysis of the schizophrenic patient: Theory of the technique* (2nd ed.). New York, NY: YBK Publishers.

Steger, M. F., Frazier, P., Oishi, S., & Kaler, M. (2006). The meaning in life questionnaire: Assessing the presence of and search for meaning in life. *Journal of Counseling Psychology, 53*, 80–93.

Sullivan, H. S. (1953). *The interpersonal theory of psychiatry.* New York, NY: Norton.

Sutich, A. (1973). Transpersonal therapy. *Journal of Transpersonal Psychology, 5*(1), 1–6.

Thyer, B. (2013). Evidence-based practice or evidence-guided practice: A rose by any other name would smell as sweet. Invited response to Gitterman & Knight's evidence-based practice. *Families in Society: The Journal of Contemporary Social Services, 94*(2), 79–84.

Townsend, P., & Kaklauskas, F. J. (2008). Therapist subjectivity in contemplative psychotherapy. In F. Kaklauskas, S. Nimanheminda, L. Hoffman, & M. Jack (Eds.), *Brilliant sanity: Buddhist approaches to psychotherapy* (pp. 39–64). Colorado Springs, CO: University of the Rockies Press.

Tracey, T. G. J., Lichtenberg, J. W., Goodyear, R. K., Claiborn, C. D., & Wampold, B. E. (2003). Concept mapping of therapeutic common factors. *Psychotherapy Research (4)*, 401–413.

Vaughan, F. (1979). Transpersonal psychotherapy: Context, content, and process. *Journal of Transpersonal Psychology, 11*(2), 101–110.

Walfish, S., McAlister, B., O'Donnell, P., & Lambert, M. J. (2012). An investigation of self-assessment bias in mental health providers. *Psychological Reports, 110*(2), 639–644.

Walsh, R., & Vaughn, F. (1993). *Paths beyond ego: The transpersonal vision.* New York, NY: Jeremy P. Tarcher/Putnam.

Wampold, B. E. (2009). Research evidence for the common factors models: A historically situated perspective. In B. L. Duncan, S. D. Miller, B. E. Wampold, & M. A. Hubble (Eds.), *The heart and soul of change: Delivering what works in therapy* (2nd ed., pp. 49–81). Washington, DC: American Psychological Association.

Wickramasekera II, I. E. (2015). Hypnosis and transpersonal psychology: Answering the call within. In H. L. Friedman & G. Hartelius (Eds.), *The Wiley-Blackwell handbook of transpersonal psychology* (2nd ed., pp. 492–512). West Sussex, UK: John Wiley & Sons.

Wilber, K. (1975). Psychologia perennis: The spectrum of consciousness. *Journal of Transpersonal Psychology, 7*(2).

Williams, A. K. (2000). *Zen and the art of living with fearlessness and grace.* New York, NY: Diane Publishing.

Yalom, I. (2002). *The gift of therapy: An open letter to a new generation of therapists and their patients.* New York, NY: HarperCollins.

Yehuda, R., Hallig, S. L., & Grossman, R. (2001). Childhood trauma and risk for PTSD: Relationship to intergenerational effects of trauma, parental PTSD, and cortisol excretion. *Development and Psychopathology, 13*, 733–753.

Chapter 5
Imaginal Mindfulness—Imaginal Intelligence: Musings on the Languages of Shadow and Light in Art, Meditation, and Clinical Practice[1]

Michael A. Franklin

Light reveals, darkness obscures. Visual artists study and utilize these features when using color, light, and shadow to articulate opposing emotions, model form, or surface unconscious meaning. What is felt can be materialized and shown to others, and if this process is trusted, corresponding existential anguish becomes surmountable as inner self-structure fragments and reassembles in creative work. Image and imagination, which are indigenous to all aspects of the art process, not only support the discovery of meaning in suffering, but also reveal pathways for creating our way out of our suffering. During such times, endarkened shadow material becomes illuminated, but, like quicksilver, images change, hide, and resurface again. Attentiveness to this mercurial intelligence, a core theme in this chapter, is discussed from various contemplative perspectives—specifically imaginal mindfulness, which is

---

[1] The following chapter has several sections related to an upcoming publication, *Art as Contemplatie Practice: Expressive Pathways to the Self*, to be published by SUNY Press in 2017.

a personally devised term that joins meditation with visual art and archetypal psychology. Thoughts, somatic sensations, and related narratives, when observed from a perspective that privileges the primacy of images in tandem with artistically manifesting corresponding content, exponentially magnify inner awareness. Not only can we see our thoughts materializing before us in languages of lines, shapes, textures, and colors, we can track this content as it unfolds within artworks that unflatten and externalize human experience. Below I address how the expressive language of art, related to the subjects of shadow and light, becomes metabolized imagery within the psyche. Imaginal, archetypal psychology is also discussed as it uniquely relates to art, imaginal intelligence, and imaginal mindfulness, which I have written about elsewhere in more detail (Franklin, in press).

Shadow, Light, Inner Diversity, and Languages of Art

Art speaks. If carefully observed, imagery in artworks reveal patiently waiting, innate intelligence. These images, perhaps consisting of tones of grey in a black-and-white photograph, ecstatic bodily movements in dance, or discordant sounds in the environment, articulate the background and foreground of wide-ranging imaginal material. When heeding these poetic cues, insights and influences from inner life instinctively emerge. Furthermore, this contemplatively engaged approach to art awakens deeper awareness into the shadowed chambers of the non-dual, inner self (Franklin, in press).

Developmentally speaking, Western psychology, including transpersonal viewpoints, spotlights the mechanisms of the ego, including ego strengths/resources, ego ideals, ego defense mechanisms, ego boundaries, and the observing capacities of the ego. Additionally, paths beyond ego, an implicit premise in transpersonal psychology, considers non-duality, or a unified view of human potential, that transcends subject–object splits (Walsh & Vaughan, 1993). Davis (2000) notes that Western psychological theory has a penchant for conditioning, "reductionism, and separateness," yet our well-being implies self-transcendence from a "conditioned personality to a sense of spiritual identity" that implies cascading degrees of non-dual unification (p. 4).

An example of how art awakens non-duality can be seen in the work of art historian Ananda Coomaraswamy. In his introduction to *The Mirror of Gesture,* Coomaraswamy (1917) observed:

> The arts are not for our instruction, but for our delight, and this delight is something more than pleasure, it is the God-like ecstasy of liberation from the restless activity of the mind and the senses, which are the veils of all reality, transparent only when we are at peace with ourselves. From the love of many things we are led to the experience of Union. (p. 9)

Entheos, meaning the God within, is the root of enthusiasm and, as this chapter argues, massages the passion to create and surface expressive life force. Visual art catalyzes soul and entheos, making inner, imaginal diversity visible at the personal, communal, or cultural level. Within this context, soul means entheos. Through amplification, Hillman suggests that the soul is an ambiguous symbol that can be searched, put on trial, or even taken on a journey. Therefore, soul is best imagined not as a thing but as layered processes of interiorized "mind, spirit, heart, life, warmth, humanness, personality, essence…courage, virtue, morality, wisdom, death, God" (Hillman, 1972, p. 23). As both oxygen and blood flow, images irrigate the psyche's systemic totality while the arts function to make these territories visible through the currents of the soul's imagination. Perhaps the most poignant example of this premise can be found in the publication of Jung's Red Book (2009). The *Liber Novus* represents a masterwork of art-based research (McNiff, 1998; Sullivan, 2010) regarding the discovery of guiding myths during times of personal and cultural crisis (Stein, 2012).

Interstices and Gobos: Contemplating Shadows and Light
In the late 1970s, I worked in Manhattan at a professional photography studio where we did high-end catalogue work. Each shoot consisted of complex lighting. The set could have 30 or more individually focused

lights, each casting intentional shadows with the aid of barn doors, scrim, or nothing at all. Sometimes we would need to "Gobo" the light, or put a piece of cardboard between the light source and the subject. Gobo stands for go-between and is a well-known phrase to studio photographers. It is a way to creatively use light and shadow for dramatic effect.

This idea of interceding between a stimulus and a behavioral response or a thought and an action, revealed through studio lighting, made psychological sense to me. To intrapersonally gobo intrusive, dysfunctional thoughts is to intentionally intervene with reframing solutions. Various contemplative practices serve a similar purpose. For example, mantra meditation can achieve a comparable result. That is, the mantra exists between an unproductive thought and corresponding, habitual response. As the mantra becomes the focus of concentration, healing sound replaces dysfunctional ruminations. Not meant as a cure but as a beginning reframing strategy, mantra recitation deflects negativity while magnetizing the psyche toward healing seed syllables. Consisting of two roots: *trāna*, "that which protects," and *manas*, "mind," mantra practices protect the mind by concentrating on sacred, consciousness-transforming phrases from spiritual languages like Hebrew or Sanskrit (Feuerstein, 2003). Contemplative practices interrupt deviant patterns and positively spackle the cracks of defeatist thoughts. By no means is this the sole purpose of mantra repetition. In fact, certain mantras both liberate and offer protection through the mental body while representing the subtle-level sonic body of a deity (Feuerstein, 2003; Khanna, 1979; Mookerjee & Khanna, 1977). Devotedly repeating a sacred mantra serves as a caring intrapersonal maneuver. Rather than thinking of 100 things, focusing on one revered sound or phrase intercedes between disturbing distractions and attention to one treasured mantra.

Illuminating Waiting Potential: Visual Mantra Practice in Art
Khanna (1979) discussed how mantras are "non-discursive symbols" (p. 36) that express transcendent elemental truths through recited sounds. An essential component of mantra recitation is repetition of the sound,

word, or phrase. Although certain Sanskrit mantras are recommended, watchwords such as rest, blue, or the name of a safe place from childhood could serve a similar purpose. Interceding by repeating such a phrase, the mantra, like the notion of the photographic gobo, pierces subtle layers of the psyche by soothing the body–mind continuum with brightening sacred sounds. In addition to the auditory quality of the mantra, repetition is essential for the benefits of the practice to manifest results.

Within the performing arts and visual arts, students also learn through repetition. Musicians play and replay great works to empathically enter the skin and mind of the composer. Visual artists create and recreate certain landscapes, color studies, or old master artworks. For example, Cezanne frequently repainted Mont Sainte-Victoire near Aix-en-Provence (Plazy, 1990). Reinterpreting this scene revealed penetrating understanding of a fresh, radical analysis of form and space on a flat, two-dimensional canvas. Like a visual mantra practice, these repetitive experiments both freed the surface of his paintings and consequently ushered in a fundamental shift in Western art that influenced many artists and facilitated the rise of cubism (Franklin, in press).

Another way to metaphorically apply interceding gobo techniques with art materials and processes is through shadow and light techniques like chiaroscuro and value scales. As fundamental representations of conscious and unconscious material, shadow and light represent a vast territory of the psyche's landscape.

Umbral De-light
When sunlight hits an object from one direction, a two-part shadow is cast, one darker, and the other lighter. The umbra is the densest, interior part of the shadow. The penumbra manifests as the outer region of a shadow. Here, the light source is partially obscured (a root word of chiaroscuro) by the obstructing body.

In creative work, when an illuminating idea emerges awareness is peaked, while the ambiguity of nameless information remains. Yet-to-be-exposed eurekas eventually emerge through further experimentation. As awareness becomes lit with ideas, the cast shadows of waiting potential drift into preconscious availability, ready for lighted discovery. This is the territory where psychological material is slightly out of awareness, but increasingly accessible for contact, especially through artistic, imaginal processes that favor poetry and artistic methods like chiaroscuro and grey-scale value studies.

Image "What I Look Like Inside." Charcoal and chalk on paper (black-and-white version); original artwork by the author.[2]

The Greek verb *poieo* means to do, create, or construct. And poetic voice is a timeless means for decoding messages of the soul's speech. Aristotle's work on poesis (to create in order to manifest), mimesis (imitative behavior for ascertaining meaning), and tekne (adept

---

2 This drawing was completed during the early stages of seeking treatment for prostate cancer. Throughout this time, a disciplined practice of combining art with meditation proved to be extremely effective. Meditation allowed me to be the witness of my mind while art allowed me to see the content of my mind. In this example, I was imagining what I looked like inside. Charcoal was chosen to model light and dark areas of imagined inner anatomy and emotional vulnerability.

technique for surfacing latent possibilities) all support discovery through creative investigation (Liddell & Scott, 1996). During Vedic times, poets were inspired by the gods and goddesses to voice indescribable spiritual experiences. Adeptly moving between the realms of mind and heart, these enlightened artists humbly engaged the revelatory faculty of the imagination to reify inexplicable meaning within divine and natural order. Fascination with light particularly interested them as a way to grasp how the hidden world paints itself from darkness into existence or "nonbeing into being" every day (Mahony, 1998, p. 71). Light was the reflection of various deities and could be understood through contemplative insight (Franklin, in press). These visionary poets, said to hold "light in their mouths," manifested what was inexpressible to most through their transcendent speech (Mahony, 1998, p. 73).

Exploring gradations of shaded lightness and dense darkness sensitizes both the artist and viewer to contemplate areas of textural contact. Chiaroscuro techniques utilize dramatic contrast in order to show three-dimensional modeling on a flat surface. Both chiaroscuro and grey-scale studies are used to model volume, thereby unflattening the surface. Highlights and lowlights as well as dramatic meetings between a dark edge and a lighter edge amp up the visual effect. This point of contact between opposite boundaried spaces raises contemplative questions about the subtleties of borders, how to negotiate sides of a viewpoint, and meet in the middle holding awareness of multiple perspectives.

Color, Light, and Transpersonal Discovery through Art

A consistent historical theme related to creativity, art, and spirituality is the subject of light (Knight, 1987; Golding, 2000; Tuckman, 1986). For obvious reasons, religious traditions reference light for its representation of nuance and contemplative vocabulary, thus offering terminology to express ineffable experiences associated with spiritual life. For example, synonyms like radiant, illumination, glimmer, and luminosity aptly apply to spiritual experiences. Light, and the lack of it, suggest hellish conditions or divine revelation as well as shifts in time. Surfaces bathed in shadow and light, when carefully observed, provide ongoing lessons on temporal phenomena. Concerning psychological states and time-based occurrences, the language of shadows—including the partial shading of penumbral gradation or the lavishly darkened umbral textures within shadows—reveals felt-sense awareness of moods like darkened illumination or illuminated dreariness. Intentionally stated within binary terms, blackened radiance suggests qualities of unconscious subtlety. Making this hidden, deteriorating transpersonal territory seen is a primary function of art. Susanne Langer, the galvanizing and distinguished philosopher of the mid 20th century, vividly suggested that a major function of all the arts was to perceptibly articulate human emotion (Langer, 1951, 1953). Further deepening her claim within the context of this chapter includes the way in which the arts coherently serve the psyche's language of image.

Karen Armstrong (1993) viewed "the image-making part of the mind," known as the imagination, as essential to contemplative life, especially when cognizing mystical experiences of God (p. 219). Analogous to the artist who pursues numinous content, the mystic, according to Armstrong, creates deliberate exercises that promote visionary access to the sacred. Intentional pursuit of what is holy seemingly proceeds first through imaginal pathways toward somatic-sensory awareness, and then toward mind-training exercises such as meditation and art.

Armstrong (1993) refers to examples of contemplative traditions like the ancient practices of hesychia, meaning "tranquility" or "inner silence" (p. 220). Acts of grasping for images or ideas could derail the early mystic's search. The mind could be reined in and stilled through various concentrative, illuminating techniques. Quieting thoughts promoted "waiting silence" (p. 220) that transcended categories and therefore granted access to reality beyond conceptual constructions of God. Armstrong notes that the Christian experiences of God at this time favored light rather than darkness as a guiding worldview.

Color and Light

The work of the Impressionists and Post Impressionists (National Gallery of Art, 1980), Rudolf Steiner (1964), and Wassily (1911/1977; Golding, 2000), for similar and different reasons, referenced connections to the artist's palette for painting light. Spiritual and artistic traditions mention light for its nuance and connection to contemplative practice. Light, or lack of it, can imply divinity or severe suffering. Daylight reveals the glow of lit surfaces. As the sun moves, so do the lighted and shadowed exteriors of objects. Impressionist painters keenly observed not only the uniquely lit moment but also studied the passage of time. Sometimes working at great speed, they quickly painted desirable moments before they changed. Attention to temporal displays of shadows and light for plein-air artists then and now becomes a form of mindfulness practice. Active, intentional blending of spontaneity with purposeful observation infers how art and meditation can be linked together.

Color emerges from light and is revealed by light. Sources can be dim or bright. Either way, light from sources like the sun produce vibrating waves at various speeds that impact human sight. Furthermore, colored objects possess pigmentation. A red house reflects red light waves to the eye while absorbing all the other colors of the spectrum. White paint used in artwork reflects from its surface an equal degree of the "color waves in light" while black equally absorbs all rays of color (Ocvirk, Bone, Stinson, & Wigg, 1981).

Derived from two Greek words, photography means to "draw by light" (Swedlund, 1974, p. 102). As energy made observable, light makes perceptible those bodies that manifested it; it is how we see. The physics of light and visual perception are complex. Briefly, as waves and particles, light travels in straight lines. Photons, Greek for light, are particles that transmit and carry light through space. Overall, photography favors the wave qualities of light and how it exposes film. Brightness, color, angles of light, opaque and transparent surfaces guide the photographer's sensibilities of when and how to respond to the moment that makes photography a valued contemplative tool. Cameras can quickly illustrate relationships between thoughts, actions, and the non-dual moment. Click, and the moment is fixed within borders for contemplative consumption. Dining with the eyes on the photograph's record of time reminds one how to relate to thoughts without attachment. The picture holds the contemplative moment like the meditator observes on the screen of the mind, without attachment, the movement of thoughts.

Clinical Connections: Bollas and The Shadow of the Object

In analytic thinking, the term object is semantically rich. At least bidirectional, the relational flow between subject and object can be observed, studied, and used to understand relational psychotherapy (Hamilton, 1989). Curiously, artists also talk about art objects, a generic term for a manifested something made with materials and processes. Either way, the relationship between the subjectified object or the objectified subject is innately woven throughout all art experiences, a point made by Susanne Langer (1951, 1953) in her seminal work examining the arts as articulate language for emotion.

There are various ways to conceive of objectified, repressed shadow material in psychotherapy. Jung's shadow archetype, which harbors personal and collective material, holds unconscious subject matter at odds with the conscious ego. This territory often shows up first in psychotherapy work as the *nigredo* stage of blackness and disintegration in alchemy (Jung, 1968). It is within shadowed material that the essence *prima materia* of personal and collective transformation can be discovered (Edinger, 1985). We all must go through our shadow material in order to arrive at the light of our basic goodness and the sanity we are born with (Trungpa, 2005).

The Shadow of the Object
Instead of using the art therapist as the only object of projection for the client, materials, processes, and products are used to surface, relive, and restructure transferred unconscious material. One way to approach these latent parts of the psyche that live in their "wordless world" is to utilize the non-verbal languages of visual art (Bollas, 1987, p. 3). In

therapy, early recordings of client object relations need a current relationship and space to materialize and transform (Hamilton, 1989). Bollas, who worked with autistic children, learned from them how to attune to the wordless world of inner, object related, or unrelated interpersonal recordings. This, he says, is the domain of the shadow of the object, reflected on the ego, and laced with developmental residue. The parent-object can cast a caring or non-nurturing shadow without the child sufficiently understanding gradations of the interaction. Yet the child knows something of the exchange, feeling it before it is cognized. The analytic approach advocated by Bollas supports reliving through language, relationship, and aesthetic experience "that which is known, but not yet thought" or the "unthought known" (p. 4).

Projective identification becomes a helpful construct in this conversation. It refers to how the client utilizes the therapist as an object of transferential holding. This bidirectional interchange transports the therapist into the mind and body of the client, thereby inducing the therapist to relive and reexperience the client's inner world. Through projection onto me as an art therapist, identification with my client's inner life occurs. Clinical applications of artistic empathy further this process of intrapersonal-interpersonal-transpersonal resonant communication by consolidating emotional material into accessible, coherent formed expressions (Franklin, 2010). Therefore, projective identification is equally alive in artistic processes and is distinctively explored in post-session response art that untangles the moving parts of the therapeutic exchange.

The inner self is its own object to relate to and is often experienced through early-life, interiorized conversations with introjected parental parts. Within these conversations, as in dreams and art, we are both subject and object in the dialogue. Organizing inner life, especially for children, is challenging. It is as if the inner self-states of childhood are stored for later examination. This journey to promote awareness is further aided by the arrival of transitional objects that effectively move internalized, nurturing histories toward a subjectified, outer object (Winnicott, 1971). This process of investing a supportive symbolic item with psychic importance lays tracks for eventual understanding of relational creativity, devastation, and rebirth. Bollas describes the aesthetic moment when the subjective self "feels held in symmetry and solitude by the spirit of the object" and nurturing bliss enclosing the relationship (Bollas, 1987, p. 31). Ineffable experiences like these result in the nurturing object's caring shadow cast on the subject's wordless, yet to be realized, felt-attachment connections.

Heartfelt experience, particularly in spiritual practices, often infers sensorial meaning long before conscious knowing. I suggest that transpersonal approaches to therapy can be aided by the ideas of Bollas and his innovative perspectives on object, shadow, and aesthetics. For the client struggling to know God, silent encounters with the Divine are to be expected. God, as numinous internalized object, casts a wide shadow of unthought, waiting, non-verbal emergent insights. Self-awareness unfolds developmentally through inner conversations with introjected parts of the Divine in measure with textures of the observing capacities of the ego. It is through these dialogues, particularly with dreams and sacred transformative symbols revealed through art, that we practice subject/Self and object/God interchanges. In a way, God practices a form of projective identification with the seeker. The practitioner utilizes God as an object of transference while numinous disclosure marinates within the mind and body of the seeker through imaginal, revelatory dialogue.

Emotional, Spiritual, and Imaginal Intelligence

Originating from Latin *intelligere*, to understand, intelligence infers styles of learning and computation, the acquisition and comprehension of knowledge, and convergent and divergent applications of this understood information. Importantly, not every novel or adaptive behavior constitutes an intelligence. Gardner (1993) widened the conversation on this subject by carefully considering as many as nine multiple forms of intelligence. Besides logical–mathematical and linguistic intelligence, Gardner first outlined five other forms of intelligence: musical, spatial, bodily-kinesthetic, interpersonal, and intrapersonal. With further research, he identified naturalist intelligence and the capacity to observe patterns within ecosystems as well as spiritual intelligence, which he later reconsidered, believing existential intelligence more appropriate when it comes to spiritual aptitude (Gardner, 1993, 2000). Concerning spiritual intelligence, control of consciousness though practices like meditation register in the kinesthetic area of aptitude. Gardner believed that feeling states of sensed experience, as in a spiritual awakening, were not related to his eight criteria for intelligence, which are outlined below (Gardner, 1993).

1. Functioning intelligence can be identified in regions of the brain through refined neuroscience studies.
2. The isolated presence of savants, prodigies, and exceptional individuals confirms, through inconsistencies and contradictions, unique forms of intelligence.
3. Identifiable modular and domain-specific capabilities are important for complex processing tasks.
4. Intelligence is developmental, with evolving states of expertise and eventual mastery.
5. Through a variety of tasks, intelligence is identifiable and measurable.
6. Although arguably uneven, psychometric instruments are useful for studying intelligence and can be suitably modified to study forms of intelligence.
7. The development and application of symbol systems, verbal and nonverbal, are part of the conveyance of information. (pp. 62–67)

Emotional Intelligence. Emotional intelligence (EQ), made popular by Daniel Goleman (1998), focuses on introspective, intrapersonal, and interpersonal awareness of emotions and their effective regulation. Skillfully identifying and labeling feelings helps to guide behavioral decision making, which is a key component of relational acuity. Empathic sensitivity for self and other is a result of an education that develops EQ.

Susanne Langer argued that the arts were a sophisticated way to give human feeling form (Julliard & Van Den Heuvel, 1999; Langer, 1953).

Furthermore, affective education and aesthetic education have in the past been highlighted as approaches for learning about emotion through the arts in schools (Rubin, 1984).

Recently, McPherson and colleagues (2016), using fMRI studies, investigated the evidential links between the neural systems of emotion and emotional expressive intent as they relate to motivation for creativity in the arts, particularly music, which was the focus of the study. They argue that art in general is likely the best approach for researching the complex neurological connections and interactions between creativity and emotion. The authors suggest that previous investigations of creativity studied areas of the brain responsible for artistic creativity. However, past studies of this functional network did not expose the unpredictable behaviors characteristic of creativity. Therefore, as this research suggests, it is essential to identify the factors of emotional intent that modulate this network and, consequently, study the diverse range of ideas inherent in creativity.

Spiritual Intelligence. Spirituality is a broad word encompassing many meanings. Often associated with its root of spirit, or the non-physical embodied soul, spirituality here equates with a sincere embrace and orientation toward numinous phenomena. Ronel (2008) approached spiritual intelligence from a theistic perspective. Additionally, Ronel and others refer to creativity as an important aspect of spiritual intelligence. From the perspective of this chapter, artistic symbols and their healing potential to catalyze opposing emotions or to reach toward abstractions of God, serve as compensatory agents that hold even more meaning when listened to and followed. Insight is rarely enough to foster behavioral changes. Direct application of meaningful connections, in this case as healing symbols from dreams or artwork, teach us most when heard and applied to daily life (Adams & Hyde, 2008; Harding, 1961).

Emmons (2000), looking through Gardner's lenses of multiple intelligences, evaluates and lists five characteristics that attempt to explain spiritual intelligence: (1) an aptitude for transcendence; (2) capacity to access spiritual states of consciousness; (3) locating the sacred in daily life; (4) accessing spirituality as a source for creative problem solving; and (5) virtuous inner awareness and corresponding outer behavior. Emmons' assertion of spiritual intelligence into the arena of scientific discourse, in measure with standard criteria for assessing an intelligence, was met with appreciation for its plausibility from Gardner (2000), and also disagreement. Gardner instead viewed existential intelligence a more apt point of convergence between the two authors.

Imaginal Intelligence. In meetings with the Dalai Lama, Goleman (2003) and other notable scholars convened discussions on how to work with and shift destructive emotions. The need for gymnasium-like emotional training was suggested as well as how to move beyond stages of brainstorming toward actual implementation of credible interventions. By trading basketballs and parallel bars for paint brushes, this gymnasium also can be found in art studios in schools, psychiatric hospitals, or community centers. Furthermore, the arts educate and integrate all of Gardner's categories of an intelligence, including intuition, sensory acuity, empathy, systemic and spatial awareness, and symbolic speech. In fact, art-centered, fluid, imaginal acuity in my view meets the criteria for further investigation as an intelligence, a core argument of this chapter. Considering various creativity tests and studies (Rothenberg & Hausman, 1976), research in neuroaesthetics (Marin, 2015; Ramachandran & Hirstein 1999), the historical cross-cultural record of imaginal practices used in art, prayer, and meditation (Diamond, 2013; Marlan, 2012; Tuckman, 1986), and the complex symbol systems that undergird private and public artistic rituals (Dissanayake, 1992; Mahony, 1998), the die has long been cast for studying art as imaginal aptitude, or imaginal aptitude through art.

Mindfulness and Imagination

In the Christmas classic, *Miracle on 34th Street*, Kris Kringle tells second-grader Susan that the Imagi-Nation is a nation all to itself. Within this inventive realm of inspiration and possibility, mindful opportunities abound.

Mindfulness can be summed up as relaxed, flexible attentiveness to the "reflective self," including non-judgmental "moment-to-moment awareness" of emerging thoughts and sensations (Davis & Hayes, 2011, p. 198). Trungpa Rinpoche (1976) addressed mindfulness and awareness in meditation and the value of creating space around distressed thoughts. A quote that I consistently return to is how "meditation is giving a huge, luscious meadow to a restless cow" (p. 49). The agitated cow in the large pasture relates to Rubin's notion of framework for freedom in art and art therapy, and to Winnicott's ideas about holding environments (Franklin, 2014; Winnicott, 1971). For example, within the borders of a canvas, there is freedom to engage in aggressive, volcanic mark making or gentle, feathery brush strokes. From edges to center, top to bottom, background to foreground, paint and canvas, film and editing, or clay and hand-building all present a framework to freely explore and sustain engagement with potent emotions. When difficult thoughts emerge, materials and processes can invoke figure-ground relationships in just about any art process to surround agitation with space. By symbolically placing room around restless thoughts reflected directly in artworks, ruminations are present yet less cramped when expressively ventilated. In art, as in meditation, there is a dynamic relationship among figure/thought and space/ground.

Imaginal Mindfulness
Imaginal mindfulness, a devised term, is a practice of non-judgmentally observing the moment-to-moment arrival and evolution of constellating narratives within surfacing imagery (Franklin, in press). A hand gesture, the sound of an ambulance siren, a cool breeze across the face, or the central figure in Munch's Scream (Shriek) are examples of imaginal terrain. As reverberations of context, mood, and scene that are alive within these examples echo throughout our awareness, mindful collaboration with the "full democracy" of the imaginal ego follows (Berry, 1982, p.60; Hillman, 1978, 1983). Intermittent, democratic, and reflexive, the "imaginal ego," a term originally coined by Henry Corbin, is exercised through practices like active imagination and theophanic prayer (Corbin, 1958/1969; Chodorow, 1997; Hillman, 1972, p. 183). Here the universal archetypal schemas of myth making abound, distinctively constellating for each person. Image is not the perceived object; rather, image is the patiently waiting narrative alive within the branches, roots, and sky before us, awaiting our receptive, collaborative

responses. We listen to the imagery of old, oak, and tree, or shrieking siren by observantly receiving the context–mood–scene of each. As harbingers of ouroboric, self–other referential process, imaginal mindfulness becomes a practice of respectful engagement with these symbolic visitations. Similar to welcoming a house guest, awareness is activated, judgment is suspended, and the present moment materializes responsive acknowledgement toward the imagery. Witnessing the movements of the mind and corresponding images awakens layers of awareness. With meditation we practice witnessing the mind, and with art we tangibly surface both witness and content of the mind.

Art is often a spontaneous process, like a visual form of free association. Mindful attention to spontaneous mark making on surfaces or attuning to fingertip sensations while pinching clay begins to awaken sensory sensitivity. From start to finish, creating with materials and processes offers opportunities to non-judgmentally witness thoughts associated with the work before us. Of us as our art, yet separate from us as created other, imaginal mindfulness reveals unanticipated layers of awareness alive in each unfolding moment.

Going Forward

Although not the exact emphasis of this chapter, shadow and light themes that are related to social justice work within communities, particularly studio settings, merit mention and further examination. The Naropa Community Art Studio (NCAS) has researched this mandate since 2001 by studying the role of the socially engaged artist and therapist (Franklin, 2016; Franklin, Rothaus, & Schpock, 2005). In my experience, community-based studio work flattens hierarchy by providing an illuminated, egalitarian space for visual free speech. When our marginalized community members, who often feel eclipsed by the diagnostic stereotypes of the medical system or the economic hardships of class-bound limitations, shed these debilitating labels, independent, liberated imagery emerges. Forged out of the fires of emancipated creativity, community forms as private matters are publically expressed and accepted by the collective. Shame is slowly traded for pride as each artist in the collective honorably participates. No longer defined as medical cases or diagnostic categories in the studio, these artists discover their birthright to claim aesthetic agency. Simply, where the arts thrive, enlightened humanistic actualizing trends flourish, which is a core focus of this chapter.

The Forever Moment:
Shadows, Light, and Concluding Thoughts

Light paints the world into existence; darkness reveals the opposite as forms fade to obscurity. Artists enjoy observing how brightness and darkness behave on surfaces, whether with pigments, negative spaces, or excavating latent content. During moments like a sunrise or sunset, there is an invitation to mindfully decelerate, engage the senses, and witness the forever moment with imaginal awareness.

If we can imagine into our suffering, then through the arts we can create our way out of our suffering. During such times, darkness, illumination, and reflection become the perfect metaphors for grasping solidity and subtlety, enlightened and endarkened limitations. Relaxed, non-judgmental, flexible attentiveness to moment-to-moment contexts, moods, and scenes remarkably exercises relationship with interiorized imaginal movements. The goal is to welcome the full democracy of the intelligent image, follow its cues, and learn from these constantly arriving others.

References

Adams, K., & Hyde, B. (2008, March). Children's grief dreams and the theory of spiritual intelligence. *Dreaming, 18*(1), 58–67. http://dx.doi.org/10.1037/1053-0797.18.1.58

Armstrong, K. (1993). *A history of God: The 4,000 year quest of Judaism, Christianity and Islam.* New York, NY: Gramercy Books.

Berry, P. (1982). *Echo's subtle body: Contributions to an archetypal psychology.* Dallas, TX: Spring.

Bollas, C. (1987). *The shadow of the object: Psychoanalysis of the unthought known.* New York, NY: Columbia University Press.

Chodorow, J. (1997). *Jung on active imagination*. Princeton, NJ: Princeton University Press.

Coomaraswamy, A. K. (1917). Introduction. In *Nandikeśvara, The mirror of gesture: Being the Abhinaya Darpana of Nandikeśvara* (A. K. Coomaraswamy & G. K. Duggirala, Trans.) (pp. 1–10). London, England: Oxford University Press.

Corbin, H. (1969). *Creative imagination in the Sufism of Ibn 'Arabi* (R. Manheim, Trans.). Princeton, NJ: Princeton University Press. (Original work published 1958)

Davis, J. (2000). We keep asking ourselves, what is transpersonal psychology. *Guidance and Counseling, 15*(3), 3–8.

Davis, D. M. & Hayes, J. A. (2011). What are the benefits of mindfulness? A practice review of psychotherapy-related research. *Psychotherapy, 48*(2), 198–208.

Diamond, D. (2013). *Yoga: The art of transformation*. Washington, DC: Freer Gallery of Art /Arthur M. Sackler Gallery Smithsonian Institution.

Dissanayake, E. (1992). Art for life's sake. *Art Therapy: Journal of the American Art Therapy Association, 9*, 169–177.

Edinger, E. F. (1985). *Anatomy of the psyche: Alchemical symbolism in psychotherapy*. La Salle, IL: Open Court Publishing Company.

Emmons, R. A. (2000). Is spirituality an intelligence? Motivation, cognition and the psychology of ultimate concern. *The International Journal for the Psychology of Religion, 10*(1), 3–26.

Feuerstein, G. (2003). *The deeper dimension of yoga: Theory and practice*. Boston, MA: Shambhala Publications.

Franklin, M., Rothaus, M., & Schpock, K. (2005). Unity in diversity: Communal pluralism in the art studio and the classroom. In F. Kaplan (Ed.), *Art therapy and social action: Treating the world's wounds*. London and Philadelphia: Jessica Kingsley Publishers.

Franklin, M. (2010). Affect regulation, mirror neurons and the 3rd hand: Formulating mindful empathic art interventions. *Art Therapy: Journal of the American Art Therapy Association. 27*(4), 160–167.

Franklin, M. A. (2014). Mindful considerations for training art therapists: Inner friendship—outer professionalism. In L. Rappaport (Ed.), *Mindfulness and the arts therapies: Theory and practice* (pp. 264–275). London: Jessica Kingsley.

Franklin, M. A. (2016). Contemplative approaches art therapy: Incorporating Hindu-Yoga-Tantra and Buddhist wisdom traditions in clinical and studio practice. In J. A. Rubin (Ed.), *Approaches to art therapy*. New York, NY: Routledge.

Franklin, M. A. (in press). *Art as contemplative practice: Expressive pathways to the self*. Albany, NY: State University of New York Press.

Gardner, H. (1993). *Frames of mind: The theory of multiple intelligences*. New York, NY: Basic Books.

Gardner, H. (2000). A case against spiritual intelligence. *The International Journal for the Psychology of Religion, 10*(1), 27–34.

Golding, J. (2000). *Paths to the absolute: Mondrian, Malevich, Kandinsky, Pollock, Newman, Rothko, Still.* Princeton, NJ: Princeton University Press.

Goleman, D. (1998). *Working with Emotional Intelligence.* New York, NY: Bantam Books.

Goleman, D. (2003). *Destructive emotions: How can we overcome them?: A scientific dialogue with the Dalai Lama.* New York, NY: Bantam Books.

Hamilton, N. G. (1989). A critical review of object relations theory. *American Journal of Psychiatry, 146*(12), 1552–1560.

Harding, M. E. (1961). What makes the symbol effective as a healing agent? In G. Adler (Ed.), *Current trends in analytical psychology* (pp. 1–18). London, England: Tavistock.

Hillman, J. (1972). *The myth of analysis: Three essays in archetypal psychology.* New York, NY: Harper & Row, Publishers.

Hillman, J. (1978). Further notes on images. *Spring,* 152–182.

Hillman, J. (1983). *Healing fiction.* New York, NY: Station Hill.

Julliard, K. N., & Van Den Heuvel, G. (1999). Susanne K. Langer and the foundations of art therapy. *Art Therapy: Journal of the American Art Therapy Association, 16*(3), 112–120. http://dx.doi.org/10.1080/07421656.1999.10129656

Jung, C. G (1968). *Psychology and alchemy.* Princeton, NJ: Bolligen Foundation, Princeton University Press.

Jung, C. G. (2009). *The red book: Liber novus* (S. Shamdasani, Ed.; S. Shamdasani, M. Kyburz, & J. Peck, Trans.). New York, NY: Norton.

Kandinsky, W. (1977). *Concerning the spiritual in art* (M. T. H. Sadler, Trans.) (pp. xiii–xxi). New York, NY: Dover. (Original work published 1911)

Khanna, M. (1979). *Yantra: The tantric symbol of cosmic unity.* New York, NY: Thames.

Knight, J. A. (1987). The spiritual as a creative force in the person. *Journal of the American Academy of Psychoanalysis, 15*(3), 365–382.

Langer, S. K. (1951). *Philosophy in new key: A study in the symbolism of reason, rite, and art.* New York, NY: New American Library.

Langer, S. K. (1953). *Feeling and form.* New York, NY: Scribner's.

Liddell, H. G., & Scott, R. (1996). *A Greek-English lexicon.* Oxford: Clarendon Press.

Mahony, W. K. (1998). *The artful universe: An introduction to the Vedic imagination.* Albany, New York: State University of New York Press.

Marin, M. M. (2015). Crossing boundaries: Toward a general model of neuroaesthetics. *Frontiers in Human Neuroscience. 9,* 443. doi:10.3389/fnhum.2015.00443

Marlan, S. (Ed.). (2012). *Archetypal Psychologies: Reflections in honor of James Hillman.* New Orleans, Louisiana: Spring Journal Books.

McPherson, M. J., Barrett, F. S., Lopez-Gonzalez, M., Jiradejvong, P., & Limb, C. L. (2016). Emotional intent modulates the neural substrates of creativity: An fMRI study of emotionally targeted improvisation in jazz musicians. *Scientific Reports, 6:* 18460; doi: 10.1038/srep18460

McNiff, S. (1998). *Art-based research.* Philadelphia, PA: Kingsley.

Mookerjee, A., & Khanna, M. (1977). *The tantric way: Art, science, ritual.* London, England: Thames.

National Gallery of Art. (1980). *Post-Impressionism: Cross-currents in European and American painting 1880–1906.* Washington DC: Board of Trustees, National Gallery of Art.

Ocvirk, O. G., Bone, R. O., Stinson, R. E., & Wigg, P. R. (1981). *Art fundamentals: Theory and Practice.* Dubuque, IA: Wm. C. Brown Publishers.

Plazy, G. (1990). *Cezanne.* New York, NY: Crescent Books.

Ramachandran, V. S., & Hirstein, W. (1999). The science of art: A neurological theory of aesthetic experience. *Journal of consciousness studies, 6*(6–7), 15–51.

Rothenberg, A., & Hausman, C. R. (1976). *The creativity question.* Durham, NC: Duke University Press.

Ronel, N. (2008). The experience of spiritual intelligence. *The Journal of Transpersonal Psychology, 40*(1), 100—119.

Rubin, J. A. (1984). *Child art therapy.* New York, NY: Van Nostrand Reinhold.

Stein, M. (2012). How to read the Redbook and why. *Journal of Analytical Psychology, 57,* 280–298.

Steiner, R. (1964). *The arts and their mission.* New York, NY: Anthroposophic Press.

Sullivan, G. (2010), *Art practice as research: Inquiry in the visual arts.* Los Angeles, CA: Sage.

Swedlund, C. (1974). *Photography: A handbook of history, materials, and processes.* New York, NY: Holt, Rinehart, and Winston, Inc.

Tuckman, M. (1986). Hidden meanings in abstract art. In M. Tuchman (Ed.), *The spiritual in art: Abstract paintings 1890–1985* (pp. 17–61). New York, NY: Abbeville Press.

Trungpa Rinpoche (1976). *The myth of freedom and the way of meditation.* Berkeley & London: Shambhala Publications.

Trungpa, C. (2005). *The sanity we are born with: A Buddhist approach to psychology.* Boston, MA: Shambhala Publications.

Tuckman, M. (1986). Hidden meanings in abstract art. In M. Tuchman (Ed.), *The spiritual in art: Abstract paintings 1890–1985* (pp. 17–61). New York, NY: Abbeville Press.

Walsh, R. & Vaughan, F. (1993). *Paths beyond ego: A transpersonal vision.* New York, NY: Tarcher-Putnam.

Winnicott, D. W. (1971). *Therapeutic consultations in child psychiatry.* New York, NY: Basic Books.

Chapter 6
Oracle of the Ultimate: Contemplative Practice and Mind/Body Assessment in Transpersonal Counseling

Ian Wickramasekera

There are innumerable modes of entry into the Buddha's teaching. Just as there are in the world difficult and easy paths—travelling on foot by land is full of hardship and travelling in a boat by sea is pleasant—so it is among the paths of the bodhisattvas.
      Nagarjuna (Inagaki, 1998, p. 142)

Just as there exist many enumerations of worlds, so also the sentient beings who are their inhabitants is inconceivable...even the karmic actions of sentient beings are inconceivable in terms of their multiple enumerations...Just so, the (number of) doctrines expounded by the Sugatas (enlightened teachers) that convert sentient beings are inconceivable to the mind.
      Druchen Gyalwa Yungdrung (Reynolds, 2006, p. 37)

Contemplative Practice in Transpersonal Psychology

Contemplative mind/body practices can be said to be an absolutely critical part of the tradition of transpersonal counseling for theoretical (Wilber, 1993) as well as clinical reasons (Cortright, 1997). Contemplative practices have been defined and understood in different ways (Mind and Life Education Research Network, 2012; Wall, Nye, &

FitzMedrud, 2013), so let me first offer a simple definition in the context of transpersonal psychology. I define contemplative practices as practices that engage a person within a direct experience of their own *innate wisdom and compassion* while also developing the capacity to manifest their innate wisdom and compassion through disciplined practice. This definition grounds contemplative practices in the experience and development of the deep potential for transcendence that transpersonal theorists assert is the innate birthright of all human beings (Cortright, 1997, Tart, 2009; Trungpa, 2005). Contemplative practices can take a myriad of forms in the tradition of transpersonal counseling, such as techniques of biofeedback, meditation, prayer, self-hypnosis, and yoga, which are some of the more popular mind/body practices that are utilized in the world today.

A contemplative practice can be said to be a perfect companion for transpersonal theorists and counselors since contemplative practices are designed to help bring about transpersonal experiences that help them to gain access to their innate wisdom and compassion (Wilber, 1993). Wilber goes so far as to assert that transpersonal psychology "depends on those who have practiced and achieved competence in a transpersonal/spiritual discipline" (p. 265). Contemplative practices are utilized in transpersonal psychology to help clients, clinicians, and theorists alike reach for and experience their innate wisdom and compassion. The same wisdom and compassion that frees a client from suffering can also magnify the healing potential of a counselor and the insightfulness of a theorist's writings. Thus contemplative practices have become a familiar part of the theory and practice of transpersonal psychology.

However, there seems to be no general agreement or well-elaborated assessment process to help one recommend a particular practice to a particular person from the thousands of potential practices that one could potentially teach a client (Cortright, 1997). This is unfortunate since it is well known in both the ancient spiritual writings and in modern day transpersonal psychology that not everyone benefits from each and every contemplative practice to the same degree. For example, individuals do seem to vary in their response to meditation, although most people reliably report experiencing a basic level of benefit in quite a number of clinical contexts (Awasthi, 2013; Shapiro & Walsh, 2003). However, a minority of people actually seem to get worse during contemplative practices such as meditation (Awasthi, 2013) and contemplative journaling (Baikie, 2008). So it is important that we help clients not only find a contemplative practice that works well for them but also one that does not have much potential to harm them. Cortright (1997) nicely summarized this problem by writing that:

> At the present time, when someone says that they work transpersonally, it may mean anything from a rigorous, grounded and clinically sophisticated approach of integrating clinical practice into a spiritual context on the one hand, to a very flaky, ungrounded, grab bag of New Age techniques and spiritual homilies. (p. 225)

The myriad ways in which the human mind can present itself seems to argue for a myriad of contemplative approaches to uniquely help individuals develop their innate wisdom and compassion. This is just what the introductory quotes to this chapter from the Bon and Buddhist traditions of Tibet seem to suggest.

Tibetans are also fond of saying that Shakyamuni Buddha gave 84,000 different types of teachings for the 84,000 different types of unique challenges that sentient beings possess (Namdak, 2016) based on their unique circumstances and phenomenology. And yet we are still tasked with discovering a way to recommend the best contemplative practice for the person we are counseling. This is not as easy a task as one might assume. Research has shown that around 50% of clients will give up using their contemplative practice within two weeks after they were taught it (Smith, 1989). After all, even the great Tibetan Saint Milarepa (1052–1135 CE) made no progress on his spiritual journey when he was initially assigned a practice of meditation that was not well suited to his needs (Lhalungpa, 1985). Milarepa describes his difficulty in practicing Dzogchen meditation (Wangyal, 2000) because of his initial inability to understand how to correctly practice a meditation technique without an object of attentional fixation.

For some counselors this whole issue is rather simple, in an unfortunate way. If you only know how to teach one contemplative practice, such as mindfulness meditation, then you really only have one choice to offer your clients and yourself. Most counselors eventually learn quite a wide variety of practices that they like to use with clients as they develop their spiritual practice and clinical skills throughout their career. However, developing an expertise with a wide variety of methods can also be a dangerous thing if you do not also have a solid plan for how you decide which techniques to use with clients. The danger is that you might accidentally slip into becoming one of those clinicians that Cortright (1997) says have fallen into the "New Age grab bag" category unless you utilize a rigorous assessment plan that ties all your methods together with case conceptualization skills. In the following sections of this chapter, we will explore how transpersonal counselors can employ rigorous phenomenological and quantitative methods of mind/body assessment to guide making recommendations for our client's contemplative practice in transpersonal counseling. We will end the chapter with a case example to help embody the powerful utility of the principles and procedures of mind/body contemplative assessment in transpersonal counseling.

Mind/Body Assessment in Transpersonal Psychology

The approach to mind/body assessment that I will be describing here is derived primarily from a number of sources in addition to my own experiences in practicing as a health psychologist for the past 15 years and in pursuing research in consciousness studies and neuroscience over the past 25 years. In particular, I have tried to integrate the largely phenomenological approach that the transpersonal community already embraces to mind/body assessment (MacDonald & Friedman, 2013) with powerful quantitative methods that may be new to many readers of this chapter. The core of what we are trying to achieve by using mind/body assessment in transpersonal psychology is to get a good sense of what each client's unique experience of their mind/body relationship is like. We would like to know how they directly experience their mind/body relationship in different contexts, as well as the relative strengths and weaknesses in their development of their mind/body ability. By mind/body ability, I mean to say the relative ability of the person to utilize the full spectrum of contemplative practices—from those that require very little development of the mind/body relationship to advanced techniques that require highly evolved imagery skills, psychophysiological integration, and/or a myriad of other metacognitive skills.

Ultimately, every client's mind/body potential is considered to be capable of the same great feats of mind/body ability that great saints like Milarepa have accomplished according to transpersonal psychology and many spiritual traditions (Cortright, 1997, Tart, 2009; Trungpa, 2005; Wickramasekera II, 2014). However, it would be foolish of us to assign methods that require a high level of mind/body ability, such as lucid dreaming (Wangyal, 1998), as a contemplative practice to people who have relatively low levels of development of mind/body ability. In the case of lucid dreaming, both the ancient Tibetan teachings and modern day psychological research has revealed that lucid dreaming is a practice that one has to work their way up to (LaBerge, 2009; Wangyal, 1998). However, there are also some fortunate people who seem to be born with very high levels of mind/body ability who develop their mind/body abilities to very advanced levels from an extremely young age. We know this from research on assessing mind/body ability, which we will review later (Pekala & Kumar, 2000; Wickramasekera II, 2005, 2015). So we will not be doing our clients any favors by not acknowledging that everyone varies in levels of mind/body ability and treating them all the same. Instead, we should be actively assessing our client's level of mind/body ability so we can recommend a contemplative practice that actually suits them.

We can make high-quality predictions with this kind of knowledge about what the best contemplative technique would be for each person. For instance, it is somewhat futile and problematic to teach a visualization technique to a person whose experience of mental imagery is extremely impoverished just because we happen to like using imagery ourselves. Meanwhile the very same client may do excellently with hypnosis if somatic sensations are emphasized rather than hypnotic imagery and the client happens to have a gift for altering body sensations, which in fact many people with medium to high mind/body ability possess (Pekala & Kumar, 2000; Wickramasekera, 2013). It is time for transpersonal clinicians to stop recommending practices to clients based mainly on their own experiences with a given contemplative practice and to embrace using mind/body assessment procedures to learn about their clients' mind/body potential.

I assert that we can derive the best overall understanding of a person's level of mind/body ability and their unique experience of their mind/body relationship by using a rigorous assessment strategy integrating both qualitative and quantitative methods. We will first begin reviewing these methods by studying some familiar phenomenological paradigms derived from humanistic psychotherapy paradigms (Rogers, 1959) and qualitative research (Moustakas, 1990). Next we will discuss a powerful quantitative model of mind/body assessment (Wickramasekera II, 2005) derived from studies in health psychology that can be readily applied to contemplative practice in transpersonal counseling. I will also endeavor to illustrate these ideas with small clinical vignettes and eventually a longer case example along the way to help elucidate the power of employing mind/body contemplative assessment methods in transpersonal counseling.

Phenomenological Mind/Body Assessment

One very simple and commonly used method of finding out about our clients' mind/body relationship in transpersonal counseling is simply to ask them about their previous experiences with different types of contemplative practices (Cortright, 1997). I always make time during a clients' initial interview to ask them questions like: "Tell me something about what you have already been trying to do to cope with your challenges?" and also "What are your favorite methods of relaxing in life, even if you haven't used them for a long time?" I will then use methods of humanistic psychotherapy (Rogers, 1959) and heuristic phenomenological inquiry (Moustakas, 1990) to process whatever they may have to say. In answer to my question, clients have often told me about their experiences with mindfulness meditation, prayer, yoga, and other commonly used contemplative practices. However, they have also told me about highly valuable and unique practices that I knew little about at the time such as *speaking in tongues* and *Ikebana*, a traditional Japanese form of flower arrangement. People often also discuss highly unique forms of what constitutes a contemplative practice for them that may not always be experienced as a contemplative practice for others. For instance, I have worked with people for whom the experience of "remaining motionless as a live model on display in a store window" could be described as a contemplative practice and also people for whom fishing was a contemplative art.

The key is to examine the person's direct experience of the practice, whatever it may be, and to assess whether they have already had an experience of discovering their innate wisdom and compassion while utilizing it. For example, a person who told me about fishing as a contemplative art, let me know that it didn't particularly matter to them whether they caught a fish or not while fishing. They explained to me that the most important thing for them was to get out in nature. They described their joyful experience of the slow passage of hours while they felt at one with the flowing water of the river and with the movement of the sun as it passed over them from dawn until dusk. The client also told me that they would only catch as many fish as they could serve their family for dinner that night. The client related that after catching their limit, they would simply stop fishing and just relax in the natural environment around them until it was time to go home.

We can often discover a person's *hidden* contemplative practices by processing their life experiences in this way. In general, anything that you find in this category of hidden practices will be very powerful, especially if you integrate it with other practices that may be similar. For instance, in the fishing example just given, I later determined through quantitative assessment that the client had a strong propensity to experience mindfulness meditation. I then combined the practices of fishing and mindfulness by suggesting that the client had already been practicing mindfulness meditation while fishing. I suggested that learning mindfulness of their breath might not only teach them a practice that they could do while not fishing, but that could also potentially enrich their contemplative experience of fishing. This worked very well for the person. The client expressed to me a feeling that he was discovering the power of something within himself that he had simply not taken seriously enough throughout his life.

It is also quite important to ask clients about any religious and/or spiritually based contemplative practices that they may have experienced in the past. This will naturally lead to a discussion of their spiritual background, which may also lead to important knowledge about what kind of contemplative practice is the best for a given client. For example, I have many times encountered clients who let me know up front that they had religious objections to engaging in any form of contemplative practice that did not come from their religious and/or cultural traditions. These clients often mention being frightened that using a contemplative practice like mindfulness or self-hypnosis might open them up to phenomena like demonic possession (Wickramasekera, 2014). I am always very happy when clients bring up these concerns to me since it likely indicates that the patient is very committed to their spiritual path. People like this may already have some sense of their deep innate wisdom and compassion and may likely have better than average mind/body ability. Many of these clients already have a contemplative practice that they have practiced but may have given it up due to feeling disempowered by challenges they have not yet overcome.

However, some of these patients with religious/spiritual objections have also not progressed far enough in their own religious tradition to have been taught a contemplative practice. In these cases, it is absolutely essential to get the client to disclose or investigate what their religion recommends as a contemplative practice for them. I have often asked these clients to ask an authority figure in their religion for instruction on a contemplative practice and/or permission for them to try a number of practices that I might know have been acceptable to other adherents of their faith. On a number of occasions, I have also asked the client for permission to speak to their religious teacher and have facilitated their getting permission to practice techniques that previously the client might have thought were off limits. Many people do not know that the Catholic Church and also more conservative Christian authorities have praised the biomedical benefits of hypnosis and mindfulness meditation and have deemed them to be helpful to people with medical and psychological problems (Wickramasekera II, 2014; Forrest, 1999). We should also seek out whether other psychosocial demographics such as ethnicity and race might have implications for contemplative practice as well.

In general, when we ask questions such as "What have you done to cope with and overcome your challenges so far?" we are getting at the deep reserves of strength that transpersonal theorists tell us we all possess without exception (Cortright, 1997, Wickramasekera II, 2004). It is very important for us to remember that as much as 40% of the outcome in counseling and psychotherapy can be attributed to the client's previous strengths (Lambert, 1992). Therefore, we would be foolish not to ask clients early on what they have done to cope with their challenges in life. Sometimes the very best thing for us to do as a clinician might be to simply empower a client to do what they already know they should be doing (Bohart & Tallman, 1999).

So often in life we just do not appreciate the riches that we already have. A traditional Tibetan tale tells the story of a poor woman whose husband died and who was despondent with grief and poverty (Wangyal, 2000). The story goes that each night that she went to bed she slept on very poor quality bedding that was supported by uncomfortable rocks beneath it. However, unbeknownst to her, the rocks she was sleeping on were actually nuggets of gold that her husband had hidden to help take care of her after his passing. In a transpersonal sense, all of us are exactly like the woman in that we often do not fully appreciate the hidden treasures that await the investigation of our own innate wisdom and compassion (Wickramasekera II, 2004).

Introducing Quantitative Assessment to Patients

Utilizing quantitative assessment can be a new experience for many transpersonal counselors. Unfortunately, some counselors may even have been taught that quantitative assessment methods are not valuable in counseling that is primarily phenomenologically based (MacDonald & Friedman, 2013). However, the approach that we are taking here is to supplement the deep personal richness of the phenomenological inquiry with the rigor and normative data that we can derive from quantitative assessment methods.

We must be very careful in employing quantitative assessment methods during transpersonal and other phenomenologically oriented paradigms of counseling. We have to explain the purpose and nature of mind/body assessment procedures to our clients without triggering negative expectations (Kirsch, 1990) that might distort our therapeutic relationship with them. Let us now review some of the more important points to cover with patients.

I explain to my clients that the purpose of mind/body contemplative assessment is to gather information that will allow me to recommend what the best clinical methods might be for them. I explain that these will be paper and pencil tests of their personality characteristics as well as direct experiences of their ability to experience different states of consciousness such as meditation, relaxation, and self-hypnosis. I explain to them that "these are not tests that you could ever possibly fail" and that "nothing is on the line here" regarding my ability to help them. The purpose of the testing is simply to determine "which methods will be best for them as a client." I tell them that I have experience with using hundreds of different methods in the past with clients and also with myself. I often mention that the Buddha once said that there are over 84,000 different types of approaches to overcome suffering (Namdak, 2016). I explain that we use these tests to help determine which of the many hundreds of methods that we could possibly try might actually be the best contemplative practice for them to start using right away. I also explain to my clients that most people find the testing procedures to be very relaxing and interesting (Pekala, 1995) since they will get a chance to experience phenomena like hypnosis and relaxation. I give every single patient this information to ensure that they have a positive clinical expectation (Kirsch, 1990) of what we are doing. It is absolutely critical that clients are prepared for mind/body assessment in this way, or it is possible they will not have the proper motivation and comfort to experience phenomena like meditation and self-hypnosis in enough depth for our purposes in mind/body assessment.

Hypnotic Mind/Body Assessment

One of the first questions that I have about every client that I see in transpersonal counseling is: "What is the client's level of hypnotic ability, and how do they uniquely experience states of consciousness like hypnosis?" I believe that it is critical to know what a person's experience of hypnosis is like even when one doesn't particularly plan to use hypnosis on that client. The reason why I believe this is critical is that we can use the large literature on the nature of hypnotic experiences and hypnotic ability (Lynn & Shindler, 2002; Pekala, 2002; Pekala & Kumar, 2000; Wickramasekera, 1988; Wickramasekera II, 2005, 2013, 2015) to guide our recommendations for contemplative practice with clients, as we shall shortly discuss. For instance, research on the High Risk Model of Threat Perception (HRMTP) has established a useful clinical guideline for using biofeedback with people who have low hypnotic ability (lows) and hypnosis for those with high hypnotic ability (highs) (Wickramasekera, 1988).

Let us start by discussing what hypnotic ability is and how it is measured since quite a few transpersonal counselors may be unaware of the many years of clinical research that have gone on in the field of hypnosis over the past 200 years (Wickramasekera II, 2013, 2015). Next we can discuss how to integrate hypnotic assessment into treatment planning and method selection in contemplative transpersonal counseling.

Abbé Faria (1756–1819) was the first scholar of hypnosis to note that individuals vary in their ability to experience hypnotic phenomena (Carrer, 2006). He was also the first scholar to ascribe these differences to the mind/body ability of the person experiencing hypnosis rather than to the magical power or the skill of a hypnotist (Forrest, 1999). Faria created the word, *epopte*, which means "those who see clearly" (Forrest, 1999), to describe people who were high in hypnotic ability in general. He described an epopte as a person who had a high level of mind/body ability that they could use to experience a wide variety of transpersonal and anomalous phenomena (Carrer, 2006). What was so amazing about Faria's ideas was that everyone else before him was foolish enough to attribute the power of hypnotic effects to the person of the hypnotist. Modern research in hypnosis has essentially proved Faria right in that we now know that hypnosis has little to do with the power of the hypnotist or even the power of suggestibility (Wickramasekera II, 2015). Instead, we now know that people's experiences of hypnosis are created by their own advanced mind/body abilities such as their attention, empathy, metacognitive skills, and psychophysiological abilities (Wickramasekera II, 2015).

In essence, Faria's theories about the mind/body abilities of high hypnotizables (people who experience hypnosis strongly) are similar to Bonpo and Buddhist ideas about the characteristics of an advanced meditator, sometimes known as a *yogi* (Wickramasekera II, 2013, 2014, 2015). One area of common ground between high hypnotizables and yogis is that both types of people have been noted to possess advanced mind/body abilities. Interestingly enough, there is an extensive literature in neuroscience demonstrating that yogis and high hypnotizables both have the ability to alter their brain functioning, consciousness, heart rate, imagery, immune system functioning, memories, spiritual experiences, and many other psychophysiological and spiritual achievements at will during contemplative practice (Shapiro & Walsh, 2003; Wickramasekera II, 2004, 2013, 2014, 2015). It is for this reason that I strongly recommend measuring hypnotic ability and hypnotic experiences with all your clients. Hypnotic assessment is one of the most valid and reliable ways of quantitatively assessing a person's general mind/body relationship, as we shall see in this section of this chapter. Hypnotic assessment allows us not only to get a sense of how developed a person's mind/body ability is relative to others but also their unique experiences of it. For instance, there are methods of hypnotic assessment that can quantify the percentile range within which a given client's experiences with imagery and/or somatic sensations (Pekala, 2002) fall when they use contemplative practices. So we can use quantitative hypnotic assessment methods to classify clients into the low, medium, and high range of mind/body ability while also collecting information about their unique experiences during contemplative practices.

The tradition of hypnosis made significant strides toward the measurement of hypnotic ability during the last century (Wickramasekera II, 2013). It also chose a theory-free way of assessing hypnotic ability as "the ability to become hypnotized, to have the experiences characteristic of the hypnotized person, and to exhibit the kinds of behaviors associated with it" (Hilgard, 1965, p. 67). Hypnotic ability is assessed simply by administering standardized hypnotic instructions to a person and then evaluating their ability to perform them, as well as their unique experiences during the procedures (Pekala & Kumar, 2000). Hypnotic ability is a very stable characteristic of individuals and has even been shown to be correlated after 15- and 25-year intervals with test–retest correlations of $r = .8$ and $r=.7$, respectively (Piccione, Hilgard, & Zimbardo, 1989). The relative stability of hypnotic ability is very impressive and rivals many other psychological constructs such as intelligence (Neisser et. al., 1996). It is known to be a partly genetically determined trait (Morgan, 1973; Raz, 2005) with a roughly normal distribution (Hilgard, 1965). Most people fall into the medium range (mediums) while something like 15% fall into either the high or low ranges and are referred to as *highs* and *lows,* respectively.

There have been more than 200 years of research and theorizing about how personality factors might be involved with hypnosis. Almost all of these assumptions have been shown to be incorrect (Barber, 2000; Bowers, 1977; Wickramasekera II, 2015), although the public still holds onto many erroneous perceptions about the nature of hypnosis. For instance, hypnotic ability is not related to suggestibility outside of hypnosis, gullibility, a histrionic personality style, or schizophrenia. Hypnotic ability is related to empathy (Wickramasekera II & Szlyk, 2003; Wickramasekera II, 2015) and also to a personality trait called *absorption* (Glisky & Kihlstrom, 1993; Tellegen & Atkinson, 1974). Absorption can be defined as a person's tendency toward being open to experiencing absorbing and self-altering events. Highs (high hypnotizables) are commonly experienced as being very empathic and experientially open to the world just like yogis and other people with high mind/body potential have been described for centuries (Wickramasekera II, 2004, 2013, 2014, 2015).

Clinical Implications of Hypnotic Mind/Body Assessment

The main utility in measuring hypnotic ability for contemplative practice and transpersonal counseling is that it gives us a good idea of a person's development of mind/body ability, as just discussed. However, we can also gain an understanding a person's unique experience of their mind/body relationship as well, as we shall see later on in this chapter. Knowledge of a person's relative development of their mind/body relationship gives us a sense of whether they possess the attentional resources, metacognitive skills, and psychophysiological abilities to practice contemplative techniques that require low, medium, or high levels of mind/body ability. For example, people with relatively low development of mind/body ability will generally not benefit as much from contemplative techniques that require good mental imagery and/or metacognitive skills to manage distracting thoughts (Benning, Rozalski, & Klingspon, 2015; Weinstein & Smith, 1992; Wickramasekera II, 2005). Even the great Saint Milarepa felt very discouraged and eventually left his first Buddhist teacher when he was taught a meditation practice that did not suit him (Lhalungpa, 1985), and he was most likely a high. So let us endeavor to be mindful of the client in front of us and their needs rather than simply teach them a method that we personally enjoy or feel comfortable using with clients.

Wickramasekera (1988, 1998) discusses an assessment model (HRMTP) of matching a mind/body practice to a client based on their overall level of mind/body (hypnotic) ability. The HRMTP prescribes biofeedback as the method of choice for people with low mind/body ability (lows) due to their tendency to possess a cognitively analytic, rigid, and skeptical interpersonal style (Wickramasekera, 1998). Lows seem to prefer the biomedical validation and scientific aura surrounding the methodology of clinical psychophysiology (biofeedback). They tend not to do as well in psychotherapy (Bowers & Kelly, 1979), and perhaps this is due in part to their tendency to be less comfortable with empathy and interpersonal relationships (Wickramasekera II & Szlyk, 2003; Wickramasekera II, 2005, 2015). Lows tend to initially prefer the biomedical validation of their stress and relaxation responses available from biofeedback equipment rather than the therapeutic empathy of their therapist (Wickramasekera II, 2005). They simply will not believe in the reality of the mind/body relationship unless one can show them that both stress and relaxation have a direct effect on their body that can be measured with biofeedback equipment. Simply telling them that they are doing well will not work as effectively as actually showing them that their heart rate, muscular tension, and other psychophysiological measures improved when they engaged in contemplative practice. Thus, they experience the biomedical validation of their stress, pain, and/or relaxation responses as a form of *machine empathy* (Wickramasekera II, 2005).

Clients with low mind/body ability are in jeopardy of falling out of treatment that emphasizes the learning of a contemplative practice due to their difficulty with psychotherapy (Benning, Rozalski, & Klingspon, 2015; Bowers & Kelly, 1979; Weinstein & Smith, 1992; Wickramasekera, 1988) and the narrow range of the practices that will likely work well for them in the initial stages of practice. They are definitely the type of person that frequently washes out of training programs that teach clients how to use contemplative practices. Previous research has demonstrated that the general public is already washing out of these programs at a rate of around 50% (Smith, 1989). My sense is that lows are even more likely to drop out of many of the most popular contemplative training methods such as mindfulness meditation since they simply lack the requisite metacognitive and psychophysiological skills to enact the techniques. We must recommend an alternative contemplative practice to lows that they can actually do well with quickly and that is suited to their interpersonal style in psychotherapy.

Lows do best with contemplative practices that require very little metacognitive skill and psychophysiological ability. I am often saddened when I hear of clinicians who only utilize the mid to higher end techniques like mindfulness meditation and hypnosis *with all of their clients*. This means that all of their clients with low mind/body ability are struggling with methods that do not suit them well at best and may likely leave them needlessly feeling like they are failures. I consider this kind of therapeutic impasse to be an iatrogenic failure since the client could do quite well with a different contemplative practice such as biofeedback and/or progressive muscle relaxation (Benning, Rozalski, & Klingspon, 2015; Bowers & Kelly, 1979; Weinstein & Smith, 1992; Wickramasekera, 1988).

Lows are actually quite easy to work with when they are taught an appropriate contemplative practice for their level of mind/body ability. Lows are also less susceptible to treatment relapses than highs (Das, 1958; Bowers & Kelly, 1979) due to their learning characteristics. I have heard many of my pain patients with low mind/body ability exclaim things like, "Maybe this relaxation is something more than just woo!" and "I always thought that stress was just in my mind until this machine showed me that it was in my body too!" We do lows no favor by treating them as if they were highs, as we previously discussed. What's even more amazing is that the average low can learn to develop their mind/body ability up to medium levels after as little as six to eight weeks of consistent training with an appropriate contemplative practice (Diamond, 1974; Lynn, 2004). I have even worked with a small number of lows who after a number of months had developed their mind/body abilities into the high range. So there really is no excuse not to use the methods that will work the best for them.

Meanwhile, the HRMTP and other clinical models (Wickramasekera, 1988; Wickramasekera II, 2005) recommend that clients with high levels of mind/body ability (highs) should be using more advanced contemplative practices. The superior metacognitive skills and psychophysiological abilities of highs are ready for any contemplative method, but they will feel the most engagement with techniques that present a challenge to them such as advanced forms of meditation (e.g., Chod & Tonglen), guided imagery, lucid dreaming, and/or hypnosis. These patients will often report feeling bored with only using biofeedback since they prefer the interpersonal relationship style of psychotherapy and actually make more progress quickly in psychotherapy than other people (Bowers & Kelly, 1979; Wickramasekera, 1988). I often begin my work with highs by teaching them mindfulness meditation since it is very easy to teach and has a high degree of research supporting its utility in a vast array of clinical circumstances in psychotherapy and medicine (Shapiro & Walsh, 2003). Many advanced forms of meditation often assume that the meditator is in a state of mindfulness while practicing it (Wangyal, 2000), and thus mindfulness can enrich any other contemplative practice that we recommend to the client as well.

Clients with medium mind/body ability often do well with a combination of biofeedback and another contemplative method that only requires a medium or low level of mind/body ability. The clinician can simply discontinue biofeedback when it no longer appears necessary to produce clinical progress. There are a number of medium-level contemplative practices that one can begin employing with mediums and/or highs such as affirmations, autogenics, holotropic breathing, mantra meditation, mindfulness meditation, and basic forms of guided imagery and hypnosis. It is also quite possible that many of your mediums will progress into the high range of mind/body ability after six to eight weeks of consistent practice.

Psychophenomenolgical Hypnotic Assessment with the PCI-HAP

The vast majority of hypnotic assessment instruments utilize standardized procedures that measure a person's ability to experience a variety of hypnotic phenomena that range in their relative difficulty for the average person to experience (Pekala & Kumar, 2000). These tests are excellent at classifying clients into the low, medium, and high ranges of mind/body ability, but they give almost no information about the client's unique experience of hypnosis. This is not ideal as there are many different types and subtypes of people with low, medium, and high levels of hypnotic ability (Pekala, 2002; Terhune & Cardeña, 2010). Even among highs, there are some whose experiences during contemplative practices are relatively less strong in mental imagery than one might expect. Therefore, the best quantitative hypnotic assessment method should give the clinician both a reliable index of their client's mind/body ability and information about their unique experiences during contemplative practice.

There is really only one instrument available that provides us with both a reliable index of a client's mind/body ability as well as a thorough assessment of their unique phenomenology during hypnosis. It is called the Phenomenology of Consciousness Inventory—Hypnotic Assessment Procedure or *PCI-HAP* (Pekala, 1995; Pekala & Kumar, 2000). The PCI-HAP is like other measures of hypnotic ability in that it assesses hypnotic ability through employing a variety of standardized hypnotic experiences created to be very unobtrusive and well tolerated even by patients with complex trauma (Pekala, 1995; Pekala & Kumar, 2000). Indeed, much of the research done on creating the PCI-HAP was done with veterans with complex PTSD and addictions at a VA Hospital. Therefore, the clinician can feel confident that most clients will enjoy their experience of testing and report that it was a comfortable and relaxing experience.

However, the PCI-HAP also collects a lot of information via its 52-item questionnaire that assesses a person's unique phenomenological experiences during hypnosis and can compare them to normative data from other patients. The PCI-HAP gathers information about the 12 major dimensions and 14 minor dimensions of phenomenological experiences that people generally experience with a wide variety of various contemplative practices such as shamanic drumming, fire-walking, hypnosis, meditation, prayer, and many other practices (Pekala & Kumar, 2000). The 12 major and 14 minor dimensions (minor dimensions in parentheses) are: altered state of awareness, altered experience (body image, time sense, perception, unusual meaning), volitional control, self-awareness, rationality, internal dialogue, positive affect (joy, sexual excitement, love), negative affect (anger, sadness, fear), imagery (amount and vividness), attention (direction and absorption), memory, and arousal. The PCI-HAP provides percentile ranks for each of these dimensions, which makes it possible to know that a given client might rank in the 90th percentile for their level of positive affect during contemplative practice. This is critical information for us as clinicians since most people have never discussed their mind/body experiences in any great depth with another person. Many of my patients have been astonished to find out that their experience of various contemplative practices is unique. We can then help them to utilize their unique responses by amplifying them in our instructions as we teach them new contemplative practices. For example, a person who experiences mostly positive emotions during mind/body practices may be a good candidate to use simple or advanced forms of compassion-based meditations designed to develop their empathy and altruistic motivations. We can also make frequent reference to experiencing a sense of well-being with them when we teach them any technique since we know that is a unique feature of their mind/body ability.

The PCI-HAP is an incredibly useful assessment instrument for assessing mind/body ability and a person's unique experiences of their mind/body relationship during contemplative practice. However, many transpersonal counselors have not been trained in how to administer a method of hypnotic assessment like the PCI-HAP or even in how to administer any kind of hypnotic intervention. In this case, it is possible for a clinician to at least approximate a client's level of hypnotic ability by administering the Tellegen Absorption Scale (TAS) to them (Wickramasekera, 1988). The TAS has only 34 brief items and is easy to administer and score (Roche & McConkey, 1990). Patients in the low range generally score less than a raw score of 9, while high scorers can be defined as scoring greater than 25. Clinicians new to hypnotic assessment can begin using the TAS to divide patients into the low, medium, and high ranges of mind/body ability while they seek out training in hypnosis from a reputable organization such as the American Society of Clinical Hypnosis, International Societies of Hypnosis, or the Society for Clinical and Experimental Hypnosis.

How to Integrate Qualitative and Quantitative Mind/Body Assessment Approaches

We are in an excellent position to make recommendations for a client's contemplative practice when we use qualitative and quantitative methods of mind/body assessment. We can gather a lot of information in our first session about potential practices that the person has already done and whether they enjoyed them or not. We can learn whether a person's ethnic, racial, religious, and other psychosocial factors might predispose them to want to do certain types of practice. Quantitative assessment will reveal to us their relative level of mind/body ability and also their unique experience of their mind/body relationship during a contemplative practice. Let me provide an amalgamated and hypothetical case example to illustrate the utility of mind/body assessment in transpersonal counseling.

Mr. No-Way was a 52-year-old cisgender White American male that I treated a number of years ago, referred to me by an anesthesiologist. The physician warned me that this client was one of the angriest patients that he had ever interacted with. I learned that my client had been through a number of terrible accidents throughout his life that resulted in severe and chronic low back pain. Mr. No-Way let me know that he had very little faith in the idea that counseling might help a person with a real pain problem. He told me that he was angry that numerous surgeries had not helped him and that his life was now ruined.

I asked Mr. No-Way what he had already tried to do to cope with the pain. He told me that nothing really worked other than not moving at all and staying in bed all day. I asked him what he did to pass the time while in bed. He discussed feeling bored and depressed, although occasionally he did enjoy watching some birds that came to a feeder near his living room window. He told me that he used to be an avid bird watcher before his pain condition made standing and walking without pain impossible. I asked him what he liked about bird watching and he replied that he felt a kind of kinship with birds. I also asked him about other relaxation and spiritually oriented pursuits, but he seemed reluctant to disclose much of anything. He also became defensive during this part of the interview and asked me several times why I would want to talk to him about bird watching so much. I explained to him that I was interested in learning the natural ways in which his body and mind had already learned to relax. I then explained to him the general scientific literature on how contemplative practices can help people with real pain problems. I also explained that we would be doing more quantitative assessment in the next session. The purpose and methods of all the assessment procedures were explained to him just as I discussed earlier in this chapter.

The client was cooperative but very skeptical that contemplative practices could actually help him in the next session. The client immediately opened his eyes as I was counting him back to the room from 5 to one during the PCI-HAP. He then loudly exclaimed, "Well I hope that was good for you because I didn't experience anything!" I thanked him for his cooperation and assured him that his efforts during mind/body assessment would help provide us with information to make his treatment more effective. He was quantitatively assessed to be in the low range of mind/body ability, which was consistent with my phenomenological assessment of him. However, his quantitative assessment did reveal that he had a minor level of ability to relax and experience some positive emotions during the PCI-HAP. His level of negative affect was also quite high, and this was consistent with my overall case conceptualization of him. I saw him as a person with low mind/body development who was suffering greatly with a chronic, very painful condition that was understandably causing him some anger. However, I also saw that he did have some previous experiences with a *hidden contemplative practice* when engaging in bird watching in the past. I was very keen on folding these relative strengths into our work together.

I recommended to the client that we start off with biofeedback and slow deep breathing as a combined contemplative practice. Mr. No-Way was amenable to this idea, although he expressed skepticism that these methods could really help him with his pain. We started treatment in the third session using these contemplative methods. He did quite well and was able to lower the muscle tension in his lower back with biofeedback. He reported to me that he was surprised that just focusing on slowing his breathing was actually having an effect on his body and making him feel better. I asked him to continue practicing for 15–20 minutes a day but said that he could also practice longer if he wished. I also suggested that he could practice in his living room so that he could watch his bird feeder while practicing.

The next week Mr. No-Way returned and stated that he was curious to see if the machine would validate that he was doing much better. He told me that he had made a breakthrough during the week while practicing in his living room and watching the birds outside. Sure enough, he was able to reduce his muscle tension much more than he had shown in the first session. It appeared that he had chronically tense muscles around his lower back. This was most likely due to him trying to hold his body motionless to stay out of pain. I gave Mr. No-Way a printout of a graph showing how his muscle tension levels had decreased very significantly during his 10 minutes of practice in our session. He left my office smiling and said that he wanted to show his graph to his wife. I heard him exclaim to his wife very loudly in the waiting room, "See, I told you that my pain was real! Now it's really going away too!"

Mr. No-Way continued to do very well and to exhibit a very high level of practice and motivation in subsequent sessions. He was now spending the majority of his day relaxing and watching the birds. He was quite giddy and happy in describing the birds to me. He was clearly much less depressed and angry than he had been a few weeks previously. I asked him what he liked best about his practice, and he described it as a feeling of *being at one with the birds*. He was happy to see that his baseline (resting) muscle tension levels had fallen over 50% since we started work together. He attributed the results to the contemplative practices that he had learned and also to the birds, which had encouraged him.

We kept working for a number of months together. I transitioned him into mindfulness meditation with bird watching as an object of meditation. It appeared to me that Mr. No-Way had advanced from being a low to a person with medium mind/body ability capable of using mindfulness. I later taught him a method of self-hypnosis for pain management that he could do with his eyes open while bird watching. The patient's pain was now under control, and he was much less angry and depressed. He returned to bird watching outside and reported using mindfulness and self-hypnosis to manage breakthrough pain. His physician later asked me how this patient had gotten better so quickly and said that Mr. No-Way "must have gone to the birds"!

The Oracle of the Ultimate

In summary, using methods of mind/body assessment can assist counselors in recommending the best contemplative practice to help a client develop their inner wisdom and compassion. Mind/body assessment helps therapists recommend a practice to a client that is consistent with their level of mind/body ability, unique mind/body experiences during contemplative practice, and their life history of contemplative activities and other psychosocial factors. In this way, mind/body assessment functions like an *oracle* that helps us to foresee which contemplative practices will likely best help our clients develop their inner wisdom and compassion. In the end, it can be said that teaching a client to connect with their *innate* and *ultimate* ability to transcend their suffering through contemplative practices is among the most helpful things that we can offer anyone in transpersonal counseling.

References

Awasthi B. (2013). Issues and perspectives in meditation research: In search for a definition. *Frontiers in Psychology, 3:613.* Published online. doi:10.3389/fpsyg.2012.00613.

Baikie, K. A. (2008). Who does expressive writing work for? Examination of alexithymia, splitting, and repressive coping style as moderators of the expressive writing paradigm. *British Journal of Health Psychology, 13*(1), 61–66. doi: 10.1348/135910707X250893.

Barber, T. X. (2000). A deeper understanding of hypnosis: Its secrets, its nature, its essence. *American Journal of Clinical Hypnosis, 42*, 208–272.

Benning, S. D., Rozalski, V., & Klingspon, K. L. (2015). Trait absorption is related to enhanced emotional picture processing and reduced processing of secondary acoustic probes. *Psychophysiology, 52*(10), 1409–1415.

Bohart, A. C., & Tallman, K. (1999). *How clients make therapy work: The process of active self-healing.* Washington, DC: American Psychological Association.

Bowers, K. S. (1977). Hypnosis for the seriously curious. New York, NY: W. W. Norton.

Bowers, K. S., & Kelly, P. (1979). Stress, disease, psychotherapy, and hypnosis. *Journal of Abnormal Psychology, 88*(5), 490–505.

Carrer, L. (2006). *Jose Custodio de Faria: Hypnotist, priest and revolutionary.* New York, NY: Trafford.

Cortright, B. (1997). *Psychotherapy and spirit: Theory and practice in transpersonal psychotherapy.* Albany, NY: State University of New York Press.

Das, J. P. (1958). Conditioning and hypnosis. *Journal of Experimental Psychology, 56,* 110–113.

Diamond, M. J. (1974). Modification of hypnotic ability: A review. *Psychological Bulletin, 81*(3), 180–198.

Forrest, D. (1999). *Hypnotism: A history.* New York, NY: Penguin.

Glisky, M.L., & Kihlstrom, J.F. (1993). Hypnotizability and facets of openness. *International Journal of Clinical and Experimental Hypnosis, 16,* 112–123.

Hilgard, E.R. (1965). *Hypnotic susceptibility.* New York, NY: Harcourt, Brace, & World.

Inagaki, H. (1998). *Nagarjuna's discourse on the ten stages: Dashabhumika-vibhasa–translation and study of Verses and Chapter 9.* Kyoto, Japan: Ryukoku University.

Kirsch, I. J. (1990). *Changing expectancies: A key to effective psychotherapy.* New York, NY: Brooks/Cole Professional Books.

LaBerge, S. (2009). *Lucid dreaming: A concise guide to awakening in your dreams and in your life.* Boulder, CO: SoundsTrue.

Lambert, M. J. (1992). Psychotherapy outcome research: Implications for integrative and eclectic therapists. In J. C. Norcross & M. R. Goldfried (Eds.), *Handbook of psychotherapy integration.* New York, NY: Basic Books.

LaBerge, S. (2009). *Lucid dreaming: A concise guide to awakening in your dreams and in your life.* Boulder, CO: SoundsTrue.

Lhalungpa, L. P. (1985). *The life of Milarepa.* Boston, MA: Shambhala Publications.

Lynn, S. J. (2004). Enhancing suggestibility: The effects of compliance vs. imagery. *American Journal of Clinical Hypnosis, 47*(2), 117–128.

Lynn, S. J., & Shindler, K. (2002). The role of hypnotizability assessment in treatment. *American Journal of Clinical Hypnosis, 44,* 185–197.

MacDonald, D. A., & Friedman, H. L. (2013). Psychospiritual integrative practices. In H. L. Friedman and G. Hartelius (Eds.), *The Wiley-Blackwell handbook of transpersonal psychology* (pp. 544–561). West Sussex, UK: John Wiley & Sons.

Mind and Life Education Research Network (2012). Contemplative practices and mental training: Prospects for American education. *Child Development Perspectives* 6(146), 153–161.

Morgan, A.H. (1973). The heritability of hypnotic susceptibility in twins. *Journal of Abnormal Psychology, 82*, 55–61.

Moustakas, C. (1990). *Heuristic research: Design, methodology, and applications.* London, UK: Sage.

Namdak, T. N. (2016). *The four wheels of Bon.* London, UK: Foundation for the Preservation of the Yungdrung Bon.

Neisser, U., Boodoo, G., Bouchard Jr, T. J., Boykin, A. W., Brody, N., Ceci, S. J., ... & Urbina, S. (1996). Intelligence: knowns and unknowns. *American psychologist, 51*(2), 77.

Pekala, R. J. (1995). A short unobtrusive hypnotic induction for assessing hypnotizability: II. Clinical case reports. *American Journal of Clinical Hypnosis, 37*(4), 284-293.

Pekala, R.J. (2002). Operationalizing trance II: Clinical application using a psychophenomenological approach. *American Journal of Clinical Hypnosis, 44*(3), 241–255.

Pekala, R.J., & Kumar, V.K. (2000). Operationalizing "trance" I: Rationale and research using a psychophenomenological approach. *American Journal of Clinical Hypnosis, 43*(2), 107–135.

Piccione, C., Hilgard, E. R., & Zimbardo, P. G. (1989). On the degree of stability of measured hypnotizability over a 25-year period. *Journal of Personality and Social Psychology, 56*, 289–295.

Raz, A. (2005). Attention and hypnosis: Neural substrates and genetic associations of two converging processes. *International Journal of Clinical and Experimental Hypnosis, 53*(3), 237 –58.

Reynolds, J. M. (2006). *The oral tradition from Zhang Zhung: An introduction to the Bonpo Dzogchen teachings of the oral tradition from Zhang Zhung known as the Zhang-Zhung snyan-rgyud.* Kathmandu, Nepal: Vajra Publications.

Roche, S. M., & McConkey, K. M. (1990). Absorption: Nature, assessment, and correlates. *Journal of Personality and Social Psychology, 59*(1), 91–101.

Rogers, C. R. (1959). A theory of therapy, personality, and interpersonal relationships, as developed in the client-centered framework. In S. Koch (Ed.), *Psychology: A study of a science* (Vol. 3, pp. 184–256). New York, NY: McGraw Hill.

Shapiro, S., & Walsh, R. (2003). An analysis of recent meditation research and suggestions for future directions. *The Humanistic Psychologist, 31*, 86–114.

Smith, J. C. (1989). *Relaxation dynamics: A cognitive-behavioral approach to relaxation.* Champaign, IL: Research Press.

Tart, C. T. (2009). *The end of materialism: How evidence of the paranormal is bringing science and spirit together.* Oakland, CA: New Harbinger Publications.

Tellegen, A., & Atkinson, G. (1974). Openness to absorbing and self-altering experiences ("absorption"): A trait related to hypnotic susceptibility. *Journal of Abnormal Psychology, 83,* 268–277.

Terhune, D., & Cardeña, E. (2010). Differential patterns of spontaneous experiential response to a hypnotic induction: A latent profile analysis. *Consciousness and Cognition, 19,* 1140–1150.

Trungpa, C. (2005). *The sanity we are born with: A Buddhist approach to psychology.* Boston, MA: Shambhala Publications.

Urbina, S. (1996). Intelligence: Knowns and unknowns, *American Psychologist, 51*(2), 77–101.

Wangyal, T. (1998). *The Tibetan yogas of dream and sleep.* Ithaca, NY: Snow Lion.

Wangyal, T. (2000). *Wonders of the natural mind: The essence of Dzogchen in the native Bon Tradition of Tibet.* Ithaca, NY: Snow Lion.

Wall, K., Nye, F., & FitzMedrud, E. (2013). Psychospiritual integrative practices. In H. L. Friedman & G. Hartelius (Eds.), *The Wiley-Blackwell handbook of transpersonal psychology*, (pp. 544–561). West Sussex, UK: John Wiley & Sons.

Weinstein, M., & Smith, J. C. (1992). Isometric squeeze relaxation (progressive muscle relaxation) vs. meditation: Absorption and focusing as predictors of state effects. *Perceptual and Motor Skills: 75*(1), 1263–1271.

Wickramasekera, I. E. (1988). *Clinical behavioral medicine: Some concepts and procedures.* New York, NY: Plenum.

Wickramasekera, I. E. (1998). Secrets kept from the mind but not the body or behavior: The unsolved problems of identifying and treating somatization and psychophysiological disease. *Advances in Mind-body Medicine, 14*(2), 81–132.

Wickramasekera II, I. E. (2004). The kalyanamitra and the three necessary and sufficient conditions of client-centered psychotherapy. *Journal of Humanistic Psychology, 44*(4), 485–493.

Wickramasekera II, I. E. (2005). Best of both worlds: How to integrate hypnosis and biofeedback with empathy and hypnotic assessment procedures. *Biofeedback, 33*(1), 31–34.

Wickramasekera II, I. E. (2013). Hypnosis and transpersonal psychology: Answering the call within. In H. Friedman & G. Hartelius (Eds.), *The Wiley-Blackwell handbook of transpersonal psychology.* West Sussex, UK: John Wiley & Sons.

Wickramasekera II, I. E. (2014). Early psychological knowledge. In T. Leahey, S. Greer, G. Lefrançois, T. Reiner, J. Spencer, I. Wickramasekera II, & E.

Willmarth (Eds.), *History of psychology* (pp. 15–42). San Diego, CA: Constellation.

Wickramasekera II, I. E. (2015). Mysteries of hypnosis and the self are revealed by the psychology and neuroscience of empathy. *American Journal of Clinical Hypnosis, 57*(3), 330–348.

Wickramasekera II, I. E., & Szlyk, J. (2003). Could empathy be a predictor of hypnotic ability? *International Journal of Clinical and Experimental Hypnosis, 51*(4), 390–399.

Wilber. K. (1993). Paths beyond ego in the coming decades. In R. Walsh & F. Vaughn (Eds.), *Paths beyond ego: The transpersonal vision* (pp. 256–266). New York, NY: Penguin Putnam.

Chapter 7
Transpersonal Dreams as Spiritually Transformative Experiences

Stanley Krippner

Reports of strange, extraordinary, and unexplained experiences related to dreams have been a topic of fascination for people throughout the millennia. For many Native American tribes, there was no distinction between nighttime dreams and daytime visions; either could portend the future or describe distant events (Krippner & Thompson, 1996). In modern times, these reports persist and have become controversial because they seem to transcend conventional notions of time and space, at least to highly educated members of Western society. However, in ancient eras, they were often attributed to divine forces and found their way into the sacred writings of various faiths. More recently, they have been subsumed under the umbrella of what has become known as "transpersonal studies."

The word "transpersonal" was first introduced into human discourse by William James in a 1905 lecture (Vich, 1988). In 1942, C. G. Jung used the German term *uberpersonlich*, which his English translators rendered as "transpersonal," in the phrase "transpersonal unconscious" as a synonym for "collective unconscious" (Vich, 1988). A few years later, the term "transpersonal" was used by Gardner Murphy (1949) and still later, in 1967, by Abraham Maslow, Stanislav Grof, and Anthony Sutich (Friedman, Krippner, Riebel, & Johnson, 2013, p. 216; Sutich, 1976). The term is now applied to a variety of human behaviors and experiences.

"Transpersonal studies" can be defined as disciplined inquiry into those observed or reported human behaviors and experiences in which one's sense of identity appears to extend beyond its ordinary limits to encompass wider, broader, or deeper aspects of humanity, life, and/or the cosmos, including purported divine elements and those that are potentially transformative (Friedman, 1983; Krippner, 1997).

One current focus of transpersonal studies is a type of dream or similar human experience in which people believe they have interacted with spiritual entities or domains, an interaction that has had long-lasting consequences. These experiences have been described in different ways—numinous (filled with *numen*, or divine power), transcendent (establishing contact with higher, or "divine," existence), or sacred (encountering something considered to be hallowed, holy, and inviolate). In 1996, Kason used the term "spiritually transformative experiences" (STEs) to describe these experiences. The term seems to be a useful one, although "transpersonally transformative experiences (TTEs) would have been more inclusive. The words "transpersonal" and "spiritual" are not synonyms, and the reference to TTEs would have rejected any underlying assumptions as to the veridicality of a "spirit" or "soul" as is implicit in the way that STEs is used. Nonetheless, the STE term will be privileged in this essay simply because it has a wider currency than the term TTE.

Spiritually Transformative Dreams throughout History

Dreams have played a major role in religious and spiritual traditions throughout the world (Cunningham, 1992; Klemp, 1999). The Carthaginian philosopher Tertullian wrote, "Nearly everyone knows that God reveals himself to people most often in dreams" (in Savary, Berne, & Williams, 1984). Christians are familiar with the biblical account of St. Joseph's dream in which the agency of Mary's pregnancy was revealed. Another biblical dream warned the Eastern Magi to return to their country without revealing the whereabouts of Jesus to King Herod. Joseph was warned in a dream to take Mary and Jesus into safety because Herod was seeking to destroy the child; in addition, the time

7. Transpersonal Dreams

when it was safe for Joseph to return to Israel was announced in a dream.

Queen Maya, the mother of the Buddha, reportedly had a dream in which a white elephant with six tusks entered her womb, indicating that she would give birth to an infant who would become a universal monarch. King Cudhodana, father of the Buddha, also dreamed about his son's path and was saddened by the separation it predicted. Gopa, Buddha's wife, dreamed of catastrophic events and shared it with her husband, who explained that world turmoil heralds a potential inner liberation. In the sixth century, the mother of Prince Shotokutaishi dreamed that a Bodhisattva asked to take shelter in her womb. She soon became pregnant and gave birth to the individual who was to establish Buddhism in Japan.

The *Talmud* contains 217 references to dreams and the *Bible*'s Old Testament contains about 15 dreams, most of which herald the beginning of vital stages in Judaism's history. For example, Joseph attained eminence by interpreting the Egyptian Pharaoh's dreams. Earlier, his father, Jacob, is said to have undergone a transformative experience as the result of a dream. Jacob was hardly an appropriate figure to be the patriarch of Israel. At one point, he had refused to feed his hungry brother, Esau, until the latter surrendered to him the rights of the firstborn. In conspiracy with his mother, Jacob undertook an elaborate deception to take advantage of his father's blindness and to cheat Esau out of a paternal blessing. Later, when Jacob made a journey, he had a powerful dream in which he saw a ladder stretching from earth to heaven, with angels ascending and descending the steps. At the top of the ladder, God stood and proclaimed that He would give all the surrounding land to Jacob and his descendants. In such a manner, the apparently unrighteous brother was chosen over the pious one. Jacob, shaken by the dream, slowly mended his ways and, years later, offered Esau his wives, sons, servants, and animals. Esau refused the gifts out of love, and the two brothers were reconciled.

Most of the followers of Muhammad dispute reports that his revelations occurred in dreams. They point out that the Prophet's personal development was so highly evolved that there was no dividing line between his "conscious" and "unconscious." His "night journeys," whatever their origins, were spiritually transformative experiences. In about the early 17th century, Muhammad was resting in Mecca when the archangel Gabriel appeared with a winged steed that carried them to a mosque in Jerusalem where Muhammad led a number of prophets in prayer. From there, he toured the circles of heaven, speaking with Abraham, Moses, and Jesus, and finally was taken by Gabriel to Allah, who began to dictate the *Koran* to him. These journeys lasted for a dozen years, during which time Muhammad would recite the words of Allah to scribes since he was illiterate. This series of spiritually transformative experiences gave birth to a major religious movement.

A spiritually transformative dream was reported by one of Muhammad's followers, Abdullah ben Zayd, and it played an important role in the development of Islam. Muhammad was eager to introduce a recognizable call to prayer for the faithful, just as the Jews were called to the synagogue with a trumpet and the early Christians to church by the sound of a rattle. During prayers, ben Zayd fell asleep and dreamed of a man dressed in green who was carrying a rattle. Ben Zayd asked if he could buy the rattle to use as a call to prayer. The man in green replied, "Call out, there is no god but God and Muhammad is his Prophet." Upon awakening, ben Zayd told Muhammad of his dream, and the Prophet instructed him to teach the exact phrase he had heard to another follower, who became the first *muezzin*.

Francis of Assisi, the 13th century monk who founded the Franciscan order, was about to have an interview with the terrifying Pope Innocent III. It is reported that he dreamed he had grown as tall as a great tree and, as Innocent looked on in dismay, restored the balance of a Vatican basilica that was on the point of collapsing. This dream gave St. Francis the courage to tell the pope that his order was badly needed to restore vigor to the Roman Catholic Church. St. Dominic, who founded a rival religious order, reported a dream of being presented to Jesus and the Virgin Mary in the company of St. Francis. The two of them were jointly entrusted with the conversion of the world.

Spiritually transformative dreams can also illuminate intrapersonal religious conflicts. St. Francis had a dream series in which his fiancée, present in the first dream, was replaced by the Virgin Mary, signifying his rejection of secular life. A 12th century Jain text tells the story of Kesara and Vasanta. One night, Kesara dreamed that she married Vasanta, and that same night he dreamed that he married her. Both were delighted with the dream message and declared their mutual love. But Kesara's parents, as was the custom, had arranged her marriage to someone else based on such traditional practices as favorable astrological signs. They considered their daughter's dream an illusion and disregarded their daughter's pleas. Saddened, Kesara and Vasanta tried to commit suicide. Fortunately, they were rescued, escaped their parents, and lived together happily.

The establishment of the Church of the Latter Day Saints was associated with dream revelations purportedly received by Joseph Smith in 1820. He dreamed that God told him to establish a church and, in 1823, the angel Moroni appeared in a dream and revealed to him the existence of the *Book of Mormon*. Bulkely (1995) observed that religion was the original field of dream study, and that dreams are major spiritual phenomena in almost all of the world's religious traditions.

In some eras, religious institutions have taken a hostile attitude toward dreamworkers and dreamworking. In some meditative disciplines, it is maintained that spiritually developed adepts do not need to dream. In the fifth century, St. Jerome's translation of the *Bible* from Greek and Hebrew manuscripts was marred by his substitution of "observing dreams" for "witchcraft" in several parts. Therefore, the new translation dogmatically stated, "You will not practice soothsaying or observe dreams." As a result, dreamwork was held in disfavor by the Roman Catholic Church for the next 15 centuries; people were discouraged from turning to their dreams for insight, consolation, or hope. It is not known whether St. Jerome or the church authorities were responsible for the error in translation, but it appears to have been deliberate because the word "witchcraft" is correctly used in other portions of the translation (Savary, Berne, & Williams, 1984).

Dreams are not the only vehicle for spiritual transformation. On his first three trips outside the palace, the Buddha saw sickness, old age, and death, asking himself, "How can I enjoy a life of pleasure when there is so much suffering in the world?" On his fourth trip, he met a wandering monk who had given up everything, and resolved to follow the same path. For six years, the Buddha practiced extreme asceticism, but no spiritually transformative experience was forthcoming. He then started to eat nourishing food, regaining his strength, and resolving to sit under a Bodhi tree until he found an answer to his question. Following temptations and conflicts, he had a spiritually transformative experience, understanding the cause of suffering and how to resolve it. For the next 45 years, he taught the three universal truths, the eightfold path, and the five precepts. Many of those who follow these teachings have reported spiritually transformative experiences themselves.

Psychological Inquiry into Spiritually Transformative Dreams

Jung spoke of the "Self" archetype as the center of the psyche. This so-called "Self" attempts to integrate all opposing elements of the psyche, transmuting them into a unique entity representing all that a person is able to become. In dreams, this process of integration (or "individuation") can appear as a flower (e.g., the Golden Flower of Taoism, the rose window of medieval Christian cathedrals); a geometric form (e.g., the circular mandala found in Tibetan Buddhism and many Native American medicine wheels); a jewel (e.g., the Blessed Pearl of Islam, the Jeweled Net of Indra); a person (e.g., Buddha, Jesus, Muhammad, Lord Krishna); or a common object that takes on new meaning (e.g., the wheel of Hinduism, the drum of the Lakota Sioux).

Although dreams have been perceived to play a role in the spirituality of individuals and groups since ancient times, modern dream research has paid little attention either to their content or to their significance in contemporary life. Interviews and conversations with individuals who report spiritual dreams, however, indicate that they often are perceived to have significance and value to the dreamers (Bulkely, 1995; Savary, 1990). These attitudes involve how the dreamers perceive the world and how they conduct themselves in it, typically in terms of manifesting greater serenity, more facile decision-making capabilities, an appreciation for aspects of life described as "divine," and an increased satisfaction with their social and professional activities. In addition to enhanced outcomes in dreamers' waking lives, there are also indications that spiritual dreams may sometimes have negative consequences, such as misguiding the dreamer into actions that result in personal distress (Robbins, 1988).

Some research studies have demonstrated a relationship between spiritually transformative experiences and positive outcomes in individuals' lives, such as psychological well-being and improved psychological attitudes (e.g., Hood, 1974; Kaas, Friedman, Lesserman, Zuttermeister, & Benson, 1991; Pollner, 1989) as well as individuals' relationship to the world–for example, investigating the purpose of life and their place in that purpose (e.g., Grof, 1988; James, 1902/1958). Since waking spiritually transformative experiences have been found to play a role in enhanced life outcome, a similar relationship with spiritual dreams, if it exists, may indicate that these dreams may also become a catalyst for enhanced quality of life.

The content and use of spiritual dreams in the lives of individuals typically have been examined in the literature of spirituality and dreaming through descriptions of personal experiences, historical anecdotes, and ethnographic dream accounts. Some of these dream accounts include specific content (perceived by the dreamer to be spiritual) such as light (Boteach, 1991; Gillespie, 1989; Sanford, 1989), divine entities (Savary, Berne, & Williams, 1984), and spiritual teachers (Evans-Wentz, 1958; Shaw, 1992). Other dream accounts include experiences perceived by the dreamer to be spiritual, such as the oncoming of death (Sanford, 1989; Wren-Lewis, 1985/1991), experiences of transcendence and awe (Busnik & Kuiken, 1996), and the entry into spiritual domains (Kelsey, 1974; Strickmann, 1988; Tedlock, 1987). Esoteric practices in dreams (Eliade, 1987; Kilborne, 1990) and Tibetan dream yoga practices (Sogyal Rinpoche, 1992) also have been considered to be spiritual.

There is some published research into what Jungians call "archetypal" dreams—for instance, dreams that reflect supposedly "universal" themes or vivid images from mythology, folklore, and/or religion (Faber, Saayman, & Touyz, 1978; Spadafora & Hunt, 1990). In addition, there is a body of research involving lucid dreams and/or meditation and dreams (Gackenbach, Cranson, & Alexander, 1986; Hunt & Ogilvie, 1988; Kelzer, 1987). However, archetypal dreams and lucid dreams are not spiritual dreams per se and most of the studies involving them did not distinguish spiritual dreams from other types of dreams. An exception is the work of Busnik and Kuiken (1996), who asked 36 men and women to report their most "impactful" dreams from the preceding month. Cluster analysis identified five groupings, one of which, "transcendence," was marked by feelings of "joy, delight, ecstasy, and awe." The overall results constituted a partial replication of an earlier study (Kuiken & Sikora, 1993).

My students and I embarked on a different kind of research procedure that would identify "spiritual dreams." To accomplish this objective, we selected content analysis, a method developed to systematically and objectively identify characteristics and themes of communications or documents and the relative extent to which these characteristics and themes pervade a given communication or document (Berg, 1989; Holsti, 1968; Weber, 1990). Since 1888 there have been many research studies using content analysis to investigate dream content (Winget & Kramer, 1979), but there has been little work on the spiritual content of dreams. We asked the research question, "Can the spiritual content of dream reports be identified and measured?"

"Dreaming" is defined by the *American Heritage Dictionary* (1993) as a sequence of images, ideas, and/or emotions that occur during sleep. Dreams are generally reported in narrative form. Hall and Nordby (1972) have noted that dream researchers need to attempt to distinguish between the dreamer's subjective experience, the dreamer's memory of the dream and reflections on the dream experience, and the dreamer's verbal, artistic, or other ways of reporting the experience.

Images, or imagery, in dreams are defined in the same way that Achterberg and Lawlis (1980) defined "imagery," as "the internal experience of a perceptual event in the absence of the actual external stimuli" (p. 27). Therefore, imagery in dreams does not have to be visual but can be auditory, olfactory, gustatory, or kinesthetic. In this investigation, the definition of dreaming was any reported imagery or other mental/emotional content that the dreamer claimed to have experienced during sleep. Self-awareness without content during sleep, as well as content reported from guided imagery, waking fantasies, meditative states, or other altered states of consciousness not occurring during sleep were excluded from this research.

"Spiritual" was defined as one's focus on, and/or reverence for, as well as openness and connectedness to, something of significance believed to be beyond one's full understanding and/or individual existence (*American Heritage Dictionary*, 1993; Elkins, Hedstrom, Hughes, Leaf, & Saunders, 1988; Krippner & Welch, 1992; Shafranske & Gorsuch, 1984). This definition was crucial to our research because, as Wilber (1999) notes, the answer to questions about spirituality depends upon how one defines the term.

The "divine," in this research, was defined as that which is regarded as holy (belonging to, derived from, or associated with religious or spiritual powers) and/or sacred (that which is dedicated to or worthy of veneration or worship) (*American Heritage Dictionary*, 1993), thus deserving the highest respect. The locus of the divine can be either outside of oneself, as when it has the nature of a superhuman entity or a deity, or within oneself, as when it is thought to reside within one's "inner," "deeper," and/or "higher" self. "Reverence," in this research, was defined as an attitude or feeling of profound awe and respect (*American Heritage Dictionary*, 1993).

Definitions of "spiritual" and "religious" and of "spirituality" and "religion" are often similar. For example, James (1902/1958) defines "religion" as "feelings, acts, and experiences of individual men [and women] in their solitude, so far as they apprehend themselves to stand in relation to whatever they may consider divine" (p. 42). However, this definition is very much like the definition of "spiritual" as given above, especially in its implied link between beliefs and action (Reese, 1997). Therefore, for clarity's sake, "religion" or "religious" was distinguished in this research from "spiritual" as pertaining and adhering to an organized system of beliefs about the divine, and the observance of rituals, rites, and requirements of that organized system of beliefs (*American Heritage Dictionary*, 1993). Spiritual, on the other hand, refers to activity and experience, especially one's direct contact with the dimensions of existence one considers "sacred" (Walsh, 1999, p. 3).

Even so, spiritually oriented dream reports can be extremely useful to science; the identification of such variables as gender, age, and cross-cultural differences can help investigators understand the roles that dreams play in human development. Faith and I (2001) looked for "exotic dreams" (i.e., anomalies) in a collection of 910 dream reports from women and 756 from men. All reports had been collected by me in seminars presented in six different countries between 1990 and 1998. Seminar participants were simply asked to volunteer a recent dream, and only one dream per participant was utilized in the analysis. When a dream report was not written in English, it was translated by a native speaker of that language. Faith and I made no pretense that the dream reports were representative of the general population of the countries investigated. Scoring guidelines were applied to the dreams, and when a report fell into more than one category, half a point was given for each category. Two raters scored each of the 1,666 dreams; inter-rater reliability was .95; in other words, the scoring guidelines were clear with minimal overlap. The categories used were those described in the book *Extraordinary Dreams* (Krippner, Bogzaran, & de Carvalho, 2002).

There were no statistically significant differences between genders: 8.5% of all female dreams were anomalous versus 7.7% of male dream reports. The country with the highest number of anomalous dreams was Russia (12.7%), followed by Brazil, Argentina, Japan, Ukraine, and the United States (5.7%). The only categories that surpassed 1% of all dream reports were lucid dreams (1.7%), out-of-body dreams (1.4%), visitation dreams (1.1%), and precognitive dreams (1.1%) (Lewis & Krippner, 2015). To be scored as a visitation dream, a deceased person or an entity from another reality had to provide counsel or direction that the dreamer felt of comfort or value. For example, a Ukrainian woman reported, "In this dream, I am afraid of dying because my neighbors start to die, one by one. I think of what a short period of time it took for so many of them to die, both men and women. I would like to live a more spiritual life, but the conditions around me do not permit it, so I must work very hard each day. Then one of my dead neighbors comes to see me and tells me that I can lead a spiritual life through my work." Of course, the existence of the deceased neighbor could not be verified, but the dream assisted the dreamer in resolving an existential dilemma in her life.

Faith and I did not create a category for "spiritual" dreams because we felt that element would overlap with the "visitation" category. Further, no attempt was made to determine if a dream was a STE. Those questions will need to be asked and answered by future scholars.

The Casto Spirituality Scoring System

Hall and Van de Castle's system of dream content analysis, with its predetermined categories and subcategories, is frequently used to detect common and recurring elements in dreams. While Hall and Van de Castle's (1966) categories do not include spiritual categories per se, they do include categories that sometimes contain spiritual content items, for example, physical surroundings, characters, social interactions, activities, achievement outcomes, environmental press, emotions, descriptive elements. The reliability of scoring, or consistency of measurement, was found by Hall and Van de Castle to be 73% for physical surroundings, 76% for characters, 70% for social interactions, 85% for activities, and 63% for emotions. Hall and Van de Castle's original normative data has been replicated in other studies; for example, Hall, Domhoff, Blick, and Weesner (1982) found few differences between the normative data of Hall and Van de Castle's original research and their own participants.

One of my students at Saybrook University, Kira Lynn Casto, developed a "spirituality" system to supplement Hall and Van de Castle's system (Casto, 1995). The "Casto Spirituality Scoring System" (CSSS), modifies several categories in Hall and Van de Castle's (1966) system to identify spiritual content (Figure 1). Their "Objects" category was altered to "Spiritual Objects"; their "Characters" category was altered to "Spiritual Characters"; their "Settings" category was altered to "Spiritual Settings"; their "Activities" category was altered to "Spiritual Activities"; their "Emotions" category was altered to "Spiritual Emotions."

Hood's (1975) Mysticism Scale was used to develop a "Spiritual Experiences" category yielding several possibilities—i.e., experiences in which there is a sense of direct contact, communion, or union with something considered to be ultimate reality, God, or the divine; experiences in which one's sense of identity temporarily reaches beyond or extends past their ordinary personal identity to include an expanded perspective of humanity and/or the universe; experiences where one appears to enter a sacred realm or condition that goes beyond the ordinary boundaries of space and linear time.

The difference between "Activities" and "Experiences" is similar to the psychological differentiation between behavior (i.e., externally observable actions, including verbal behavior) and experience (i.e., reported lived events that are phenomenological). The phrase, "I was angry at God" would be scored for "spiritual emotion." The phrase, "I told God that I was angry" would be scored for both "Spiritual Emotion" and "Spiritual Activity." The phrase, "I was angry at God and this reaction produced a red glow in my heart that sent intense heat throughout my body" would be scored for "Spiritual Emotion" and "Spiritual Experience." The phrase, "I told God that I was angry this reaction produced a red glow in my heart that sent intense heat throughout my body" would be scored for "Spiritual Emotion," "Spiritual Activity," and "Spiritual Experience."

These content definitions could apply to dreams reported from individuals representing a wide variety of spiritual backgrounds and could also be used to assess spiritually transformative experiences. One dreamer might report dreaming about "an intense ecstatic experience accompanied by white light conveying a blessing by Jesus Christ," another might report an intense ecstatic dream experience accompanied by white light that is felt to be a precursor to "the Nirvana described by the Buddha," and still another might report an intense ecstatic dream experience accompanied by white light that represents the arrival of Oxala, the African-Brazilian *orisha* (i.e., deity) of purity. All three dreams would be scored for "Spiritual Experience," for "Spiritual Activity" (e.g., the blessing, the description, the arrival), for "Spiritual Object" (e.g., the white light), and "Spiritual Character" (e.g., Jesus Christ, the Buddha, Oxala), despite the disparate traditions represented.

SPIRITUAL OBJECTS: Objects used for focus and reverence, to open and connect one to something of significance that is believed to be beyond one's full understanding and/or individual existence.

SPIRITUAL CHARACTERS: People, animals, or beings that are meaningfully connected to something of significance that is believed to be beyond one's full understanding and/or individual existence and that one associates with a sense of reverence.

SPIRITUAL SETTINGS: Places where one feels meaningfully connected to something of significance believed to be beyond one's full understanding and/or individual existence and that are associated with a sense of reverence.

SPIRITUAL ACTIVITIES: Activities used to open and connect one to something of significance believed to be beyond one's full understanding and/or individual existence and that are associated with a sense of reverence.

SPIRITUAL EMOTIONS: Felt emotions that are regarded as meaningfully related to something of significance that is believed to be beyond one's full understanding and/or individual existence and that are associated with a sense of reverence.

SPIRITUAL EXPERIENCES: Experiences in which there is a sense of direct contact, communion, or union with something that is considered to be ultimate reality, God, or the divine; and/or experiences in which one's sense of identity temporarily reaches beyond or extends past his or her ordinary personal identity to include an expanded perspective of humanity and/or the universe; and/or experiences where one appears to enter a sacred realm or condition that goes beyond the ordinary boundaries of space and linear time.

Figure 1. Casto Spirituality Scoring System

To evaluate reliability, the scores of two judges using the CSSS had been compared before this study was initiated (Casto, Krippner, & Tartz,

1999). A content item was not judged to be "Spiritual" unless it had received scores from both judges. Each dream was compared for presence or absence of each content category. Correlations reported by the two judges using the CSSS were .946 for "Spiritual Objects," .943 for "Spiritual Characters," .918 for "Spiritual Settings," .946 for "Spiritual Activities," .993 for "Spiritual Emotions," and .929 for "Spiritual Experiences." The reliability of the CSSS as a whole was .946, which indicates high reliability between scorers. An agreement between raters was counted if both raters scored a spiritual dream element for a particular dream or if both raters did not score a spiritual dream element for a particular dream. An example of a dream report that neither judge scored as having spiritual content was:

> I am playing with my friend, but something is chasing us. It was like my father or a huge shadow. My friend could run with a great deal of speed, but I could not move quickly enough. I was about to be captured, but my friend was safe because he was able to run faster.

Examples Using the Casto Spirituality Scoring System
Casto (1995) once worked with a female client who reported a spiritually transformative experience following a dream:

> In my dream, I was lying on my side, facing a wall. I propped myself up on my elbow as I stared at a white flickering illumination of a Madonna that was facing the same wall, praying. I stared at it, gathering my wits for a few moments. I was not afraid. I was awestruck. It occurred to me that this was some kind of message from my Mom, who only months ago had died. I wanted it to be a message from her, so I waited for the Madonna to speak to me. But it only faced the wall, oblivious to me. It wore a white flowing robe with a drape over its head. And then the face changed into my face. It was my face as a teenager. I watched in amazement as the figure clenched its fists to its breasts and threw its head back to scream this silent, anguished scream. I thought,

"My goodness, that's me. That's how I feel." I was startled by this but I immediately felt like the world or God or my Mom had recognized my pain. I then actually woke up in bed.

Casto and her client worked with the dream, finding indications that the dreamer's life options were limited or blocked in some way. Such phrases as "it only faced the wall," "the figure clenched its fists to its breasts," and "this silent, anguished scream" suggested that something was holding her back. Perhaps the dreamer's grief was blocking her actions but at the same time providing a comforting link with her mother. The anguish that the dreamer recognizes in herself appears to be a breakthrough in the grieving process that accompanied her mother's death, especially since it seemed to bring to her an acknowledgement that her pain is recognized by presences beyond herself. The discussion of this dream helped Casto's client work through the grief surrounding her mother's death, and released the energy required to explore options and make plans for the future.

Adele brought a dream to me that had originally recurred for about three years when she was a child, and now had returned. The setting of the dream was a hilly countryside, and the dreamer was seated outside a cave that seemed to be sacred. As she waited expectantly, a faceless monk in a black robe entered the sacred cave, chanting, "In time I come for everyone." Adele's feelings were fear, respect, and reverence. This dream report became a spiritually transformative experience, allowing Adele to examine the existential issues surrounding death, as it occurred at a time in her life when the realization that she might lose family members became acute. Eventually, Adele resolved these fears by focusing on the feelings of respect and reverence in her dreams, concluding that death is part of the life process, and that an awareness of its inevitability enhances the immediacy and enjoyment of each daily activity.

A clinical psychologist used the Casto scale when working with a client who reported a dream that triggered a spiritually transformative experience. The client was in his late 20s when he dreamed that he was a young man, and everything was bright and new. Suddenly, he changed into an old man, and life's freshness seemed to have faded. Now the only certainty that the future held was death. The dreamer thought that if he meditated, he would become eternal. He had begun to meditate when the myth of Gilgamesh came to mind. He then realized that his attempt was futile, since, like Gilgamesh, he would have to die. But, like Gilgamesh, he resolved to make himself useful to society and live in the present moment.

This dream was transformative in affecting therapeutic change in this client. One of the dream's main themes is the realization of death's imminence accompanied by fear. Another theme is the dreamer's attempt to escape his demise through spiritual practices, but his realization that this goal is futile. Finally, the dream encouraged the dreamer to take an active role in his life in contrast to his usual passivity. The client followed up this insight in therapy by molding his interpersonal relationships in a more positive manner and by becoming an active member of society, participating in organizations committed to positive social change.

These three dreams illustrate the way that symbols, metaphors, and mythic elements convey meaning in spiritually transformative dreams. They were scored for "Spiritual Characters" (e.g., the Madonna, the "faceless monk," Gilgamesh), "Spiritual Settings" (e.g., the "sacred cave"), "Spiritual Activities" (e.g., praying, meditating), "Spiritual Emotions" (e.g., "I was awestruck," "feelings of respect and reverence"), and "Spiritual Experiences" (e.g., "I immediately felt like the world or God or my Mom had recognized my pain"). Each dream played an important role in shifting the dreamer's attitudes and behaviors in more positive directions.

This study had asked if the spiritual content of spiritually transformative dream reports could be identified and measured. On the basis of the high reliability scores obtained by the judges, we can give a tentative affirmative answer to this question. Insofar as the validity of the CSSS is concerned, Casto (1995), in her original study, found that dreamers with identifiable spiritual content in their dream claimed to have had concomitant experiences in their daily lives.

Previous work with content analysis (e.g. Munroe, Nerlove, & Daniels, 1969) supports the contention that dream life mirrors waking life, championed by Alfred Adler (1938), Calvin Hall (Hall & Nordby, 1972), and others. If this is the case, the CSSS could be used to study the spiritual development of historical and contemporary personages who have reported spiritually transformative experiences, the spiritual states of clients undergoing transpersonally oriented psychotherapy or counseling, the incidence of spiritual dream content in certain demographic groups, and cross-cultural studies of spiritual activity and interest (e.g., Heinze, 1991; Krippner & Thompson, 1998).

Conclusion

This study provided data that answered the research question positively, and showed that the spiritual content of spiritually transformative dreams can be identified and measured, using the CSSS system based on a specific definition of "spiritual." The CSSS has already been used to identify spiritual elements in ayahuasca sessions (Krippner & Sulla, 2000), and we hope it will have other uses as well. The role played by spiritually transformative experiences in religious history as well as in the lives of ordinary people is an exciting area for those researchers interested in the field of transpersonal studies.

References

Achterberg, J., & Lawlis, G. F. (1980). *Bridges of the bodymind: Behavioral approaches to health care*. Champaign, IL: Institute for Personality and Ability Testing.
Adler, A. (1938). *Social interest: Challenge to mankind*. London, England: Farber and Farber.
American Heritage Dictionary. (1993). [Computer program: Microsoft Bookshelf]. Redmond, WA: Microsoft.
Berg, B. L. (1989). *Qualitative research methods for the social sciences*. Boston, MA: Allyn and Bacon.
Boteach, Y. S. (1991). *Dreams*. Brooklyn, NY: Bash.
Bulkely, K. (1995). *The wilderness of dreams*. Albany, NY: State University of New York Press.

Busnik, R., & Kuiken, D. (1996). Identifying types of impactful dreams: A replication. *Dreaming, 6*, 97–119.

Casto, K. L. (1995). *Contemporary spiritual dreams: Their content and significance.* Unpublished doctoral dissertation, Saybrook Institute, San Francisco, CA.

Casto, K. L., Krippner, S., & Tartz, R. (1999). The identification of spiritual content in dream reports. *Anthropology of Consciousness, 10*, 43–53.

Cunningham, S. (1992). *Sacred sleep: Dreams and the divine.* Freedom, CA: Crossing Press.

Elkins, D. N., Hedstrom, L. J., Hughes, L. L., Leaf, J. A., & Saunders, C. (1988). Toward a humanistic-phenomenological spirituality: Definition, description, and measurement. *Journal of Humanistic Psychology, 28*(4), 5–18.

Eliade, M. (1987). Dreams. In M. Eliade (Ed.), *Encyclopedia of religion* (pp. 482–492). New York, NY: Macmillan.

Evans-Wentz, W. Y. (1958). The doctrine of the dream-state. In W. Y. Evans-Wentz (Ed.), *Tibetan Yoga and secret doctrines* (pp. 215–223). Oxford, England: Oxford University Press.

Faber, P. A., Saayman, G. S., & Touyz, S. W. (1978). Meditation and archetypal content of nocturnal dreams. *Journal of Analytical Psychology, 23*, 1–22.

Friedman, H. (1983). The Self-Expansiveness Level Form A: Conceptualization and measurement of a transpersonal construct. *Journal of Transpersonal Psychology, 15*, 37–50.

Friedman, H., Krippner, S., Riebel, L., & Johnson, C. (2012). Models of spiritual development. In L.J. Miller (Ed.), *The Oxford Handbook of Psychology and Spirituality* (pp. 207–220). Oxford, UK: Oxford University Press.

Gackenbach, J., Cranson, R., & Alexander, C. (1986). Lucid dreaming, witnessing dreaming, and the Transcendental Meditation technique: A developmental relationship. *Lucidity Letter, 5*(2), 34–40.

Gillespie, G. (1989). Lights and lattices and where they are seen. *Perceptual and Motor Skills, 68*, 487–504.

Grof, S. (1988). *The adventure of self-discovery: Dimensions of consciousness and new perspectives in psychotherapy and inner exploration.* Albany, NY: State University of New York Press.

Hall, C. S., Domhoff, G. W., Blick, K. A., & Weesner, K. E. (1982). The dreams of college men and women in 1950 and 1980: A comparison of dream content and sex differences. *Sleep, 5*, 188–194.

Hall, C. S., & Nordby, V. J. (1972). *The individual and his dreams.* New York, NY: New American Library.

Hall, C. S., & Van de Castle, R. L. (1966). *The content analysis of dreams.* New York, NY: Appleton Century Crofts.

Heinze, R. I. (1991). *Shamans of the 20th century.* New York, NY: Irvington.

Holsti, O.R. (1968). Content analysis. In G. Lindzey & E. Aronson (Eds.), *The handbook of social psychology: Vol. 2. Research methods* (Vol. 2; pp. 597–601). Reading, MA: Addison-Wesley.

Hood, R., Jr. (1974). Psychological strength and the report of intense religious experience. *Journal for the Scientific Study of Religion, 13*, 65–71.

Hood, R., Jr. (1975). The construction and preliminary validation of a measure of reported mystical experience. *Journal for the Scientific Study of Religion, 14*, 29–41.

Hunt, H. T., & Ogilvie, R. D. (1988). Lucid dreams in their natural series: Phenomenological and psychophysiological findings in relation to meditative states. In J. Gackenbach & S. LaBerge (Eds.), *Conscious mind, sleeping brain: Perspectives on lucid dreaming* (pp. 389–417). New York, NY: Plenum.

James, W. (1958). *The varieties of religious experience*. New York, NY: Mentor. (Original work published 1902)

Kaas, J. D., Friedman, R., Lesserman, J., Zuttermeister, P. C., & Benson, H. (1991). Health outcomes and a new index of spiritual experience. *Journal for the Scientific Study of Religion, 30*, 203–211.

Kason, Y. (1996). *A farther shore: How near-death and other extraordinary experiences can change ordinary lives.* San Francisco, CA: Harper Collins.

Kelsey, M. T. (1974). *God, dreams, and revelation: A Christian interpretation of dreams* (Rev. ed.). Minneapolis, MN: Augsburg.

Kelzer, K. (1987). *The sun and the shadow: My experiment with lucid dreaming.* Virginia Beach, VA: A.R.E. Press.

Kilborne, B. (1990). Ancient and native peoples' dreams. In S. Krippner (Ed.), *Dreamtime and dreamwork* (pp. 194–203). Los Angeles, CA: Tarcher.

Kiuken, D., & Sikora, S. (1993). The impact of dreams on waking thoughts and feelings. In A. Moffit, M. Kramer, & R. Hoffman (Eds.), *The functions of dreaming* (pp. 419–476). Albany, NY: State University of New York Press.

Klemp, H. (1999). *The art of spiritual dreaming.* Minneapolis, MN: Eckenkar.

Krippner, S. (1997). Foreword. In D. Rothberg & S. Kelly (Eds.), *Ken Wilber in dialogue: Conversations with leading transpersonal thinkers* (pp. ix–xi). Wheaton, IL: Quest Books.

Krippner, S., Bogzaran, F., & de Carvalho, A. P. (2002). *Extraordinary dreams and how to work with them.* Albany, NY: State Univeristy of New York Press.

Krippner, S., & Faith, L. (2001). Exotic dreams: A cross-cultural study. *Dreaming, 11*, 73–82.

Krippner, S., & Sulla, J. (2000). Identifying spiritual content in reports from ayahuasca sessions. *International Journal of Transpersonal Studies, 19*, 59–76.

Krippner, S., & Thompson, A. (1996). A 10-facet model of dreaming applied to dream practices of sixteen Native American cultural groups. *Dreaming, 6*, 71–96.

Krippner, S., & Welch, P. (1992). *Spiritual dimensions of healing: From tribal shamanism to contemporary health care.* New York, NY: Irvington.

Lewis, J., & Krippner, S. (2015). Cross-cultural aspects of extraordinary dreams. In M. Kramer & M. Gluckman (Eds.), *Dream research: Contributions to clinical practice* (pp. 188–197). New York, NY: Routledge.

Meissner, W. W. (1990). The role of transitional conceptualization in religious thought. In Psychoanalysis and Religion. J. H. Smith & S. A. Handelmann (eds.) (pp. 95-116) Baltimore MD: John Hopkins Press.

Meissner, W. W. (1984). *The psychology of religious experience.* New Haven CT, Yale University Press.

Munroe, R. L., Nerlove, S., & Daniels, R. (1969). Effects of population density on food concerns in three East African societies. *Journal of Social Psychology, 125,* 405–406.

Murphy, G. (1949). Psychical research and personality. *Proceedings, Society for Psychical Research, 49,* 1–15.

Pollner, M. (1989). Divine relations, social relations, and well-being. *Journal of Health and Social Behavior, 30,* 92–104.

Randour, M. L. (1993). *Exploring sacred landscapes: Religious and spiritual experiences in psychotherapy.* New York, NY: Columbia University Press.

Reese, H. W. (1997). Spirituality, belief, and action. *Journal of Mind and Behavior, 18,* 24–51.

Robbins, P. R. (1988). *The psychology of dreams.* Jefferson, NC: McFarland.

Sanford, J. A. (1989). *Dreams: God's forgotten language* (2nd ed.). San Francisco, CA: HarperCollins.

Savary, L. M. (1990). Dreams for personal and spiritual growth. In S. Krippner (Ed.), *Dreamtime and dreamwork* (pp. 89-92). Los Angeles: Tarcher.

Savary, L. M., Berne, P. H., & Williams, S. K. (1984). *Dreams and spiritual growth: A Christian approach to dreamwork.* New York, NY: Paulist Press.

Shafranske, E. P., & Gorsuch, R. L. (1984). Factors associated with the perception of spirituality in psychotherapy. *Journal of Transpersonal Psychology, 16,* 231–241.

Shaw, R. (1992). Dreaming as accomplishment: Power, the individual and Temne divination. In M. C. Jedrej & R. Shaw (Eds.), *Dreaming, religion and society in Africa* (pp. 36-54). Leiden, Netherlands: E. J. Brill.

Sogyal Rinpoche. (1992). *The Tibetan book of living and dying.* San Francisco, CA: HarperCollins.

Spadafora, A., & Hunt, H. (1990). The multiplicity of dreams: Cognitive-affective correlates of lucid, archetypal, and nightmare dreaming. *Perceptual and Motor Skills, 71,* 627–644.

Strickmann, M. (1988). Dreamwork of psycho-sinologists: Doctors, Taoists, monks. In C. T. Brown (Ed.), *Psycho-sinology: The universe of dreams in Chinese culture* (pp. 25–46). Washington, DC: Woodrow Wilson International Center for Scholars.

Sutich, A.J. (1976). The emergence of the transpersonal orientation: A personal account. *Journal of Transpersonal Psychology, 8*, 5–19.

Tedlock, B. (1987). Dreaming and dream research. In B. Tedlock (Ed.), *Dreaming: Anthropological and psychological interpretations* (pp. 1–30). New York, NY: Cambridge University Press.

Vich, M. (1988). Some historical sources for the term "transpersonal." *Journal of Transpersonal Psychology, 20*, 107–110.

Walsh, R. (1999). *Essential spirituality*. New York, NY: John Wiley & Sons.

Weber, R. P. (1990). *Basic content analysis* (2nd ed.). Newbury Park, CA: Sage.

Wilber, K. (1999). Spirituality and developmental lines: Are there stages? *Journal of Transpersonal Psychology, 31*, 1–10.

Winget, C., & Kramer, M. (1979). *Dimensions of dreams*. Gainesville, FL: University of Florida.

Wren-Lewis, J. (1991). Dream lucidity and near-death experience: A personal report. *Lucidity, 10th Anniversary Issue, 10*, 75–79. (Original work published 1985)

Chapter 8
Exploring the Lived Experience of Meditation Instructors

Xiaodan Zhuang
Daphne M. Fatter
Peter G. Grossenbacher

> Meditation is not so much a particular delimited experience, but is rather *a way of seeing through* experience, always eluding any attempt to pin it down conceptually. (Welwood, 1977, p. 2)

Two fundamental areas of study in transpersonal counseling are transformative processes and transcendence of the self. Meditation practice has been enthusiastically embraced by the transpersonal traditions as it deeply embodies these aspects of the human potential and journey. There are many different kinds of meditation, with numerous specific practices that can lead to personal development and self-transcendence. For example, mindfulness practice (foundational to many forms of meditation) helps practitioners gain greater familiarity with themselves and their experience, often initiating a path of progressive transformation that leads beyond conceptual knowing. Likewise, insight practice, with its emphasis on directly encountering mind, readily engenders dissolving the solid sense of self.

Because of meditation's potential for deep inner change, it is well suited for gaining perspective on and understanding many of the subtler ways that humanity manifests. Through slowing down the speedy pace of conceptual thinking, meditation enables wakefulness and finding peace with things as they are. By learning to let go of clinging to our small ideas of who we are or what is real, moment-to-moment engaging with awareness opens into experience of spacious aliveness. Meditation thus transcends the personal; it cultivates living and knowing in the larger space of interconnection and interbeing. During and consequent to meditation, "the subject-object duality merges in a larger field of awareness" (Welwood, 1977, p. 4). The profundity of this transpersonal experience can be transformative, leading many people to develop keener sensitivities, appreciation, and connection with life on Earth.

Meditation has been passed from generations of teachers to generations of students for thousands of years, often offered only to monastics or individually selected students. In the 21st century, meditation has become widely accessible, effectively removing traditional restrictions on who can learn and teach meditation. Though many teachers of meditation come from Asia, an increasing number are native Westerners who learned meditation from Asian teachers or from an earlier generation of Western teachers. Countless individuals have now devoted much of their lives to helping others gain the freedom from intrapersonal limitations afforded by meditating.

Meditation affords equal opportunity for working with both the light and the shadows encountered in one's own mind and being. Meditation instructors are uniquely positioned and equipped to see this rich range of experiential content, first within themselves as meditators and then, as teachers, in their students. Such experienced and wise people constitute a rich reservoir of perspective and understanding that can illuminate both the challenges and enriching qualities that so often manifest along paths of meditative and transpersonal development.

Together, the authors of this chapter bring many decades of personal experience with meditation practice and teaching meditation in Theravadan Buddhist, Tibetan Buddhist, and Taoist traditions. For several years, the three of us have worked together in the Naropa University Consciousness Laboratory in Boulder, Colorado, a training and research facility where we delve into the lived experience of meditation and contemplative spirituality. In addition to examining how meditation contributes to growing engagement with awareness, compassion, and transformation of personal worldview, this research program also explores the teaching of contemplative practices.

Our own experience provides an intimate familiarity with teaching meditation, comprising three first-person perspectives, each entailing numerous observations and insights. Meditation instruction invites connection with greater awareness and being fully present in this intimate fashion with other people, while also holding a position of caretaking their being. In these ways, meditation instruction is truly unique. Fulfilling this responsibility without sinking into self-aggrandizement involves a sense of trust based on not knowing what will happen or what to do. This mode of being feels incredibly wakeful, and engages a level of experiential awareness that is intrinsically transpersonal.

This chapter reports on selective results of our qualitative empirical study of meditation instruction, conducted via semi-structured interviews with eight experienced meditation instructors drawn from a variety of traditions. The meditation instructors interviewed in this study included four instructors teaching Buddhist meditative traditions, two teaching Hindu meditative traditions, one teaching the Diamond Approach, and one teaching a Judeo-Christian meditative tradition. These interviews specifically addressed: defining meditation, skills developed through meditation, effects of meditation, instructional approaches, preparation before instructing, internal experience during instruction, information provided to students, and motivation to teach meditation. A more comprehensive report of this study's results, not detailed here, will soon be available (Fatter, Zhuang, & Grossenbacher, in preparation). By virtue of the generous participation of these accomplished teachers, their experience and insights offer an important empirical window into meditation instruction that reveals transpersonal aspects of meditation practice and teaching.

In order to establish and sustain rapport in a manner that supported deep reflection on lived experience, we conducted the eight interviews with a contemplative procedure that allowed for natural silences and contemplation by interviewee, interviewer, and another researcher present in the role of silent observer. Audio-recordings were transcribed and coded for thematic relevance, and were analyzed accordingly. Of the many aspects of meditation instruction addressed in this interview, in this chapter we share instructors' insights into pedagogical theory, teaching technique, and their intrapersonal process of instructing meditation in order to highlight the transpersonal themes of their lived experience,

Pedagogical Theory

Our interview questions prompted teachers to share their understanding of meditation, skills valuable to meditation learners and teachers, and integration of meditation into daily life.

Defining Meditation

Instructors' definitions of meditation varied from referring to meditation as a process, a state of being, or a practice that can be situated relative to daily life. Meditation was described as proceeding from *directed awareness*, in which attention focuses solely on the breath, to *choiceless awareness*, where attention focuses on stimuli in students' internal or external environment. Similarly, meditation was referred to as a natural process of unfoldment that increases awareness and a sense of expansiveness; a practice of discovery that cultivates presence and investigates the functioning of awareness; and a spiritual practice in which prayer can strengthen connection with the divine. One instructor referred to meditation as "learning to work with what arises in the moment" and "an alignment of body, breath, and mind."

Skills in Meditation and in Teaching Meditation

Practitioners reportedly develop diverse skills through practicing meditation. Skills that can aid meditation instruction include observation, turning inward, awareness of physical and mental presence, openness, curiosity about one's experience, self-compassion, and equanimity. Just as communication skills are founded upon and facilitated by interpersonal attunement, so, too, does interpersonal attunement rest on the supporting foundation of personal embodiment.

We find that a skilled instructor holds a level of perspective for the meditation student until the student gains greater perspective about their own experience in meditation for themselves. For example, an instructor brings compassion, tolerance, equanimity, and an invitation to greater awareness beyond what is familiar.

Integration of Meditation into Life

Meditation practice can serve as a means of integrating the transpersonal into life by transforming consciousness and one's lived experience beyond self-centering. While individual instruction varies by meditation style and instructor, instructed techniques include focusing on physical posture and sensory experience; helping to align the student's body, breath and mind to establish "a point of stillness"; and exploring and experiencing a student's energy field as well as the instructor's own energy field. One instructor encourages students to bring awareness to their judgment process, and to identify how they have aligned with their superego.

Integrated transpersonal development looks different for each person, and instructors discussed providing instruction about the various ways to integrate meditation practice into life. These practices range from meditation practice itself, to reading, breathing, and awareness exercises; attention re-directing exercises; working with chakras; and other practical activities to continuously heighten students' awareness in daily life. Four instructors mentioned teaching ways to integrate meditation practice into daily life by addressing life issues such as forgiveness and conflict resolution, and increasing awareness until the boundary between practice and one's daily life disappears. Instructors noted that students tend to separate meditation from daily life, which can interfere with fully integrating meditation benefits.

Pedagogical Technique

Interviews also focused on how instructors go about their teaching. Reported pedagogies included directly meeting the minds of students right where they are, and leveraging the immersive power of personal relationship and community.

Meeting Students Where They Are and as They Develop

Instructional approach. Overall, instructional approaches vary considerably, though most instructors endorsed a non-authoritarian teaching style with an emphasis on holding students' immediate experience and facilitating self-exploration in the process of learning meditation.

Three instructors highlighted meeting students where they are and letting them experience the practice for themselves. Two described providing only minimal structure to empower students, and taking an intuitive and experiential approach that provides atmosphere, invites learners to discover what arises along their own personal path, and helps students track their own process. One noted the difficulty and value in using language directed to the students' immediate experience, allowing students space to discover insights on their own rather than the instructor "excitedly jumping to the punch line." Another shared that "The teaching becomes more effective when it is actually presented and it becomes relevant for the student... at the time." Only one instructor reported being directive in her instruction, but she still welcomes questions. In addition, some instructors also provide conceptual and narrative information to facilitate understanding of meditation through story-telling, integrating psychological knowledge, or sharing their own experience learning meditation.

Beliefs and devotion. The transpersonal engages lived experience rather than just beliefs or philosophy (Cortright, 1997). Instructors varied widely in their pedagogical approaches to incorporating belief or devotion into teaching meditation. In terms of incorporating belief, three described instructions that involves little belief because ideas are limited, beliefs inhibit learning, or belief had completely transformed into experience. One instructor regarded all beliefs as problematic.

In dealing with students' beliefs, instructors mentioned teaching without addressing philosophy, encouraging students to explore their own belief, and focusing on cultivating love and wisdom instead of belief. Instructors also found that sometimes students hold inaccurate beliefs about meditation or look for confirmation of their own belief in meditation. Four suggested that students tended to hold certain beliefs about meditation at the beginning—such as one's mind should be empty during meditation, meditation ought to be easy and natural, or meditation is the ultimate medicine for their suffering. Three explained that students' strong beliefs, ideas of meditation, or self-centered views can interfere with learning by disrupting the momentary experience, prompting students to try to convince the instructor to adopt their own beliefs, or making meditation a selfish act.

Conversely, three instructors explained that concepts such as beliefs facilitate learning, especially for "left-brained" students, and students appreciate relevant information, with the caveat that "on the absolute level, concepts are just smoke dissolving into space." Some instructors encourage curiosity toward one's beliefs, noting that understanding the difference between expectation and real experience can help students grow.

With regard to devotion, two instructors endorsed supporting students' personal devotion as possibly helpful to learning, something that practitioners can return to in times of need or crisis. Three reported not intentionally teaching devotion to students (despite their own devotion), while one supports whatever students are devoted to, whether it's being a better parent or a vision of enlightenment. Another instructor asserted that students with devotion encountered more difficulty learning because they were looking for something outside themselves.

Instructor–Student Relationship and Community

The relationship as a co-creative journey. All instructors discussed the pivotal role of the relationship with one's meditation instructor in learning meditation. As with many relationships, the student–instructor relationship takes time to develop. It can start on a fairly superficial level, with both sides accumulating understanding of the other over time; usually, they will encounter miscommunication, conflicts, and other kinds of difficulties; and by working through these issues, the relationship deepens. As the relationship grows, many instructors disclose aspects of their personal meditation experience to benefit students' learning, and some achieve non-sexual intimacy with their long-term students. According to our participants, an ideal student–instructor relationship is like "the mountain to the cloud," always together and unified. Some even suggest the student–instructor relationship itself to be one essential goal of the learning process. The sense of unity between student and instructor is highly regarded by our participants.

From a transpersonal viewpoint, one's meditation instructor can serve as a guide to facilitate experiencing the personal realm with new eyes and learning how to move beyond the personal realm to experience the transcendence of self. Instructors stated that instruction itself can be a "co-creative journey" that sheds light on the spiritual nature of the relationship between instructor and student. One explained instruction as "two people paying attention together and staying focused on how to achieve a deep reunion with the divine" rather than a means of relaying "how to" practice a meditation technique. Another noted that there can be "a lot of love that's beyond anything that people know, between a teacher and student."

Ethical concerns in the journey. An essential part of teaching meditation includes cultivating and managing the ongoing relationship between the instructor and the student, while maintaining ethical standards in this relationship. When positive projections onto instructors seem healthy, the instructor can abide with and gradually disassemble them, whereas over-idealization can be harmful and creates the possibility of power abuse.

According to our interview results, there are at least four kinds of ethical issues involved in the instructor–student relationship and meditation instruction. The first pertains directly to relationship and intimacy: holding genuine care for students' well-being and approaching students with a "pure mind" are highly important. To maintain these stances, instructors may need to examine their own motivation and ego needs related to being in a teaching role, consult with one's own teacher or peers or receive supervision, and stay close to one's lineage in general. Instructors also need to refrain from social and sexual contact with students, maintain appropriate boundaries with students, make the purpose of touch transparent and relate it to the learning of practice, and explicitly define the relationship to minimize unspoken agreements and/or lack of clarity about the teacher–student relationship.

The second ethical issue involves power and control in the relationship. To minimize harm, instructors need to keep focus on students' needs, be aware of their own needs, refrain from telling students how to live their lives, and refrain from devaluing other meditation traditions. For students who are from another culture or have previous experience in other meditation traditions, instructors agree that it is important to validate their experience and practices and respect their cultural norms if different from the culture the instructor identifies with. As one instructor mentioned, there is no need to be afraid of conflict, but instructors need to refrain from a "them vs. me" mentality in dealing with conflict.

The third issue concerns money. Instructors need to be transparent about costs of retreats or other trainings and how teachers are paid, and avoid overcharging or undercharging. In addition, maintaining students' safety when they are a threat or danger to self is very important.

Instructors' Lived Experience

Our eight interviews yielded many hours of deep conversation about instructors' personal experience of teaching, and delved into their transpersonal motivations as well as challenges that they encountered.

Instructors' Internal Experience While Instructing

One instructor shared that "what I teach, I need to be, and to the depth that I can be, to that depth I can teach." This quote echoes the importance of instructors' own practice of meditation serving as a guidepost in their instruction. In addition, it reflects the mutually reinforcing relationship between an instructor's own transpersonal development and their ability to teach. Instructors shared their lived experience preparing for and during meditation instruction.

Preparing for instruction. Generally, we found many ways that instructors prepare for instruction, including observing, reading and studying meditation and psychology, practicing meditation, taking seminars and intensives, setting altruistic intentions to connect with and benefit students, and praying to their teacher and lineage for guidance. Seven instructors endorsed meditating before instruction as an important part of their preparation that helps to ground themselves from the vicissitudes of their daily life, quiet their mind, and open their heart to teach. This reflects the embodiment that instructors commit to when teaching. In addition, two observed that instructing itself provides preparation for instructing in the future, which reveals the self-reinforcing nature of teaching meditation.

We found that the way instructors prepare for instruction changes over time, indicating that meditation instructors are also on their own path of spiritual transformation that involves their teaching. For example, two instructors emphasized previously going through the material; however, now they focus more on internal preparation, such as setting intentions and meditating. One instructor observed not needing to "become something" to prepare for instruction, which reflects the transpersonal notion of being true to one's authentic nature rather than trying to mold oneself into a construct of who one thinks he/she should be—an important component of spiritual development (Cortright, 1997).

Internal experience while instructing. We found that instructors stressed the role of awareness during instruction, describing the process of constantly recognizing and acknowledging what is arising in the moment. One explained that the instructing process is "primarily attending to one's own participation, with another channel paying attention to things like timing or feedback that might be arising." The majority of instructors shared that they meditate while providing instruction, which enables them to receive real-time feedback about what is arising in the moment and adjust their instruction accordingly. Another instructor shared the view that "to the degree that I respond to what's arising in the moment, to that degree the teaching is alive." This suggests that as instructors attune their own awareness of what occurs in the present moment, they are able to use this moment-to-moment information and dual awareness of timing, feedback and other instructional aspects to adjust and guide their instruction. The instructors' ability to gather feedback in instruction from multiple domains of present-moment awareness exemplifies the multidimensional consciousness of the transpersonal realm (Cortright, 1997).

Three instructors emphasized a sense of connectedness—whether with others, their own inner core, or their crown chakra—invoking the transpersonal notion of connectedness within oneself and spiritual unity with others. Similarly, when asked about relating meditation instruction to what students already know, two instructors reported doing so explicitly, starting with their lived experience of embodiment and asking students questions to articulate their experience, which reminds students of their natural ability to connect with the divine.

Transpersonal Motivation and Rewards
All instructors asserted that teaching meditation had affected them. Six stated that providing instruction helped them to deepen their own meditation practice because they had more incentive to learn, and started to understand the practice from a teaching perspective. One instructor asserted "you learn best by teaching." To increase awareness during instruction, three noted paying more attention to their own experience all the time. Two instructors emphasized gaining life meaning, purpose, and spiritual inspiration through teaching meditation. Other reported effects included feeling more confidence, and discharging the responsibility of passing on Dharma.

Instructors described their motivation to teach meditation as aspiring to benefit people through teaching in their lineage, or to give something back for teaching received. In addition, instructors found motivation stemming from personal transformational experience with meditation and an understanding that whatever arises in one's experience has value. Five expressed strong connection and commitment to a lineage, most including strong personal devotion, whereas two explained that devotion was not part of their practice. One instructor described that devotion came from being in his own instructor's presence. Two indicated that they trust their life will be provided for if they follow the lineage in their teaching, and one explained that devotion is critical and can facilitate students' motivation via a teacher reflecting who students are at a profound level.

Seven instructors acknowledged receiving rewards, especially intangible rewards, from their instruction—including a sense of fulfillment in connecting with people, participating in their growing process, meeting incredible people, serving a higher purpose, world travel, and a continuous sense of awe. One reported that rewards changed over time, from being highly regarded by students to the inner satisfaction of serving the ultimate reality. Four explicitly stated that financial reward was insignificant to them. One instructor shared that spending time with people who practice meditation, have done "inner work," and have developed a "capacity for loving" is a tangible reward for providing instruction.

Resistance. Seven instructors shared that students' resistance can be one of the biggest challenges in instructing meditation. We understand resistance as an unconscious process aimed at protecting the individual from perceived threat (e.g., disturbed homeostasis), and it typically arises in contemplative training that exposes the intrinsic vulnerability of a person's sense of self. Just as resistance takes many forms in spiritual development, it can also manifest during the learning process of meditation in many different ways such as: students changing the subject when conversing with instructors, showing agitation when sitting, arriving late for class, refusing to sit in a certain way, not progressing in meditation practice, or explicitly expressing their resistance.

Instructors' opinions about resistance ranged from "not a big thing," to "the most important ingredient," to being considered as potentially life changing. While specific techniques varied, instructors' general approach toward student resistance was to support students in developing awareness of their own resistance in order for them to fully experience their resistance and learn to deal with it.

While resistance is rarely explicitly discussed in transpersonal literature (Eades, 1992; Walach, 2008), this strategy of intentionally allowing one's felt sense of an experience like resistance to be present and experienced employs the phenomenology of transpersonal experience (Valle, 1989). The transpersonal theorist Assagioli understood that part of spiritual development may involve resistance to spiritual change and transpersonal experiences (Assagioli, 1937, 1965, 1991). Assagioli proposed that this resistance may take the form of overly attributing importance to oneself, one's ideas or belief system, and consequently refusing to let go of the ideas, attitudes, or beliefs that seem core to one's personality, ultimately limiting spiritual development.

Assagioli's theory about resistance relates to another challenge named by half the instructors—working with students' preconceptions, including unrealistic views of the meditation learning process and purpose, which interfere with learning. Instructors shared that students may have conflicts with an instructor who does not confirm their beliefs or may cling to self-centered views, which can disrupt both their own and sometimes other students' practice. Two instructors shared that they take proactive approaches by explaining the learning process or confronting students' beliefs, which reportedly can solve the problem. Another two said they had no success in handling these situations, which reflects that instructors, too, have limitations.

Similarly, students' digression from practice is another common instructional challenge. Students may avoid attempting to meditate or deepen their practice because they love talking about things in their mind rather than practicing, feel they have no time to practice, or simply lack interest in practicing. These may also be forms of resistance. Avoiding dealing with painful feelings or with developmental wounds through talking about spiritual ideas or beliefs, otherwise known as spiritual bypassing (Welwood, 1984), may be another challenge during instruction.

Uncertainty. We found that uncertainty is another common challenge, which many manifest rather uniquely in meditation instruction compared with other types of instruction or clinical intervention. As a tool that can be used for self-exploration (Haimerl &

Valentine, 2001; Shapiro, Carlson, Astin, & Freedman, 2006), meditation provokes uncertainty in oneself and brings an important aspect of "not knowing" into both instructing and the learning process. The ability to acknowledge, allow, or even welcome uncertainty in others and oneself provides transpersonal guidance important for effective meditation instruction. Three instructors said they simply acknowledge the uncertainty and return to being receptive. Another reported actively clarifying it, whereas another shared relying on it: "when we rely on our inner guidance, then uncertainty is welcome because through uncertainty I can become open, I can become available to the guidance to come in and show the way."

While one's ability to tolerate uncertainty is implicitly part of spiritual growth, instructors vary in how they approach working with uncertainty with students. Meditation practitioners forge a self-discovered path of authentic development marked by both sudden insights and gradual deepening into the totality of their own being. Repeated discoveries of experiential content and process can hone skills in discovering that form the foundation needed for experiential confidence or "faith" in the efficacy of meditation, traditionally described as accruing with meditation experience. This "not knowing" way of learning tolerates uncertainty and staves off urges to settle on any particular conceptualization, thereby leaving room for more extensive processes to unfold.

Strong emotions. Another widely named challenge concerns intense emotions emerging during meditation, as well as associated psychological issues and life crises. On one hand, strong emotions are a natural part of experience that meditation training can bring into the light. On the other hand, intense experience may be evoked by an instructor's quick-paced facilitation, which can expose students to issues they are not well prepared for or reveal an uncovered psychiatric issue. Instructors explained that they may facilitate students' awareness needed to work through an intense emotion via meditation instruction, recognizing when the emotion is within a normal range. As discussed in Fatter, Zhuang, and Grossenbacher (in preparation), psychological crises are a risk in meditation practice. Three instructors mentioned incidents in which a student experienced a psychological crisis during instruction, for which they provided extra support and guidance, including referring the students to mental health professionals.

Instructors may experience strong emotions themselves, including being emotionally triggered or feeling incredible awe. When being emotionally triggered, instructors try to maintain empathy and compassion toward the student, and may talk with peers later to differentiate any of their own projection (countertransference) onto the student. One instructor noted failing to address getting triggered during instruction and later apologized to the student for his reactivity. Another described how a sense of separation from the student helped to maintain stableness during the triggering experience. In the case of awe, instructors shared that they simply let themselves experience the emotion and accept the experience. One shared that meditation instructors draw a lot of unhealed parental projections (transference) from their students and that dealing with projection is a critical skill for instructors and an opportunity for the equanimity that meditation practice helps develop (Siegel, 2007).

Instructional challenges happen universally in meditation instruction in both mindfulness-based interventions in clinical settings (McCown, Reibel, & Micozzi, 2010; Segal, Williams, & Teasdale, 2001), and in non-clinical meditation instruction, as discussed by all of our instructors. Instructors have used multiple resources to deal with difficult situations, including faith, compassion practice, cultivating non-attachment, peer support, and setting a strong interpersonal boundary with students. Instructors addressed a need for their own self-care and stated that mentorship, continued training, and supervision by their own instructor or community of peers can help in coping with instructional challenges and support their own spiritual journey as meditation teachers. With regard to peer support, one instructor explained that having a "spiritual friend" helps to balance being a teacher and a practitioner by also being a student "to own the part of me that struggles." Future instructor training may benefit from explicit training on self-care and community resources for support.

Transpersonal Qualities Revealed in Meditation Instruction

The practice of meditation reveals multiple dimensions of consciousness and enables access to "altered states of consciousness" for growth, healing, and unity with our essential spiritual nature (Cortright, 1997). Meditation encourages increasing awareness of the personal realm and also enables one to move beyond the personal realm to the transpersonal (Cortright, 1997). Much of what is learned in meditation does not consist of conceptual content but encompasses embodying transpersonal qualities through lived experience. Across meditative disciplines, after the initial benefits of verbal instruction are realized, ongoing practice brings further discovery through direct experience. For example, in certain Buddhist meditation practices, meditators discover a great deal of what actually happens in their mind that would otherwise remain unconscious through observation of their own experience. Gaining skill in observing one's own mental processes (metacognition) opens gateways to further learning.

In addition to providing a pathway for further discovery and learning, direct experience is the doorway into the transpersonal. From a developmental perspective, practicing meditation can induce new states, which can increase with frequency and thereby develop into new traits (Cahn & Polich, 2006). Because such state changes may fluctuate, rather than simply ratcheting from one state to another unidirectionally, newly developed states may occur intermittently. Such developmentally common lapses from, say, bliss or equanimity, can be interpreted negatively by practitioners as backsliding, and their response hinges on their attitude toward themselves and toward meditation. An important part of practice for successful learning is adopting the approach of relaxing with things as they are. This equanimity requires awareness, acceptance, gentleness, and being open to authentic experiencing.

These qualities are readily learned when modeled by the instructor, so it is imperative that instructors exhibit such abilities in order to transmit them to learners and to avoid the pedagogically devastating disconnect between verbal instruction and evident manifestation (which easily leads students to perceive teachers as faking or lying). An instructor needs to be authentic in order to inspire students to discover their own truth.

Non-dual Perspective
One of the transpersonal qualities that meditation practice reveals is a non-dual worldview. Personal worldview encompasses a person's framework of motivations, values, attitudes, knowledge, beliefs, goals, and plans, which can contribute to intention (Koltko-Rivera, 2004). Worldview includes understanding of mind and the purpose of meditating, which may be influenced by a meditator's personal learning history, including experience related to meditation. Meditation provides a practice and platform to develop the self as well as move beyond the self (Cortright, 1997). As such, meditation enables bridging both personal and transpersonal worldviews by inviting unfabricated experience of ordinary consciousness and moving beyond any construct of our own personal worldview to a lived experience of non-duality.

Many instructors hold a non-dual, transpersonal worldview, whereas students may start practicing meditation with a more dualistic personal worldview. Learning meditation can involve introduction to another world that has always been present, which becomes apparent through a transpersonal perspective and is the non-dual reality that students may never have imagined to be real. Truly transpersonal teaching moves as a skillful and elegant dance between the two worlds that we both live in and manifest from the infinite mind. From this perspective, instruction and meditation are not separate, as evidenced by instructors' descriptions of their lived experience in providing meditation instruction.

Awareness
Awareness is evident in each person's lived conscious experience, an experiential foundation that is potentially accessible for everyone. Depending on the type of meditation being practiced, attention may be focused on a meditation object appearing as *content of awareness*, including any breathing, verbal recitation (mantra), visual experience (imagery or perception of a candle flame, shrine, graphical depiction,

etc.), auditory experience (imagery or perception of music, chanting, bell, drum, etc.), emotion, bodily sensation, thought, entirety of current experience, awareness itself, and so on. Moment-to-moment awareness is non-verbal experience that involves an intentional quality of focus on the present experience (Gunaratana, 2002). The instructor's attuned moment-to-moment awareness and sense of connectedness shed light on the depth and breadth of instructor awareness during instruction. Similar to the co-created intimacy between psychotherapist and client (Tennes, 2007), an intersubjective level of awareness may include instructors' own internal experience during instruction, a student's experience, and the co-created energy field between instructor and student.

In addition, similar to a transpersonal model in psychotherapy, beyond an intersubjective level of consciousness lies a transpersonal level of consciousness (Cortright, 1997). As such, meditation instructors may be experiencing non-dual consciousness from which they provide meditation instruction. For example, instructors may experience no separation between their own internal experience, the student's experience, and the energy field within which they sit. Instructors can then naturally use this transpersonal non-dual lived experience to guide their meditation instruction.

Non-duality and awareness also can converge in meditation practice as transpersonal experience of spiritual oneness. For example, an instructor shared that during meditation practice one becomes increasingly aware of union with the divine that was already there prior to practicing meditation. Thus, as awareness moves beyond the personal to the transpersonal, non-duality can be experienced as unification with the divine.

Conclusion

Much has been learned from our interviewing diverse meditation teachers, including the nature of the path of learning meditation, the catalytic role that meditation plays in people's lives, and the importance of lineage.

Path of Discovery

Perhaps more so than in some other domains of instruction, we find great disparity between instructors' and students' understanding of pedagogy and curriculum in meditation. For example, instructors explicitly value the role of discovery that can naturally unfold for meditation students as a result of meditation practice, whereas beginning students themselves are not well positioned to understand this until repeated experience of discovery. Similarly, disparate levels of understanding between instructors and students also appear in other aspects of meditation pedagogy, such as appropriateness of the instructor disclosing the range of their own experience during meditation, and the relevance of detailed descriptions of the student's emotional life (deemed more relevant by students than instructors).

Instructors bring an understanding of meditative development informed by their own developmental path, including elements such as non-conceptual or non-dual experience that lie beyond a student's conception. Other aspects of curriculum that lie beyond students' mental reach and experiential familiarity may include: observing one's own mental processes, developing a capacity for non-judgmental witnessing of moment-to-moment experience, working skillfully with difficult emotions, and integrating meditative skills into daily life.

Catalyst for Further Development

Learning meditation and teaching meditation provide catalysts for further learning and spiritual development. Fatter, Zhuang, and Grossenbacher (in preparation) find mutually reinforcing relationships between instructors' personal meditation practice, instructor development, and experience teaching meditation. Instructors' lived experiences, pedagogical theory, and teaching techniques discussed in this chapter also suggest that there is a mutually reinforcing relationship between instructors' personal meditation practice, development of an instructional approach, experience instructing meditation, and spiritual development. In addition, instructors illustrated that the mutually reinforcing relationship between transpersonal development and the instructor's ability to teach students occurs only as far as the instructor's own lived experience within meditation.

Meditation practice fosters familiarization with subjective experience and psychological processes, which can guide introspective exploration that leads to further spiritual learning on life's path. For example, depending on the style of meditation, meditation practice may emphasize becoming familiar with one's own cognitive processes. By developing a more intimate relationship with the nature of their mind, a meditation student can gain awareness of their own learning processes and elements that detract from or support effective learning. Similarly, non-dual states and transpersonal qualities of authenticity and awareness can grow into traits, and thereby lead practitioners into embodying the transpersonal realm (Cortright, 1997).

The Importance of Lineage

Perennial philosophies, spiritual lineages, and wisdom traditions have historically served to transmit specific meditative practices to access non-dual lived experience and a transpersonal worldview. As meditation becomes more integrated into mainstream Western culture, lineage-based meditation instruction is no longer the only means to learn teachings and practices that foster such transpersonal experience as non-duality. While seven of eight instructors interviewed were teaching within lineage contexts, one reported no specific lineage affiliation. This particular instructor shared being fairly new to teaching meditation and observing a "veil about teaching and teachers," with some teachers encouraging secrecy and silence in discussing meditation instruction. Each lineage has its own historical and cultural story that impacts how meditation is taught and learned. Future research should investigate the relationship between instructional approaches, instructor background and characteristics, and lineage to better understand the role of lineage and the practice of meditation instruction.

Meditation instructors want to lift the veil over teaching meditation. They want peer interaction, highlighting the need for community support among teachers of diverse spiritual traditions, just as meditation students benefit from community supporting their meditation practice. Instructors' lived experience during instruction has opened our eyes to a transpersonal dimension of consciousness, including a better understanding of instructors' non-dual attention that guides instruction. This chapter has also uncovered pedagogical theory and technique among a diverse group of meditation instructors that increases our understanding of ways meditation is conceptualized and taught. Further, these teachers' perspectives have shed light on the transpersonal nature of student development across meditation traditions.

References

Assagioli, R. (1937). Spiritual development and its attendant maladies. *Hibbert Journal, 36*, 69–88.
Assagioli, R. (1965). *Psychosynthesis: A manual of principals and techniques* (1st ed.). New York, NY: Hobbs, Dorman & Company.
Assagioli, R. (1991). *Transpersonal development. The dimension beyond psychosynthesis* London, Eng: Harper Collins.
Cahn, B. R., & Polich, J. (2006). Meditation states and traits: EEG, ERP, and neuroimaging studies. *Psychological Bulletin, 132*, 180–211. doi:10.1037/0033-2909.132.2.180
Cortright, B. (1997). *Psychotherapy and spirit: Theory and practice in transpersonal psychotherapy*. Albany, NY: State University of New York.
Eades, W. M. (1992). A revisioning of resistance within a transpersonal context. *Journal of Psychology and Christianity, 11*(1), 33–43.
Gunaratana, B. (2002). *Mindfulness in plain English*. Somerville, MA: Wisdom Publications.
Haimerl, C. J., & Valentine, E. R. (2001). The effect of contemplative practice on intrapersonal, interpersonal, and transpersonal dimensions of the self-concept. *Journal of Transpersonal Psychology, 33*(1), 37–52.
Koltko-Rivera, M. E. (2004). The psychology of worldviews. *Review of General Psychology, 8*(1), 3–58. doi:10.1037/1089-2680.8.1.3
McCown, D., Reibel, D., & Micozzi, M. S. (2010). *Teaching mindfulness: A practical guide for clinicians and educators*. New York, NY: Springer.
Segal, Z. V., Williams, J. M. G., & Teasdale, J. D. (2001). *Mindfulness-based cognitive therapy for depression: A new approach to preventing relapse.* New York, NY: The Guilford Press.
Shapiro, S. L., Carlson, L. E., Astin, J. A., & Freedman, B. (2006). Mechanisms of mindfulness. *Journal of Clinical Psychology, 62*(3), 373–386.
Siegel, D. J. (2007). *The mindful brain: Reflection and attunement in the cultivation of well-being*. New York, NY: W.W. Norton & Company.

Tennes, M. (2007). Beyond intersubjectivity: The transpersonal dimension of the psychoanalytic encounter. *Contemporary Psychoanalysis, 43*(4), 505–525.

Valle, R. S. (1989). The emergence of transpersonal psychology. In R. S. Valle & S. Halling (Eds.), *Existential-phenomenological perspectives in psychology. Exploring the breadth of human experience* (pp. 257–268). New York, NY: Springer.

Walach, H. (2008). Narcissism: The shadow of transpersonal psychology. *Transpersonal Psychology Review, 12*(2), 47–59.

Welwood, J. (1977). Meditation and the unconscious: A new perspective. *Journal of Transpersonal Psychology, 9*(1), 1–26.

Welwood, J. (1984). Principles of inner work: Psychological and spiritual. *Journal of Transpersonal Psychology, 16*(1), 63–73.

Chapter 9
Transpersonal Psychology in Education and Management/Leadership: The Creation of a New Evolutionary Paradigm

Pat Luce

Robert Schmitt

This chapter flows from the research and lived experience of the authors, who were co-presidents of the Institute of Transpersonal Psychology (now known as Sofia University) from 2000 to 2006. Pat has a global range of experience as a director of organizational development, management, and training in industry. She also has years of experience as a faculty member of a university graduate school and as a spiritual director.

Besides his years of faculty and spiritual direction experience, Bob has been president of three colleges, dean at two graduate schools, Jesuit master of novices, and is now on the faculty of Saybrook University.

This chapter is divided into three major sections. The first section focuses on one approach to transpersonal education and its assumptions and values. The second section focuses on transpersonal management and its assumptions and values. The third section will describe specific transpersonal experiences with two short stories that illustrate themes from the previous sections. The environment we describe, in which transpersonal practices and teachings were applied, led to exciting possibilities, including a new paradigm of transpersonal management that embraced the integration of masculine and feminine principles, energies, and perspectives.

Transpersonal Education

As stated above, this essay is based on our work at the Institute of Transpersonal Psychology (now Sofia University), an accredited graduate school in Palo Alto, California. Our curriculum was built around six areas of focus: physical, intellectual, emotional, spiritual, social, and creative expression.

Transpersonal education is an application of transpersonal psychology. To better understand transpersonal psychology, we need to remember its relationship to the larger field of psychology. This discipline of psychology studies key elements of human living, including behavior, experiences, and cognition. Theoretically, the word *psychology* means the study of the soul, or the study of the essence or source of human living. In reality that is not what most psychologists have studied.

Speaking in general terms, psychology—conceived and born in an era of natural sciences—imitated the empirical sciences. It emphasized that knowledge of human beings should be based on what can be measured and replicated in controlled situations. At the beginning of modern psychology's development, as Meissner (1984) stated, there was mutual antagonism between psychology and anything to do with religion, spirituality, or experiences of transcendence. Despite William James's study of mystical experiences and his conclusion that people with unitive or spiritual experiences demonstrate very healthy traits, many people took Freud's position that religion is an illusion based on neurotic needs (Randour, 1993, p. 5) and religious illusions were a dragon to be slain with the hard sword of science (Meissner, 1990, p. 98).

It should be noted that important psychologists like Jung, Adler, and Assagioli were open to and explored the realm of the transcendent, including Exceptional Human Experiences (EHEs) such as lucid dreaming, visions, out-of-body experiences, hunches, deep intuition, psychic functioning, and synchronicities, as well as other aspects of religion and spirituality. Even Freud stated at one point that people seeking psychotherapy are on a spiritual search. However, on the whole, the field of psychology stayed in the realm of the secular and avoided or pathologized the realm of the transcendent or spiritual. A group of psychologists founded transpersonal psychology to study aspects of human life and experience being ignored by the psychology of their day.

Scholars have given a variety of definitions to transpersonal psychology. We adopt here the three themes proposed by Hartelius, Caplan, and Rardin (2007). First, transpersonal psychology is a beyond-ego psychology—a psychology that includes and honors exceptional human experiences and multiple ways of knowing. Second, transpersonal psychology is also an integrative/holistic psychology—a psychology that seeks to include all dimensions of being human. It assumes that the totality of a person is greater than the sum of their parts. Finally, transpersonal psychology is a psychology of transformation—a psychology that studies and supports the transformation of individuals, groups, and society.

It is true that modern psychology has become more conscious of its treatment of religion and spirituality. Within this new framework, psychology is harvesting great insights into human functioning as well as healing, but it still often leaves out key experiences and issues of development that are essential for a thorough psychological study and understanding of human beings. Transpersonal psychology responds to that deficiency. It offers psychologists and clients an alternative paradigm to traditional psychology.

Here are four major differences in these two approaches that help inform transpersonal education:

1. Traditional psychology focuses on *pathology* while transpersonal psychology focuses on *health* (including extraordinary well-being).
2. Traditional psychology develops healing practices based on a medical model that sees the healing power coming primarily from the knowledge and skill of *the therapist*. Transpersonal psychology develops healing and life-nurturing practices based on a model that sees the healing power coming primarily from within *the client*.
3. Traditional psychology assumes only *one way of knowing*, an intellectual and analytic way based on the physical sciences. Transpersonal psychology assumes that there are *many ways of knowing* that include altered states of being, body-based knowledge, and creative expressions of art.
4. Traditional psychology ignores or *pathologizes the spiritual dimension* of human experience while transpersonal psychology *considers the spiritual dimension critical* to human development and well-being.

In the 1990s, the faculty at the Institute of Transpersonal Psychology (ITP), under the leadership of William Braud, sought to define and evaluate transpersonal education at ITP. The following paragraphs draw from presentations that William Braud and Bob Schmitt gave at the 2000 Annual Meeting of the Western Association of Schools and Colleges (WASC) and at the 2001 Conference of the American Psychology Association (APA). Transpersonal education at ITP has two dimensions: (1) the subject taught (transpersonal psychology) and (2) the way it is taught. In this section we focus on the way it is taught by describing and reflecting on the educational model developed at ITP, a model that can be applied to teaching other subjects as well as transpersonal psychology.

This form of education rests on a set of assumptions (Braud & Schmitt, 2000, 2001). A major assumption is that *who* a person becomes is more important than the academic knowledge one acquires. The theory and academic knowledge that a psychologist learns is like a knife.

It can do great harm or great good. The person behind the knife is extremely important. Does the person have the self-knowledge and compassion that is critical to see with clear eyes and a loving heart?

This assumption builds on the classical distinction made by John Henry Newman (1854) between real knowledge and notional knowledge. Notional knowledge is knowledge that one knows only from the neck up. An example would be the kind of knowledge one memorizes to pass an exam and then forgets 30 minutes after the exam. Real knowledge is knowledge that changes the person. That is the kind of knowledge ITP sought.

Against this background, the faculty developed a curriculum that focused not only on traditional subject areas (e.g., group process) but also on multiple ways of knowing (Braud & Schmitt, 2000, 2001). They eventually focused on six areas of study: physical, intellectual, emotional, spiritual, social, and creative expression. Each of these areas offers distinct ways of knowing. Each gives information that is important for understanding ourselves and others. For example, how many times has your body told you what was really going on in an interaction by gifting you with a headache or tight shoulders?

Creative expression is another example as it opens us up to other ways of knowing that are non-verbal. Most of us have had the experience of doing a painting, a collage or working with clay. New insights emerged that we did not know by simply sitting still and analyzing.

In the 1990s, the faculty established four key goals of their transformative education (Braud & Schmitt, 2000, 2001). Those goals were mindfulness, discernment, compassion, and appreciation of differences. They developed ways to measure these four values as a means of evaluating the curriculum. These assessment tools were redesigned on an ongoing basis. With Bob as dean, the faculty developed a longitudinal study to assess the transpersonal nature of the program by examining the experiences and changes of students (Braud, 2006). The project's design included complementary quantitative and qualitative research methods and honored both nomothetic and idiographic aims. Quantitative methods focused on changes in how students responded to certain questions at the beginning and end of a two-year period of study while qualitative methods sought to assess an individual student's experience of the impact of this education on their life. Quantitative results indicated significant changes in measures of the following qualities: decrements in egocentric grasping and striving, increments in acceptance, greater self-transcendence, increased spiritual perspective, "thinner" and more permeable boundaries, increased present-centeredness, and increased inner-directedness. Substantial positive changes also were reported in areas of values, meaning, spirituality, attitudes, beliefs, intellect, body, emotions, spirit, creative expression, community, openness, and connectedness. In the project's qualitative components, the students reported increased awareness and changes in personal growth, mindfulness, body-related areas, academic/scholarly areas, appreciation of interconnectedness, appreciation of differences, compassion, discernment, transformation, openness, surrender/acceptance, and professional areas; some reported experiencing regression, cognitive dissonance, and disillusionment (Braud & Schmitt, 2000). (For more detail on this research, see William Braud's [2006] description, pp. 147–148).

Here are some of the findings after years of experience with the program:

1. This type of education, with its emphasis on various spiritual paths, is much more sensitive to different cultures than traditional Western psychology.
2. The experiential component of the curriculum—for example, students being required to take Aikido or another form of body movement—is critical for helping students become sensitive to body knowledge both in themselves and others.
3. An experientially oriented curriculum better prepares students to understand clients than a curriculum dedicated to learning theories and fitting clients into those boxes.
4. The growth of new information is so rapid that educators now recognize that most information that students learn has lost at least half of its value in 18 months. In such a world, whole-person learning makes more sense than ever. People need to learn how

to adjust and pay more attention to present realities, not interpret the world using past categories.

We have presented an individual school's effort to create and evaluate a form of transpersonal education. We celebrate and honor that there are other schools offering related forms of education under different titles (e.g., spiritual education, integral education, transformative education, and humanistic education). Our hope is that we can keep learning from one another. Before going on to the next section, we offer a few reflections. First, identifying key characteristics in transformative learning (e.g., mindfulness, compassion, appreciation of differences, and discernment) is extremely helpful in focusing and evaluating one's efforts. Second, focusing courses on different ways of knowing (e.g., emotional, physical) enabled students to receive a more holistic education. Third, evaluating the success of transpersonal education is not easy. Bob had faced the same challenge as a Jesuit novice director. He had to evaluate the effectiveness of a two-year spiritual formation program he had inherited from the previous director. It is much easier to evaluate a student's notional knowledge rather than real knowledge—that is, what a person knows rather than who he or she is becoming. We encourage further discussion among related forms of education on this topic. Let us learn from one another and manifest a truly holistic approach.

Transpersonal Management and Leadership

As co-presidents of a school founded on a transpersonal pedagogy, we experienced first-hand that the truly effective leader is one who leads from the core. The basic theme in transpersonal education and management is the same—that the values and attributes, which we are calling transpersonal, live at the core of a person and empower a person to be truly effective. At the heart of this approach is a conscious realization of our interconnectedness and of the transpersonal reality of a Higher Force some call Divine and some call one's Higher Self. We seek to live in harmony with this Higher Power to be what Schmittt (1995) calls *life servants* rather than *life fixers*.

In that context, we discuss here qualities in transpersonal education that are at the core of transpersonal management. We assume that transpersonal management and leadership create a transpersonal atmosphere throughout the organization and are seen in the work and communication style of all groups—not just of students, but also Board of Trustees, faculty, and administration. Using the term of William James (1902/1985), all groups appreciate and honor *Mores* in terms of *knowing*, *doing* and *being*. These Mores can be recognized as alternate modes of knowing—as states of consciousness, a sense of identity, and phases of development beyond those usually considered by organizational management. The transpersonal also manifests as ongoing processes of expansion, inclusion, and integration in the course of one's growth and development.

The transpersonal in management and leadership shows up in how staff and managers, board and faculty, alumnae and students interact with one another and the surrounding community. As a transpersonal manager works for a true integration of body, mind, and spirit, he or she brings that deep wisdom and true knowledge to the tasks of visioning, problem solving, decision making, listening, initiating, communicating, and planning. This "rubbing off" in a sense seems to occur with the professional staff even when they have not been directly participating in the school curriculum. It appears in the environment and can be absorbed or integrated into the work practices and behavior of all those participating in that environment when an open and non-defensive nature is part of the commonly held attitude. The main values or principles for which the school is striving seem to permeate the entire organization to one degree or another. The four key values or qualities that foster transpersonal management and education are: mindfulness, compassion, appreciation of differences, and discernment.

Mindfulness has the characteristics of:

- *Being present in time*: This is critical for working with "what is" and requires truly observing the whole scene. This observation must include both "what is going on" outside as well as inside.
- *Capacity to identify and disidentify appropriately*: An example of disidentification is recognizing one's feeling of fear but saying that one is not that fear. It is essential to identify your reactions to a situation but then to step back from that feeling and not get sucked into identifying with it.
- *Self-awareness*: This is being aware of your feelings—for example, what your body is saying when it's tense and how it stifles rather than supports a flow of energy and creativity.
- *Self-observation*: This entails being able to step out of one's self and observe what is going on and what part you are playing in the scenario.

Compassion has the characteristics of:

- *Empathy*: On a personal level, this includes taking the subjective into regard, listening to the circumstances, feelings, and situations of others as people rather than as cogs in a machine.
- *Service*: Administration is the Latin word for "minister to" or serve. Managing effectively is a selfless job rather than an egocentric or self-gratifying job. It is to give of one's self.
- *Personal presence*: This requires that you are present to those with whom you work as a person rather than as a dictator or machine. Your humanness is accessible.
- *Civility*: This entails treating everyone with respect and honor, and recognizing the divine in each person.

Appreciation of differences has the characteristics of:

- *Openness to change*: This is being able to hear and acknowledge another person's or persons' point of view, being willing to let go of what has been, and embracing what can be.
- *Flexibility*: This means being able to change directions when it is called for, not being frozen or maintaining a narrow view because of fear or selfish motives.
- *Inclusivity*: This includes recognizing each person's contribution and gift and incorporating it into the whole picture, not discriminating because of biases or blind spots.

Discernment has the characteristics of:

- *Mature judgment*: This is making decisions out of a deep thoughtful process that involves gathering information from outside sources and deeply listening to one's own inner guidance.
- *Integrity*: This includes making judgments that are not governed by fear or outside pressure, but emanate from the true core of one's own being and values.

These qualities and values were introduced not only into all courses in the ITP curriculum but were discussed as goals for the entire school within the strategic plan. They were explained in terms of the above definitions at board, faculty, management, and staff meetings as goals we were trying to achieve not only within our educational curriculum but as goals held by the school in its overall strategic plan.

As co-presidents, we strove to model these goals in all interactions, writings, and speeches. The results became evident in several categories. The personal interactions of community members were noticeably smoother and reverberated through every phone call, discussion, and decision. The faculty and staff turnover was measured at less than 5% after five years. This allowed cross-training in every department, making individual functions stronger and less vulnerable to change. As became apparent in student surveys, there was also a higher satisfaction rate among students regarding their personal interactions with staff and faculty. Our experiences were that when these qualities and values are present in one's leadership style, they allow one to be open to a flow of information that results in William James' description of the "More."

We would add another dimension to this transpersonal model. It is that of balancing the best of each of the so-called "masculine" and "feminine" principles. This combination brings together *male* values such as individuality, autonomy, rights, justice, and agency with *feminine* values such as relationship, intuition, deep listening, and empathy. Embracing the best of all the basic tendencies and transforming them in order to create balance and harmony points to Wilber's (2000a, 2000b) idea of transcending and including as humanity continues to evolve consciousness. We are at a point in evolution where the importance of balancing the best aspects of both value spheres moves us out of a brutal state of affairs that is no longer effective but counterproductive and abusive to human life, nature, and the planet to a new state of affairs that helps bring healing and wholeness to all life.

Having male and female co-presidents was a symbol of this effort for balance. It is important to note that each of us brought our mixture of feminine and masculine qualities. It was not experienced that Bob held all the masculine qualities and Pat the feminine, but together there was a greater balance and a focus on partnership. We see this focus on partnership (collaboration) as a key component of a transpersonal approach. It is worth noting a growing recognition in the mainstream world of the value of working together (see Eisner, 2010, for examples and reflections).

In summary, we would emphasize that the values and approach in transpersonal education give great insight into what is meant by transpersonal management. In a strongly hierarchical world, many still assume that such an approach is unrealistic. We suggest that our years at ITP—during which we believe ITP flourished financially, academically, and "transpersonally"—offer a case study of the value of a transpersonal approach to management.

Two Stories

This section contains two short stories that demonstrate the following kinds of transpersonal experiences: life guidance through meditation and inner knowing, visions, and synchronicities. The first incident occurred in the admissions office at ITP and is narrated by Pat.

One particular interview that stands out in my mind took place on a beautiful day in May. A young man from New Hampshire applied to the PhD program. He had taken a fascinating journey before arriving at the school. He had been born with part of one arm missing. Three years before he applied to the school, he and a friend decided to sail across the Atlantic Ocean on a small ship. His friend was the real captain, although they charted their course and carried out their plans together.

"About two weeks into the trip, my friend began to complain about chest pains," the young man explained. "He was such a young person that a heart attack was the last thing I ever thought could happen to him. Within a short period of time, he was in full cardiac arrest and there was nothing I could do about it. He died in my arms. Although I was petrified of sailing alone, I turned our ship around and headed back to port, trying to manage the sails, ropes, and equipment with one arm. I have never experienced the presence of God so powerfully in my entire life. I knew that someone was guiding me and strengthening me as I prayed for help."

We often conducted group interviews of two or three applicants at a time. The second person who had signed up to come in for an interview at this exact time and day was also a young man. He was born in the south of the United States, the oldest son of an African-American sharecropper. After the early death of his father, he took over the support of his mother and six brothers and sisters by farming the small plot of land on which they lived.

"I was so young, and wondered why this had happened to me. One day, while I was operating a large and cumbersome piece of equipment, I lost my grip and the machine slipped. In an instant, I had lost a major part of my hand and arm. As the blood rushed out of my body I wondered if I would ever survive, when in a flash I heard a voice telling me that everything was all right and I would be fine. I felt surrounded and protected by a divine presence and knew I would be okay." Tears slid down his cheeks as he told his story. He still felt this immense love as deeply as he had when the accident happened. The interviewing team sitting in the room had goose bumps.

Since the accident, he had worked his way through college and traveled all over the world, studying many foreign languages. Coming to the school was the next stop on his spiritual journey.

Both men never commented on the fact that they had the same physical challenges until one of the interviewers made a remark about it. Yet, in some mysterious way, they had chosen the same day, time, and interviewing space to come together to support each other in this synchronistic way. They became good friends.

The second story is about the amazing spiritual journey we took to become co-presidents of ITP. Pat tells the first part of the story.

It started with a vision. I had just delivered my second son and was returned to my room. Suddenly the whole room seemed to be filled with light. As I raised my head to see what was going on, Christ walked right through the wall in front of me. He was made out of light—pure light—with a real body. He was holding a beautiful basin in his hands. He stopped in the frame of the door where I realized that a second being of light, a woman with a veil that nearly covered her eyes, held a pitcher from which she poured water into the basin that Christ was holding in his hands. As the water fell through the air, it seemed to be made of rainbows, as if being filtered through a crystal. Waves of love and peace flowed through me as I watched this amazing picture in front of me.

For over 30 years I searched and wondered about the meaning of the pitcher and basin and the two people who were holding them until one day on a 30-day retreat at Mercy Center in Burlingame, California— on the anniversary of the vision—I shared the story with my spiritual director. "Well," she said, "the thing that seems so obvious to me is that it has a masculine and feminine theme. The Christ figure is holding the open and receptive vessel and the feminine figure is holding the more action-oriented vessel." Suddenly my eyes were opened, and I began to experience this play between masculine and feminine—an integration of yin and yang, Shakti and Shiva, Christ and Sophia—and it seemed to carry into every aspect of my life. Later on I began to realize that the Divine was revealing an important message for all humanity. The integration of masculine/feminine aspects of creation is essential for human consciousness to evolve. But I realized that for this to occur humanity's eyes have to be opened to recognize the feminine as divine. This reality was about to be impressed on our hearts in the most surprising and profound way we could imagine.

Bob now continues the story. After much reading and research Pat and I had begun to collaborate together to bring forth a shared vision of masculine and feminine approaches united in our work. I had been dean at ITP for 13 years. Pat had worked in Silicon Valley in training and management, and we had also worked together as teachers and spiritual guides.

In the springtime of 2000, ITP was going through a difficult transition, and we both felt like we needed a break. We noticed that the Sophia Foundation of North America, founded by Robert Powell and Karen Rivers, was leading a pilgrimage to Chartres Cathedral in France, so we decided to join them for a week. Fifty pilgrims arrived at Chartres on the 21st of May, 2000. We had come from all parts of Europe, Canada, and America to worship at one of the most sacred places of the Divine Feminine. The beautiful spires of Saints Michael and Gabriel—symbolizing the sun and the moon—pierced the sky. The theme of Virgo Paritura, the Virgin who is giving birth, was about to birth us into one of the most profound and astonishing happenings of our lives. Toward the end of the pilgrimage, Pat had the sense that something new—"a new birth" —was waiting for us at home.

When we returned, we noticed that two doves had made a nest outside our family room window and had given birth to a little dove. We noticed that the male and female doves took turns sitting on the eggs while the other searched for food. We thought this might be the meaning of the "new birth." But as we began to reconnect, we heard that the president of ITP had resigned and the school was in troubled waters.

One day during meditation Pat experienced being urged to apply to be co-presidents of ITP. She told this to me, and I was quite frankly shocked. I had been told previously that the school saw me as a dean, not the president. "But you didn't apply for *co*-president," Pat laughed. "I'm telling you that it has already happened in the etheric dimension and will be manifested in the physical dimension." With laughter on my part, we applied, went through a series of interviews, and, with tremendous guidance along the way, were appointed as co-presidents on July 1.

The first international transpersonal conference we attended was in Assisi and was infiltrated with doves—doves on the brochure, doves on the table decorations. Even the cab driver had two doves hanging from his mirror. This was the Divine Feminine confirming to us that she was leading us and had offered an example of synchronicity. We were filled with joy and knew that we would model, in a position that had been traditionally held in a patriarchal way, a new way to be—a sacred dance between the masculine and feminine, being able between us to value and demonstrate the interconnection between gifts of action, logic, rationality, and organization and gifts of welcoming, listening, receptivity, and intuition.

We have shared in some detail these two stories because they express a way of being and seeing that loses something when discussed in abstract terms. Both stories encourage us to look for and trust in a Life Force bigger than we, and our plans, are. It is important, then, to be present not just to what is going on in the other person(s) and ourselves but in the whole situation and context. A transpersonal approach calls for a spirit of willingness to be surprised and to be called beyond what we expect. It calls us to a spirit of gratitude and trust.

Conclusion

In this chapter we have shared a lived experience of transpersonal education and management/leadership rather than experience focused on theory. A key theme has been that the transpersonal qualities at the center of our pedagogy are the same qualities at the heart of our transpersonal leadership as co-presidents.

We believe that what we call transpersonal education and leadership is not just for transpersonal schools but will be needed increasingly in the 21st century. More people are recognizing this, although they may not use the word "transpersonal." For example, a growing number of organizations and business schools are recognizing the need for a new style of leadership. McDonald (2015) in his *New York Times* article gives examples of how many times prominent business schools use the word leadership on a single page (e.g., MIT's Sloan: 47 times). He also suggests a list of leadership competencies that fit extremely well with what we describe above. These competencies focus on: (1) self-awareness that includes realistic self-confidence and emotional insight; (2) self-management that includes resilience, emotional balance and self-motivation; (3) empathy that includes cognitive and emotional empathy and good listening; and (4) relational skills that include compelling communication and team playing.

Donald Rothberg (1999) says of transpersonal education: "ultimately the intention of transpersonal education is no less than spiritual transformation, the cultivation of wisdom and love, the opening of heart and mind, the deep communion with life" (p. 56). We say the same transformation is needed in the world of management and leadership. Our encouragement is that at this stage of human development and evolution we dialogue with like-minded people within and outside the field of transpersonal psychology. Our world needs to develop educational and leadership approaches that are nourished by the qualities and approaches we have described in this chapter.

References

Braud, W. (2006). Educating the "more" in holistic transpersonal higher education: A 30+ year perspective on the approach of the Institute of Transpersonal Psychology. *Journal of Transpersonal Psychology, 38*(2), 133–158.

Braud, W., & Schmitt, R. (2000, April). *Educating the whole person: Assessing student learning and transformative changes in an academic-experiential graduate psychology program.* Paper presented at the 76th Annual Meeting of the Association of Colleges and Universities, Western Association of Schools and Colleges, San Diego, CA.

Braud, W., & Schmitt, R. (2001, August). *A Transformational Research Project.* Paper presented at the 109th Annual Convention of the American Psychological Association, San Francisco, CA.

Brooks, D. (2015, April 12). A moral bucket list. *New York Times Sunday Review*, pp. 1, 6.

Brown, B. (2014). The future of leadership for conscious capitalism. Retrieved from https://integrallife.com/v/search??keys=barrett+brown

Cacioppe, R. (2000a). Creating spirit at work: Re-visioning organization development and leadership (Part I). *The Leadership and Organization Development Journal, 21,* 48–54.

Cacioppe, R. (2000b). Creating spirit at work: Re-visioning organization development and leadership (Part II). *The Leadership and Organization Development Journal, 21,* 110–119.

Davis, A. (1997). Liquid leadership: The wisdom of Mary Parker Follett (1868–1933). *A Leadership Journal: Women in Leadership—Sharing the Vision, 2*(1), 11–17.

Eisner, M. (2010). *Working together: Why great partnerships succeed.* New York, NY: Harper Collins.

Ferrer, J. N. (2010). *Revisioning transpersonal theory: A participatory vision of human spirituality* [Kindle DX Version]. Albany, NY: State University of New York Press.

Goleman, D. (2005). *Emotional intelligence: Why it can matter more than IQ.* New York, NY: Random House.

Hartelius, G., Caplan, M., & Rardin, M. A. (2007). Transpersonal psychology: Defining the past, divining the future. *The Humanistic Psychologist, 35*(2), 135-160.

Hendricks, G., & Ludemon, K. (1996). The last piece. *Across the Board, 33*(4), 12–13.

James, W. (1985). *The varieties of religious experience.* New York, NY: Penguin. (Original work published 1902)

Kouzes, J., & Posner, B. (1993). Credibility: How people gain and lose it. Why people demand it. San Francisco, CA: Jossey Bass.

Lewis, T., Amini, H., & Glennan, R. (2001). A general theory of love. New York, NY: Random House.

McDonald, D. (2015, April 12). Can you learn to read. *New York Times, Educational Life,* p.17.

Newman, J. (1854). The idea of a university [Kindle DX Version]. A public domain book.

Rothberg, D. (1999). Transpersonal issues at the millennium. *Journal of Transpersonal Psychology, 31* (1), 41–67.

Rowe, N., & Braud, W. (2013). Transpersonal education. In H. Friedman & G. Hartelius (Eds.), *The Wiley-Blackwell handbook of transpersonal psychology* (pp. 666–685). West Sussex, UK: John Wiley & Sons.

Schmitt, R. (1995). The spiritual director as life servant. *Presence: An International Journal of Spiritual Direction, 1*(2), 13–30.

Tett, G. (2015). *The silo effect: The peril of expertise and the promise of breaking down barriers.* New York, NY: Simon and Schuster.

Wilber, K. (2000a). *A brief history of everything.* Boston, MA: Shambhala Publications.

Wilber, K. (2000b). *Integral psychology: Consciousness, spirit, psychology, therapy.* Boston, MA: Shambhala Publications.

Chapter 10
The Transpersonal Potential of Psychedelics

Charles Walter Angelo

The use of psychedelics for medical healing and personal growth is experiencing renewed interest amid a wave of new research over the last decade as government restrictions and drug schedule classifications have changed and lessened (Cooper, 2016). Among some familiar with this new movement, enthusiasm is high regarding the potential for healing and growth through the appropriate and healthful use of these medications. Likewise, many others are avowedly against this form of investigation and believe the risks outweigh potential benefits. Personal values, beliefs, and clinical orientation may influence each person's stance and openness, and anecdotal evidence can sway individual views. Some may know or have heard of a soldier suffering with PTSD making marked improvement through the use of ayahuasca or MDMA, while others have seen close family members or friends dramatically lose functioning after recreationally using psychedelics.

This chapter aims to review current research and perspectives into the risks and benefits of psychedelics. Included are a personal account and recommendations for reconsideration of the legal status and the continued investigation of psychedelics and the experiences they engender. The potential psychological healing benefits of psychedelics are largely untapped, and it is exciting to be part of this renewed scientific inquiry and cultural curiosity regarding their transformational effects.

Psychedelics are among the most direct and powerful tools available for exploring transpersonal realms of consciousness. The psychedelic experience is a reliable means of transcending ego and experiencing non-duality (Grof, 1974). Through relationships with psychedelics, humans experience physical, emotional, psychological, and spiritual benefits. Interactions with psychedelics have had a profound impact on the evolution of human consciousness (Doyle, 2011; McKenna, 1992; Winkelman, 2013). This chapter provides evidence that this evolutionary impact continues and has the potential to facilitate personal as well as global transformation.

Psychedelics are plants, fungi, or chemicals that induce altered states of consciousness when ingested, smoked, or otherwise introduced into the bloodstream. They affect all categories of mental function: sense of self, body awareness, perceptions, emotions, and cognition (R. Strassman, personal communication, March 23, 2016). The psychedelic substances explored in this paper are naturally occurring, with the arguable exception of lysergic acid diethylamide (LSD), which is synthesized from a naturally occurring fungus. Psychedelics have been used for thousands of years by cultures around the world, often as integral companions in their spiritual traditions (Pahnke, 1966; Tindall, 2013; Trichter, Klimo, & Krippner, 2009; Walsh & Vaughan, 1993).

Psychedelics are intensifiers or expanders of normal everyday consciousness (Segall, 2013). As an experimental tool, psychedelics have provided the fields of consciousness and transpersonal studies with the equivalent of what the telescope provided to astronomy (Metzner, 1999; Segall, 2013; Watts, 1965). Segall (2014) also argues that psychedelics influenced the emergence and development of transpersonalism in the 1960s.

The psychedelics explored in this chapter are ayahuasca, psilocybin mushrooms, peyote, and LSD. Ayahuasca is a tea brewed from a mixture of plants used by indigenous cultures in the Amazon rainforest. It contains dimethyltryptamine (DMT), a powerful psychedelic compound that is also produced in the human brain (Doyle, 2011). Psilocybin mushrooms are psychedelic fungi commonly referred to as "magic mushrooms." Peyote is a cactus native to Mexico that

10. The Transpersonal Potential of Psychedelics

contains the psychedelic alkaloid mescaline (Ratsch, 2005). LSD is a derivative of lysergic acid, which occurs naturally in the ergot fungus. It was first synthesized in a laboratory by Swiss chemist Albert Hoffman and played a major role in the American counterculture movements of the 1960s (Andrei, 2015).

Many terms have been used to describe the substances referred to in this chapter as psychedelic, such as psychotropic, psychoactive, entheogenic, ecodelic, and hallucinogenic. The term psychedelic stems from Greek, meaning "mind manifesting," and the Greek mystery traditions that existed during the pioneering of modern philosophical thought almost certainly used psychedelics in their ritual rites (Segall, 2013). Throughout this chapter, the term psychedelic will be used to refer to these substances, as both a noun and an adjective (i.e., ingesting a psychedelic versus having a psychedelic experience). It can be assumed that the any of the other terms listed have the same meaning.

Personal Experience

While my experiences using psychedelics have been positive and led to my interest in this area of science, I understand that this is not universal and others have had negative effects. I had my first psychedelic experience when I was 22 years old and consumed psilocybin mushrooms with some friends. The experience was intended to be recreational but quickly transformed into an experience of great transpersonal, mystical significance for me. I was reawakened to a sense of childlike awe and deep respect for the interconnected natural world of which I am a part. The effects of the mushrooms faded as the hours passed, and the intensity and immediacy of these feelings faded as well. The lessons and insights I gained that evening and the feelings they evoked, however, remain real, true, impactful, and accessible to me years later.

Before this experience with mushrooms, I did not consider myself particularly spiritual and tended to accept the materialist, reductionist explanations of reality that dominate my culture's anthropocentric view of the world. This first psychedelic experience dramatically shifted my views, showing me that the world can be experienced in ways more broad and deep than I had imagined. It assisted me in rediscovering within myself a deep desire to live in harmony with the natural world. It sparked in me a curiosity about the existence of the universal consciousness that simultaneously underlies and infuses all of reality, and about my place in this world. Ingesting psychedelic mushrooms provided me with one of the most intensely happy and positive experiences of my life. It fits the description of what Maslow (1962) defined as a "peak experience," and its power has had lasting benefits in my life.

My subsequent experiences with psychedelics have continued to raise profound questions for me about reality and how I perceive it, as well as to evoke intense and transformative peak experiences. I feel that my personal healing process has been deepened and accelerated by psychedelics. I am a more open-hearted, physically healthy, and emotionally mature person today as a direct result of their use.

As noted earlier and discussed later in this chapter, there are risks involved in psychedelic use. However, when compared to the most popular and culturally accepted means of altering consciousness in U.S. modern culture (alcohol), psychedelics are a less dangerous and more beneficial option (Johansen & Krebs, 2015).

Psychedelics and Human Cognitive Development

"Our very psychology as human beings was shaped by the experiences induced by the psychedelics and their intrinsically religious effects, as well as a range of other cognitive, social and personal dispositions they produced" (Winkelman, 2013, p. 98). It is as if the human brain and psyche were wired to interact with psychedelics and, according to Winkelman, modern humans would not be capable of what they are without having interacted with psychedelics throughout the centuries. Winkelman posits that cognitive capacities such as abstract thought, symbolism, and spiritual capacity were made possible because of psychedelics' effects on neural transmission in the human brain. The serotonergic system of the human brain is more sensitive to psychedelics than the brains of other hominids, opening the door for deeper connection and unity with nature.

Present day psychedelic use continues to expand the horizons of human experience, broadening human capacity for spiritual experience and relationship with the natural environment (Segall, 2014). Used within the appropriate context, psychedelics have the potential to contribute to increased ecological awareness on individual and collective levels (Dickins, 2013). This chapter proposes that the complex cognitive developments resulting from psychedelic use have furthered the evolution of the human species, especially in terms of spiritual development, and will continue to do so.

Spirituality and Transpersonal Experiences

Although spirituality, mysticism, and religion are challenging terms both to define and measure, it is clear that people consistently have what they describe as religious, mystical, and spiritual experiences on psychedelics. These experiences can bring people into contact with what they perceive to be divine consciousness, spark the formation of new worldviews, and "show dramatic similarities to the deep spiritual realizations described by such traditions as Taoism, Sufism, Vedanta, Yoga, and Christian mysticism" (Walsh & Vaughan, 1993, p. 90).

Due to their direct effect on the way we perceive and experience life, psychedelics are valuable to our understanding of consciousness and its relationship to the human brain. Mystics of many traditions have said that consciousness underlies physical reality, not the other way around. This view is supported by the phenomenology of the psychedelic experience.

Grof (1974) reports on the wide variety of spiritual experiences had by the subjects of his LSD studies and emphasizes that their benefits were multidimensional. These

> profound transcendental experiences … in addition to having a very beneficial effect on the subject's physical and emotional wellbeing, are usually central in creating in him a keen interest in

religious, mystical, and philosophical issues, and a strong need to incorporate the spiritual dimension into his way of life. (p. 105)

The limited research results up to the present time show that it is quite possible generally, and quite likely under controlled circumstances, for spiritual experiences on psychedelics to lead to beneficial and long-lasting positive changes in worldview, behavior, and thought. These spiritually rooted changes can better equip humans to face a whole range of challenges.

Doyle (2011) suggests that the predominant insight arising from the psychedelic experience is "the sudden and absolute conviction that the psychonaut is involved in a densely interconnected ecosystem for which contemporary tactics of human identity are insufficient" (p. 20). The ego transcendence available within the psychedelic experience, therefore, can lead to connection and identification with the wider circles of nature and the cosmos. The subjects of Harris and Gurel's (2012) ayahuasca study generally reported that "everything is connected and alive" (p. 213) as one of their major lessons from the experience. Trichter et al. (2009) reported that "ayahuasca ceremony participants tend to, after their experience, be more empathic and feel more connected to others, nature and their sense of god or the divine" (p. 133).

Through the psychedelic experience, people acknowledge the world's aliveness that can assist them in moving beyond a strictly materialistic view of reality. In addition, when one feels intimately connected to something that is alive—for instance, a particular ecosystem—one is more likely to relate to it, form emotional bonds with it, and take action to protect it.

The psilocybin subjects of Pahnke's (1966) Good Friday experiment similarly experienced significant feelings of interconnectedness, or what was categorized in the experiment as "unity." This category encompassed feelings of ego transcendence, the loss of separation between self and the external world, and feelings of oneness among the participants. The control subjects who did not receive psilocybin in the study had no significant change in their feelings of unity. In his long-term follow-up to Pahnke's experiment, Doblin (1991) reported that among the subjects who received psilocybin, feelings of unity related to the experience had persisted over the decades, and that it continued to help them "recognize the arbitrariness of ego boundaries" (p. 12). Griffiths, Richards, Johnson, McCann and Jesse (2006) also found that psilocybin had a positive effect on participants' sense of unity.

Interspecies Communication

> The modern literature on psychedelic studies is full of reports of an increased awareness of nature, and some writers consider the phenomenology of the psychedelic experience to be eminently suited to fostering an ethos of communication with and empathy for non-human nature. (Callicott, 2013, p. 41)

One method through which psychedelics make people aware of their interconnectedness with the non-human world is through direct communication. Valuable messages can be received during the psychedelic experience that provide beneficial tools to individuals and to humanity. Maria Sabina, a well-known Mexican medicine woman, explains how the spirit of the psychedelic mushroom communicates with her:

> The sacred mushroom takes me by the hand and brings me to the world where everything is known. It is they, the sacred mushrooms, that speak in a way that I can understand. I ask them and they answer me. When I return from the trip that I have taken with them, I tell what they have told me and what they have shown me. (Sabina, 1979, p. 130)

This type of intimate communication is not unique to the mushroom. Lawlor (2013) reports that the Huichol people of Mexico communicate not only with the spirit of the peyote cactus but also with various other aspects of their environment through its ingestion. The

Western subjects in Harris and Gurel's (2012) study note that they have communicated directly with the spirit of ayahuasca:

> When asked whether they had a personal relationship with the spirit of ayahuasca, 74% of subjects replied "yes." The spirit of ayahuasca was most often described as a wise teacher, grandmother or healer from a higher spiritual dimension and intelligence who provides guidance and loving, comforting, protective support. (Harris & Gurel, 2012, p. 213)

Communication between humans and nature has profound implications for the potential of psychedelics to be of benefit to humans both individually and collectively. During psychedelic experiences, people receive direct answers to questions, personal messages, and detailed informational downloads that often correspond to ancient esoteric systems of knowledge (Grof, 1974; Walsh & Vaughan, 1993).

The content and depth of these messages can be life changing, especially when one considers the paradigm-shattering experience of being communicated to directly by an intelligent entity in the form of a plant. The authenticity of these interactions may be questioned by many people and by mainstream culture at large. However, few who have a direct experience of this nature doubt its genuineness, and the collective effect of millions of these individual experiences has the potential to positively shift human culture. The psychedelics often have something specific to teach to their users as well.

> When asked whether they received any messages or instructions during their recent ayahuasca experience, subjects cited a rich array of positive spiritual advice. Themes included: love yourself more, open your heart to yourself and others, empower yourself, another's pain is your pain, normal waking consciousness is just one of many realities, love what is... Many subjects felt they had received a large "download" of complex insights and information that was described as far too complex and extensive to describe in a questionnaire. (Harris & Gurel, 2012, p. 212)

Such messages, when heeded by those receiving them, lead to changes such as increased self-esteem, improved relationships with others, and increased compassion for others and the world. These changes have beneficial effects on families, communities, and societies. Although further research into these phenomena is needed, psychedelics seem to be capable of connecting people to profound transpersonal realms, where they can receive direct, personal, relevant, and useful messages.

Additional Benefits

"Many studies of both the historical and contemporary use of entheogens have suggested that the states they induce can have profoundly positive, even life-changing, effects upon individuals..." (Trichter et al., 2009, p. 123)

Psychedelics are not toxic, they are not physically addictive, and they do not physiologically harm the body or the brain (Johansen & Krebs, 2015). When used in a controlled setting, they are very unlikely to cause psychological problems in healthy individuals (Johansen & Krebs, 2015). The risk of harm associated with psychedelic use is due almost exclusively to factors not involving the nature and actions of the substances themselves.

In addition to not directly causing harm, psychedelics have been proven to effectively address a number of harmful conditions, such as alcohol and tobacco addictions (dos Santos et al., 2016). These researchers also reported that ayahuasca, psilocybin, and LSD have proven effective in treating depression and anxiety related to terminal illness.

Krebs and Johansen (2013) and Johansen and Krebs (2015) reported that there is no significant link between psychedelic use and mental health problems. In fact, the opposite is true; Krebs and Johansen (2013) found that psychedelic users have lower rates of mental health problems. Psychedelic use is also associated with decreased risk of suicidal thoughts, plans, and attempts, and therefore could support suicide prevention efforts (Hendricks, Thorne, Clark, Coombs, & Johnson, 2015). The promising potential of psychedelics in the realm of mental health is likely due to their ability to foster ego-transcendence, allowing individuals to view personal problems like addiction and depression from a perspective beyond the limited, egoic personality.

Psychedelics can also be used as tools for practical problem solving and for enhancing artistic and intellectual creativity. Their use has influenced major advancements in such diverse fields as film, computer science, and biotechnology (Brown, 2008). This may be due to increased brain network connectivity produced by psychedelics. For instance, psilocybin mushrooms cause brain regions that are typically disconnected to crosslink and communicate with one another while retaining organizational features (Petri et al., 2014).

Harris and Gurel (2012) reported on a wide variety of benefits resulting from the ayahuasca experiences of their subjects. These benefits include feeling more grateful, compassionate, content, tolerant, patient, forgiving, accepting, kind, self-confident, calm, centered, and aware of the needs of others. They reported an increase in spiritual awareness, improved relationships, reduced fear of death, desire to make a positive difference in the world, and a greater clarity regarding life purpose. These feelings led to positive life changes for nearly all of the subjects.

Doblin (1991) confirmed Pahnke's (1966) conclusion that the subjects of his psilocybin experiment had received significant and lasting benefits from the experience:

> Each of the psilocybin subjects felt that the experience had significantly affected his life in a positive way and expressed appreciation for having participated in the experiment. Most of the effects discussed in the long-term follow-up interviews centered around enhanced appreciation of life and of nature, deepened sense of joy, deepened commitment to the Christian ministry or to whatever other vocations the subjects chose, enhanced appreciation of unusual experiences and emotions, increased tolerance of other religious systems, deepened equanimity in the face of difficult life crises, and greater solidarity and identification with

foreign peoples, minorities, women and nature. (p. 14)

The Good Friday experiment lasted a single evening, and every psilocybin test subject that was interviewed reported profoundly positive effects, immediately, in the months following the experiment, and over 20 years later. By the standards of mainstream psychotherapy, these results after one session are nothing short of extraordinary. They suggest that controlled psychedelic use has the potential to revolutionize the field of psychotherapy.

The results also suggest that psychedelics can guide people toward becoming the greatest version of themselves. In Jungian depth psychology, this process is known as individuation, and it is driven by creating a conscious relationship with the content of one's unconscious (Hill, 2013). According to Hill, this is done by lowering the ego's control over consciousness. This is accomplished by the use of psychedelics, making them effective tools for working with shadow aspects of the psyche.

Schroll (2013) introduced the idea of *internal pollution*, a culturally conditioned egoism that exists within individuals and the collective, contributes to the global environmental crisis, and can only be effectively addressed through deep self-examination. This type of self-examination, or shadow work, is a standard aspect of the psychedelic experience. Schroll stresses that this personal work must underlie collective work to address global environmental issues.

Psychedelics cause the disintegration of cultural conditioning and the formation of new rituals, values, and stories (Segall, 2014). This stripping away of cultural conditioning creates space in the consciousness of an individual for fresh perception and original thought, effectively clearing the internal pollution. According to Schroll (2013), from this space of clarity an individual is better equipped to creatively face and overcome personal as well as global challenges.

Psychedelics provide people with a unique and powerful means to examine their worldview, and in some cases, a remarkably immediate spark to transform that worldview. This provides an opportunity to shift attitudes and behavior in profoundly beneficial ways. However, these shifts are by no means an automatic part of the psychedelic experience. These substances can provide people with information, spiritual insights, and new and profound perspectives on life. It is then the responsibility of each individual to integrate and utilize the insights and lessons of these experiences to make changes in their lives (Callicott, 2013; Metzner, 2013; Pahnke, 1966; Smith, 1964; Watts, 1965).

Risks and Concerns

Dark, painful, scary, and sometimes overwhelming emotional experiences can occur during psychedelic use. This phenomenon, known colloquially as a "bad trip," is rare but important to consider. One of the psilocybin test subjects in the Good Friday experiment had such an experience and was administered a tranquilizer due to the intense struggles (Doblin, 1991). This shows that it is possible to have a "bad trip" even in a somewhat controlled environment. Further research is needed to better understand these difficult experiences in order to maximize the chances of avoiding them or, better yet, utilizing them for growth within a supportive context. In the case of the Good Friday experiment, perhaps more skilled facilitation would have assisted that test subject in successfully navigating a spiritual emergency.

Hallucinogen Persisting Perception Disorder (HPPD) is another rare phenomenon that can result from psychedelic use (Halpern & Pope, 2003). Generally known as "flashbacks," HPPD is characterized by perceptual distortions that take users back into the psychedelic experience after it has chemically ended. These perceptual distortions can be one-time events or can persist for months or years, and they can be unpleasant or even terrifying. According to Halpern and Pope, HPPD is not well understood because of the limited amount of research that has been conducted. Once again, more research is needed to understand this aspect of the psychedelic experience.

Precipitation of psychopathology in predisposed individuals is another potential risk of psychedelic use (Walsh & Vaughan, 1993). Screening potential psychedelic users for such prior psychopathology would be ideal for reducing the risk of such negative reactions. Another reason for negative psychedelic experiences, according to Walsh and Vaughan (1993), is the use of impure substances, which will remain a concern as long as psychedelics are illegal. Legalization and government regulation of these substances would address the issue of impurity. While recent studies dispute the perception that psychedelic use is linked to mental illness (Krebs & Johansen, 2013; Johansen & Krebs, 2015), because of the similar neurobiology in psychosis and psychedelic use further research should continue (Gonzalez-Maeso & Sealfon, 2009).

A person's state of mind, temperament, and expectations going into a psychedelic experience (set), as well as the environment in which it takes place (setting), are determinant factors in how positive and potentially beneficial the experience will be (Leary & Clark, 1963). By properly preparing participants and the environment where the experience takes place—for instance. through intention setting and making sure the atmosphere is comfortable—risks involved with psychedelic use can be minimized (Metzner, 2013). If set and setting are not taken into account, the risk for negative experiences with psychedelics is increased.

Due to decades-long legal prohibition of psychedelics, there is a lack of understanding culturally about how to use them safely. Illegalization has been ineffective in stopping people from using psychedelics (Global Commission on Drug Policy, 2014). The risks of psychedelic use can be all but eliminated when they are used correctly, and it appears to be impossible to prevent people from using them. Therefore, it makes sense to educate the population regarding their safe use.

Along with concerns about the psychedelic experience itself, there are also concerns regarding the environmental and cultural impacts of psychedelic use, especially within the context of an increasingly globalized world. Molnar (2013) points out that Westerners traveling around the world to take part in indigenous psychedelic rituals provide an example of cultural appropriation. Dobkin de Rios (2009) refers to this as "borrowed mysticism." Molnar (2013) also raises the question of whether psychedelic plants and their spirits are displaced when they are used outside of their indigenous habitats. She also cites issues of over-harvesting and the resources used in transportation as concerns of modern psychedelic use.

Metzner (2013) comments that traditional psychedelic use has always been a carefully structured experience in which the importance of ritual is paramount. In many modern cases, this traditional form of sacramental use has devolved into recreational use. It is common for the modern use of psychedelics to be void of ritual and reverence, important components according to ancient traditions (Rothenberg, 2003). This is another area where education about appropriate psychedelic use can be of value.

The Future of Psychedelics

In recent decades, psychedelics have been moving out of the shadows to a significant extent, reflecting a shift that is occurring in the collective consciousness. The psychedelic research of the past decade has garnered groundbreaking discoveries in diverse fields of science, philosophy, and consciousness (Brown, 2008). Promising evidence exists for both the myriad potential beneficial uses and minimal risks of psychedelics.

Much of the psychedelic research that has been carried out is limited in one or more areas, such as sample size, repeatability, and adherence to scientific advancements that have occurred in the decades since the war on drugs made psychedelics illegal. However, the limited evidence we have for the benefits of psychedelics justifies further research into their potential.

The evidence also justifies the legal reclassification of psychedelics. As schedule I substances, psychedelics such as LSD, psilocybin, and peyote are currently considered to have no accepted medical use and a high potential for abuse (Drug Enforcement Administration [DEA], 2012). According to the evidence presented in this chapter, the potential medical uses of psychedelics are promising, and their potential for abuse is low. Therefore, the DEA's current classification of psychedelics as Schedule I substances reflects an inaccurate portrayal of their uses and dangers and should be changed to better reflect the reality of the situation.

There is evidence that full and regulated legalization of psychedelics would be of benefit to society as well as individuals. In 2001, the country of Portugal legalized personal possession of all drugs and implemented harm reduction measures (Global Commission on Drug Policy, 2014). Safety and public health in Portugal have seen great improvements in the years since this policy was implemented (Hughes & Stevens, 2010).

Not only would legalization revolutionize the way that psychedelics are studied and used, it would also address numerous social and political problems that the war on drugs has been failing to address for decades, and has in fact made worse. According to the Global Commission on Drug Policy's (2014) report:

> Harsh measures grounded in repressive ideologies must be replaced by more humane and effective policies shaped by scientific evidence, public health principles and human rights standards. This is the only way to simultaneously reduce drug-related death, disease and suffering and the violence, crime, corruption and illicit markets associated with ineffective prohibitionist policies. (p. 6)

Another area of potential development is in the creation and implementation of appropriate methods for the safe and effective use of psychedelics. The Good Friday experiment showed that a framework of religious worship is effective in containing the psychedelic experience and maximizing its benefits. The high level of successful integration of the experience among the psilocybin subjects in the study suggests that this was the case. In other words, the set and setting were appropriate.

Such utilization of religious ceremony in the West to contain the psychedelic experience can be compared to the organized, ritualistic ways that psychedelics have been used by indigenous cultures for thousands of years. These cultures have advanced systems based on administering psychedelics and guiding the experience to maximize their benefits. Western science can investigate and learn from these ancient cultures in order to develop and refine cultural parameters for safe and effective modern psychedelic use.

Conclusion

Existing research confirms that psychedelics provide a wide range of benefits, many of which are transpersonal and/or spiritual in nature. The range of benefits brought about by psychedelics can contribute to the overall well-being and evolution of individuals, especially in regard to their relationships with themselves, other people, the natural environment, and the divine.

One common result of psychedelic use and its range of benefits is the shifting of consciousness toward a more ecologically aware and interconnected view of the world, and a corresponding desire for individuals to take action toward living in greater balance with the natural environment. Therefore, psychedelics hold great potential in assisting humanity to address the global ecological crisis.

It is also clear that there are risks inherent to the use of psychedelics. There is a small segment of the population for which psychedelic use is not appropriate due to preexisting psychopathology. It is critical to ensure that psychedelics are used within the proper context in order to maximize benefit and minimize harm. When these simple precautions are taken, the risks of psychedelic use can be all but eliminated. It is clear based on the evidence presented in this chapter that the benefits of the psychedelic experience, along with the manageability of the risks involved, warrant further research into the use of psychedelics as well as a reconsideration of their legal status.

More research is needed to determine the extent to which psychedelics may be effectively utilized in modern society. For a number of decades, research in these areas has been very limited, if not impossible, due to the illegal status of the substances (Doblin, 1991). However, the scientific community and society at large seem to be shifting toward a more open, curious, and level-headed dialogue concerning psychedelics:

...controversies and problems associated with uncontrolled use

> quickly led to the illegalization of psychedelics and cessation of scientific research on their clinical and spiritual potential. Given the recent resurgence of scientific interest, and government approval of limited human studies of psychedelic effects, a less hysterical assessment of psychedelics is likely to emerge in the coming years. (Lerner & Lyvers, 2006, p. 147)

Areas of further study may include research into the therapeutic benefits of psychedelics for a wide range of psychological and emotional ailments, including trauma, depression, anxiety, addiction, attention deficit disorder, obsessive-compulsive disorder, posttraumatic stress disorder, anger management issues, etc. Future research could also examine physical benefits of psychedelics, as well as how they affect abilities such as problem solving, artistic creativity, conflict resolution, and language learning, among others. More research into the effects of psychedelics on spiritual and transpersonal development would also be likely to produce rich results. If the trend of resurgent psychedelic research continues, it is likely to bear scientific fruit in many fields, helping to expand human knowledge and consciousness.

It is clear that humanity is facing many problems, including a global environmental crisis of unprecedented severity. Our survival is in question, and it seems that a global shift in consciousness is necessary in order to change our current trajectory of self-destruction. A shift in global consciousness is made up of many shifts in individual consciousness. The time has come to use all of the tools available to facilitate such shifts, and psychedelics are one of the most effective tools we have.

> We as a species must change or be changed if we and other species on this planet are to survive. The starting point for that transformation into becoming a part of, rather than apart from, our ecosystem is our own individual consciousness. (Luke, 2013, p. 7)

References

Andrei, M. (2015, January 12). First LSD study in 40 years shows medical promise. *ZME Science*. Retrieved from http://www.zmescience.com/medicine/lsd-psychotherapy-12012014/

Brown, D.J. (2008). MAPS special issue: Technology and psychedelics. *Multidisciplinary Association for Psychedelic Studies 18*(1), 3–5.

Callicott, C. (2013). Interspecies communication in the western Amazon: Music as a form of conversation between plants and people. *European Journal of Ecopsychology 4*, 32–43.

Cooper, M. (2016). The Psychedelic Renaissance: Horizons, the Fifth Annual Conference on Psychedelic Research. *Einstein Journal of Biology and Medicine, 28*(1), 36–38.

Dickins, R. (2013). Preparing the Gaia connection: An ecological exposition of psychedelic literature 1954–1963. *European Journal of Ecopsychology 4*, 9–18.

Dobkin de Rios, M. (2009). *The psychedelic journey of Marlene Dobkin de Rios: 45 years with shamans, ayahuascaros, and ethnobotanists.* Rochester, VT: Park Street Press.

Doblin, R. (1991). Pahnke's "Good Friday Experiment": A long-term follow-up and methodological critique. *Journal of Transpersonal Psychology 23*(1), 1–28.

Dos Santos, R., Osório, F., Crippa, J., Riba, J., Zuardi, A., & Hallak, J. (2016). Antidepressive, anxiolytic, and antiaddictive effects of ayahuasca, psilocybin and lysergic acid diethylamide (LSD): A systematic review of clinical trials published in the last 25 years. *Therapeutic Advances in Psychopharmacology, 6*, 1–21.

Doyle, R. (2011). *Darwin's pharmacy: Sex, plants and the evolution of noösphere.* Seattle, WA: University of Washington Press.

Drug Enforcement Administration (DEA) of the US Department of Justice (DOJ), Office of Diversion Control. (2012). Definition of controlled substance schedules: Schedule I substance. *Drug Abuse Prevention and Control* (Chapter 13). Retrieved from http://www.dea.gov

Global Commission on Drug Policy (2014, September). *Taking control: Pathways to drug policy that work.* Retrieved from http://www.gcdpsummary2014.com/#foreword-from-the-chair

Gonzalez-Maeso, J., & Sealfon, S. C. (2009). Psychedelics and schizophrenia. *Trends in neurosciences 32*(4), 225–232.

Griffiths, R., Richards, W., Johnson, M., McCann, U., & Jesse, R. (2006). Mystical-type experiences occasioned by psilocybin mediate the attribution of personal meaning and spiritual significance 14 months later. *Journal of Psychopharmacology 22*, 621–632.

Grof, S. (1974). *Realms of the human unconscious: Observations from LSD research.* New York, NY: Viking Press.

Halpern, J.H., & Pope, H.G. (2003). Hallucinogen persisting perception disorder: What do we know after 50 years? *Drug and Alcohol Dependence 69(2)*, 109–119.

Harris, R., & Gurel, L. (2012). A study of ayahuasca use in North America. *Journal of Psychoactive Drugs, 44*(3), 209–215.

Hendricks, P., Thorne, C., Clark, C., Coombs, D., & Johnson, M. (2015). Classic psychedelic use is associated with reduced psychological distress and suicidality in the United States adult population. *Journal of Psychopharmacology, 29*(3), 280–288.

Hill, S.J. (2013). *Confrontation with the unconscious: Jungian depth psychology and psychedelic experience.* London, UK: Muswell Hill Press.

Hughes, C.E., & Stevens, A. (2010). What can we learn from the Portuguese decriminalization of illicit drugs? *British Journal of Criminology, 50*(6), 999–1022.

Johansen, P., & Krebs, T. (2015). Psychedelics not linked to mental health problems or suicidal behavior: A population study. *Journal of Psychopharmacology, 29*(3), 1–10.

Krebs, T., & Johansen, P. (2013). Psychedelics and mental health: A population study. *PLos ONE* 8: e63972.

Lawlor, D. (2013). Returning to Wirikuta: The Huichol and their sense of place. *European Journal of Ecopsychology 4*, 19–31.

Leary, T., & Clark, W.H. (1963). Religious implications of consciousness expanding drugs. *Religious Education 58*(3), 251–256.

Lerner, M., & Lyvers, M. (2006). Values and beliefs of psychedelic drug users: A cross-cultural study. *Journal of Psychoactive Drugs, 38*(2), 143–147.

Luke, D. (2013). Ecopsychology and the psychedelic experience. *European Journal of Ecopsychology, 4*, 1–8.

Maslow, A. (1962) *Toward a psychology of being.* Princeton, NJ: Van Nostrand.

McKenna, T. (1992). *The archaic revival.* San Francisco, CA: Harper Publishing.

Metzner, R. (1999). *Ayahuasca: Human consciousness and the spirits of nature.* New York, NY: Thunder's Mouth Press.

Metzner, R. (2013). Entheogenic rituals, shamanism and green psychology. *European Journal of Ecopsychology, 4*, 64–77.

Molnar, E. (2013). The responsible use of entheogens in the context of bioregionalism. *European Journal of Ecopsychology, 4*, 78–89.

Pahnke, W. (1966). Drugs and mysticism. *International Journal of Parapsychology, 8*(2), 295–313.

Petri, G., Expert, P., Turkheimer, F., Carhart-Harris, R., Nutt, D., Hellyer, P.J., & Vaccarino, F. (2014). Homological scaffolds of brain functional networks. *Journal of the Royal Society, 11*(101).

Ratsch, C. (2005). *The Encyclopedia of Psychoactive Plants: Ethnopharmacology and Its Applications.* Rochester, VT: Park Street Press.

Rothenberg, J. (2003). *Maria Sabina: Selections.* Berkeley, CA: University of California Press.
Sabina, M. (1979). Maria Sabina: Mesoamerica/Mazatec. In J. Halifax (Ed.), *Shamanic voices: A survey of visionary narratives* (pp. 129–135). New York, NY: Arkana, Penguin Books.
Schroll, M. (2013). From ecopsychology to transpersonal ecosophy: Shamanism, psychedelics, and transpersonal psychology. *European Journal of Ecopsychology, 4,* 116–144.
Segall, M.D. (2013). Participatory psychedelia: Transpersonal theory, religious studies, and chemically-altered (alchemical) consciousness. *Journal of Transpersonal Research, 5*(2), 86–94.
Segall, M.D. (2014, August 18). The psychedelic eucharist: Is there an alchemical solution to the ecological crisis? *Footnotes2Plato.* Retrieved from: https://footnotes2plato.com/2014/08/18/the-psychedelic-eucharist-is-there-an-alchemical- solution-to-the-ecological-crisis/
Smith, H. (1964). Do drugs have religious import? *The Journal of Philosophy, LXI*(18).
Tindall, R. (2013). Snake medicine: How animism heals. *European Journal of Ecopsychology, 4,* 47–63.
Trichter, S., Klimo, J., & Krippner, S. (2009). Changes in spirituality among ayahuasca ceremony novice participants. *Journal of Psychoactive Drugs, 41*(2), 121–134.
Walsh, R., & Vaughan, F. (1993). *Paths beyond ego: The transpersonal vision.* New York, NY: Putnam.
Watts, A. (1965). *The joyous cosmology.* New York, NY: Random House.
Winkelman, M. (2013). Shamanism and psychedelics: A biogenetic structuralist paradigm of ecopsychology. *European Journal of Ecopsychology, 4,* 90–115.

Chapter 11
Transpersonal Sexuality: A Paradigm Beyond the Normative

Satori S. Madrone
Debra L. Azorsky

> Sex is an emotion in motion.
> (Mae West, as cited in Louvish, 2007, p. 405)

In the 1960s and 1970s the sexually repressed U.S. culture of the 1950s exploded. A sexual revolution emerged. It is the nature of revolution to illuminate what is not currently being expressed, and this sexual revolution, similar to other sexual revolutions in history, was revealing a shadow of sexuality that could no longer be contained by cultural constraints. In this rebellion, people demanded their right to name, define, and experience their own sexuality. The shadow that emerged is a sexuality without spirituality and a sexuality disconnected from pleasure.

Periodically, humans' wild, untamed sexual energies rise up to be noticed, acknowledged, and experienced. This eruption is usually met by an equally forceful cultural resistance that attempts to suppress it. In spite of cultural opposition, change does happen, and the ends of the continuum are extended. Today the pendulum of cultural displays of sexuality swings from the Folsom Street Fair, a weekend dedicated to bondage, discipline, and sadomasochism (BDSM), to Purity Balls where girls offer their virginity to their fathers for safekeeping until marriage.

This chapter briefly summarizes some of the recent academic studies of sexuality and the biopsychosocial model currently used to describe our understanding of human sexuality. It provides a review of some of the work by those who risked being ostracized academically and professionally from Western academia in order to further the cultural knowledge and understanding of sex and sexuality. Pioneers such as Alfred Kinsey (Kinsey, Pomeroy, & Martin, 1948), William Masters and Virginia Johnson (1966), as well as our contemporaries, Helen Singer Kaplan (1974), Bernie Zilbergeld (1978), Beverly Whipple (Whipple, Ladas, & Perry, 1982), and Gina Ogden (2002) have paved the way and continue to blaze a path to greater understanding and acceptance about who we are as sexual beings.

Of most interest, however, is to consider the implications and potential advantages of incorporating a transpersonal perspective back into the understanding of sexuality. A transpersonal view of sexuality dismantles the experience of "otherness" and forms a dynamic of inclusion, and the freedom to question and explore one's internal and external experiences and expressions expands the sexual self into greater wholeness and interconnection. Further, when a phenomenological lens is placed on the biopsychosocial model of sexuality, advancement of a paradigmatic, visionary shift is required. We recommend a toroidal model as the best currently available frame for reflecting sexuality. Transpersonal psychology holds a unique opportunity to transform the current conventional thinking about sexuality, bringing a transpersonal model of sexuality to the forefront of modern U.S. culture.

Historical Perspectives on Sexuality

> One would certainly think that there could be no doubt about what is to be understood by the term "sexual." First and foremost, of course, it means the "improper," that which must not be mentioned. (Freud, 1943, p. 266, as cited in Masters, Johnson, & Kolodny, 1988, p.4)

11. Transpersonal Sexuality

Academic perspectives on sexuality and its intrinsically spiritual nature have been historically coupled with humanity's deepest roots. Descriptions of indigenous traditions, creation stories, and mysticism—such as cross-cultural applications of tantra, seasonal fertility festivals, or goddess-centered worship—are common in history and cultural texts. According to anthropologists such as Eisler (1996), these reports date back to civilizations where the "female vulva was revered as the magical portal of life" that contained the potential for spiritual awakening, transformation, and physical renewal (p. 16). Male genitalia were also esteemed as the penultimate symbol of life's fundamental energy. Indigenous and ancient civilizations' conceptions of sexuality and spirituality were non-dualistic and non-pathological: A split between body and spirit did not exist, and sexuality and spirituality were merged. In this state of wholeness, the body of human beings and the body of the Earth itself were intrinsic to the ongoing reproductive survival of all things and did not need justification or sanction. Until recently, science was not the only authority for naming, defining, and validating reality.

The advent of Christianity demonized women's sexuality as having a perverse power over men. Eve's body in particular was pointed to as the cause of the removal of Adam and Eve from the Garden of Eden (Bloch, 1992). Later the Cartesian–Newtonian scientific revolution exacerbated the duality of body and mind, placing body in a decidedly inferior position. After some 2,000 years of these powerful narratives, sexuality and spirituality are now curiously split, a separation that perpetuates many of the challenges people in the modern U.S. society have with viewing sexuality and themselves as sacred. Perhaps by repossessing a definition of sexuality in which human beings are seen as innately holy and sacred, to be revered and respected, ancient and indigenous perspectives on sexuality and spirituality could simply be reclaimed. A transpersonal sexuality, re-owning our natural, inherent spiritual essence, would reorder what has become a chaotic and damaging perspective of who we are.

From 1897–1928, Havelock Ellis published seven volumes of *Studies in the Psychology of Sex*, recognizing that sexual values and beliefs were influenced by culture and society, and that human beings expressed a wide variety of sexual proclivities and behaviors (see for example, Ellis, 1906/1937). Ellis' research and conclusions were radical for Victorian society, particularly because his work included research about women's sexual experiences (Kelly, 1995).

In 1938, Alfred Kinsey, frustrated by a lack of academic acknowledgement for his work in the field of biology, agreed to team-teach a course on marriage and the family at Indiana University. In the 1940s, college students flocked to Kinsey's class to participate in his research, eager to discuss their experiences of sex and sexuality and try to relinquish the cultural shame they had inherited from their parents. In 1948 and 1953, Kinsey and his colleagues published *Sexual Behavior in the Human Male* and *Sexual Behavior in the Human Female*, respectively. They compiled over 11,000 interviews with men and women, stirring a cultural awakening about the sexual behaviors of both sexes that included masturbatory practices, pre-marital sexual experiences, same-sex attractions and experiences, and many other previously unspoken aspects of sexual behavior.

As Kinsey neared the end of his life, William Masters was beginning his research on sexual functioning and was joined by Virginia Johnson in 1956. Masters and Johnson (1966), through the development of new, scientific instrumentation, discovered a distinct four-phase experience of sexual arousal. These phases—excitement, plateau, orgasm and resolution—simultaneously documented women's ability to have multiple orgasms. Masters and Johnson published this research, thereby furthering the U.S. culture's knowledge and understanding of how our sexual bodies function.

With Ellis' (1906/1937) cultural perspective, Kinsey's (Kinsey et al., 1948) focus on behavior, including attitudes and beliefs, and Masters and Johnson's (1966) focus on physiology as it relates to behavior, the foundation for a biopsychosocial model of human sexuality was born. George Engel, a professor of psychiatry and medicine, suggested combining sociology and psychology with models of biology and created the "biopsychosocial" model in 1977 (Lindau, Laumann, Levinson, & Waite, 2003). The more comprehensive nature of this model allowed for human sexuality to be viewed through multiple lenses.

However, as sexuality became increasingly relegated to the factual and measurement-based world of science over time, its spiritual identity was extracted, and the distilled version of sexuality became structured, compartmentalized and further de-sacralized. While the innate, spiritual nature of sexuality has never been absent, it is now time to refocus our cultural lens on designing a fluid, holistic, and toroidal framework from which to fully embrace what has always been, in truth, intact.

Definitions and Aspects Influencing Sexuality

The World Health Organization (WHO; 2006) has provided a global and inclusive definition of sexuality:

> ...a central aspect of being human throughout life encompasses sex, gender identities and roles, sexual orientation, eroticism, pleasure, intimacy and reproduction. Sexuality is experienced and expressed in thoughts, fantasies, desires, beliefs, attitudes, values, behaviours, practices, roles and relationships. While sexuality can include all of these dimensions, not all of them are always experienced or expressed. Sexuality is influenced by the interaction of biological, psychological, social, economic, political, cultural, legal, historical, religious and spiritual factors.

Sexuality is also known to be an intrinsically entwined matrix comprising many factors: sensuality, intimacy, sexual and gender identity, sexual development and functioning, reproductive and sexual health, and sexualization. Each of these terms will be briefly defined to set the stage for the discussion following:

- *Sensuality,* or our ability to feel sexual, includes our awareness and feelings about our bodies, our body image, and our experience of being in our bodies. Pleasure resides at the core of how we experience touch and is our first sense in exploring the world.

- *Sexual intimacy* is our ability to be emotionally and sexually close to another as well as our ability to accept and enjoy the closeness of others. Within sexual intimacy there is also emotional risk taking, empathy, and vulnerability.
- *Sexual orientation* describes how our attraction is oriented. We may have fluid, dynamic, and changing attractions to and experiences with others (Diamond, 2008).
- The categories of sexual and gender identity in modern Western society are in the midst of their own expansive awakening. *Sexual identity expression* is currently used to describe how we experience ourselves both internally and externally as sexual beings, and in some people's experience this may be incongruent with their culture's accepted parameters. This often creates challenges in the development of healthy self-esteem, especially if one lives in a cultural environment that is hostile to one's identity.
- *Gender identity*, as with orientation and identity expression, is not limited to biology and reflects the male to female phenomenological compatibility with one's genitalia. According to Davis, Zimman, and Raclaw (2014), transgendered individuals may experience social dysphoria, or significant discord between their biological bodies and cultural expectations of binary gender identity. Gender identity is often a scripted norm created by the culture in which one lives, and many find this script limiting, internally inconsistent, and invalidating.
- *Sexual development* includes such wide variation that it begs for an opportunity to flourish without cultural constraint. Sexual development is highly differentiated and encompasses all areas of sexual evolution in social, psychological, biological, and spiritual arenas for each and every person.
- *Sexual function* includes how our sexual bodies function with regard to what society deems healthy, proper, and "normal," and, as such, continues to be a source of self and cultural judgment, shame, and isolation.

- *Reproductive and sexual health.* The importance of factual information regarding reproduction, the right to choose pregnancy or not, as well as factual information about sexually transmitted infections (STIs) and HIV/AIDS is critical. According to David Satcher (2001), former U.S. surgeon general, sexual health is a human right, and all human beings should be informed about their right to sexual pleasure and protection from harm.
- *Sexualization* is an aspect of sexuality where people behave sexually to influence, manipulate, and control another person. These behaviors range from flirtation and seduction to the much darker end of the spectrum that involves sexual harassment, rape, and incest.

With at least these nine aspects of sexuality, and assumedly infinite varieties within each aspect, the number of possible combinations and permutations is staggering. This is the primary reason for considering a new model for describing human sexuality. Even though the dynamic, bilateral, biopsychosocial model explains human development in points in time, showing the interplay between various components of who we are and the experiences that we have both internally and relationally with others and our world (Lindau, Laumann, Levinson, & Waite, 2003), it remains inadequate because of the multidimensional and interactive parts of true sexual capacity. The currently applied cultural binary perspective applied to sexuality has become a hindrance rather than a useful construct.

From a sociocultural perspective, binary ideologies are frequently used to differentiate and categorize human traits and characteristics by placing two supposedly oppositional qualities as distinct ends on a line, identified as a continuum (Davis, Zimman & Raclaw, 2014). An example of this is our idea that maleness/masculinity is the opposite of femaleness/femininity, and that any other identity or expression is seen as some composite of the two, a quantifiable dot on the male–female spectrum. This offers an incomplete and inaccurate picture when it comes to those who do not identify or express either quality or those whose dot on the line moves depending on a variety of internal and external factors. We are multidimensional beings of limitless qualities who attempt to quantify our sexualities through the rules of a linear lens composed of linear ideologies that lie on a spectrum of extremes, with our position somewhere represented within a bell curve. Moving away from binary spectrum thinking toward a multidimensional construct, such as that represented by a torus model, allows greater room for limitless identities and expressions, leading to greater accuracy and a more complete view of sexual identity and functioning.

Toward a New Definition—Beyond the Normative
Even though there has been significant progress in the last 100 years toward having a healthier and more accurate understanding of sexuality, today we realize that sexual diversity is too vast to be contained by a dot along a defined, binary line. A more inclusive and holistic conception of sexuality is needed to describe sexual experience that reflects the expansive, non-normative reality of human beings, who are each an *n* of 1. Current theoretical models, standard bell curve ideologies, and culturally restrictive expectations do not support people in their discovery or development of this important aspect of themselves. Cultural conditioning drives people to internalize shame and inadequacy when they don't live up to the culture's expectations about adhering to normative views of sexuality, and the judgments that follow propel them to strive toward conformity even if it doesn't fit (Brown, 2004; Fessler, 2007; Davis, Zimman & Raclaw, 2014).

For those of certain sexual subcultures, social intolerance does not allow "alternative" sexualities to be safely expressed or even legally supported. Instead of seeking to change the social rules about how to live and view ourselves as sexual beings, people often turn toward denial and suppression, giving rise to an unconscious shadow that manifests as harmful thoughts and behaviors. For the collective health of our community, it is imperative to task ourselves with asking questions that invite expressions of living and being that are no longer viewed as "alternative" but are merely seen as part of what is "normal."

As various identities expand beyond categories, including fluidity within or between them, it is becoming increasingly apparent that our culture lacks appropriate language or tools to adequately appreciate, understand, or study the complexity of human sexuality (Diamond, 2008). If a significant number of our population do not belong within normative standards of sexuality, perhaps it is time to collectively establish a different understanding of "normal." Currently, "normative" is a cultural value that continually shifts, and, as such, it simply isn't a helpful or useful construction. When it is personally applied, it lends limited—if any—benefit to one's personal discovery of sexuality, including identity, preferences, desires, and relational experiences. Individuals and groups that vary from the prescribed sexual norms are deeply impacted when their sexual identities and experiences are denied or pathologized, leading to significant emotional and psychological suffering. On the group level, a cultural "shadow" is created where isolation, disconnection, silence, and suffering are acted out in socially destructive ways.

Overwhelmingly the culture in the United States seems to be trapped in a *consensus trance* (Tart, 1987) and seems to have agreed to accept the limitations, dimensions, and constructs of sexuality through the mechanism of an assumptive habitual default. Entranced, we bypass engaging conscious awareness of what is actually true about our sexualities in the present in order to reaffirm past assumptions about what we think sexuality "is" and "should be" by cutting and pasting these falsifications onto our sexual encounters. The resulting stories of sexuality are then swallowed whole as introjects and core beliefs that ineffectively guide how we live and who we think we are. Our habit of entranced living fuels repression and sexual stagnancy, and prevents us from evolving into fully expressed and connected sexual beings.

Common core beliefs in the white, European, Christian U.S. culture center around feeling that we are not okay as we are, that something is wrong with us. Perhaps we are unworthy, or there is something inherently bad about us and we don't deserve sexual pleasure in the way that we enjoy giving and/or receiving it (Brown, 2004; Nagoski, 2015). If our sexual expression and experiences—or merely our cognitions—vary from the entranced social script, our perceived failure to conform to implicit and explicit social rules brings with it shame and guilt, and we are likely to turn away from and deny our own pleasure and sexuality. While it may look differently depending on the culture in which we live, embracing an inclusive, non-normatively-defined sexuality supports our autonomy and empowers us not only to disagree with our culture's sexual narrative, but allows us to create a unique personal vision of our sexuality and its place in our lives.

Introducing a Transpersonal Sexuality
The overall implication of a paradigmatic shift is to move away from cultural definitions of normative sexuality that pathologize certain sexual behaviors, expressions, biologies, identities, functions, and development. Applying a transpersonal perspective to sexuality, on the other hand, validates our uniqueness as holistic human beings and allows us to realize that where we land on the bell curve can't accurately describe the profundity of who we are as sexual beings. Rather, the transpersonal perspective is one that awakens conscious discernment and is able to stand outside of dualistic parameters of cultural coding and ascertain what is appropriate for the individual's expression of self in the moment.

Hartelius, Rothe, and Roy (2013) rebranded the transpersonal, viewing the individual holistically as intimately relational and deeply in contact with an expansive and transformational world. It is from this evocation of fluid potential that the idea of the transpersonal is key to creating new meaning for a sexuality that simultaneously engages present-centered experience, receptivity, and expression. In addition, when the WHO's (2016) global definition of sexuality is joined with Hartelius et al.'s vision of the transpersonal, we can begin to see the formation of a transpersonal view of sexuality that supports sexually fluid expressions and experiences and allows for expansion into spiritual, as well as non-spiritual, realms. When defining sexuality from an inclusive spiritual lens, sexuality becomes harder to quantify as it shifts to include a timeless, energetic expression—a fluid experience that evolves beyond a continuum and is not linearly enacted or explained. As in the quantum world, it is simultaneously both a line and a wave, and perhaps a point as well. Perhaps transpersonal sexuality is not containable or fixed, but rather tidal and limitless.

A Paradigm of Innate Wholeness

The transpersonal perspective we have been considering here is a non-pathological view of sexuality that allows space for the process of untangling oneself from feelings of shame, dysfunction, and disconnection that may be lifelong, especially given how culturally pervasive and deeply embedded these beliefs may be (Brown, 2004; Nagoski, 2015). Even with these feelings present, perhaps we can begin to incorporate something more into our sexuality that evolves alongside the unwanted patterns, beliefs, and painful feelings. Perhaps we can move forward from the Self instead of from what feels incomplete or lacking, starting to awaken to the reality that we are moving toward a new version of wholeness instead of seeking pieces that we need to acquire to be whole, something more than who we already are.

Transpersonal sexuality is not relegated to the esoteric and the metaphysical. It is not about striving to achieve an impossibly perfect sexuality, and it is not about being someone else in a different life with better circumstances and a prettier past or a better partner. Our sexuality is not something outside of ourselves to attain or achieve but something to open to within what has always existed and is innate. We can take a dialectical stance of accepting who we are in the moment as complete, while also engaging in conscious development of who we are as developing transpersonal sexual beings.

Non-duality

Intrinsic within the transpersonal is the non-dual, which appears foreign to our current cultural ideas of relationship and the belief that humans are separate from one another and are having separate experiences. Duality creates opposition and reinforces ideas of "good" versus "bad" sexual experiences, whereas a holistic view holds both views simultaneously. Mindful awareness invites us to wisely discern what we choose to accept and allow into our expression. Although we might not always be engaged with it, we are always in possession of transpersonal sexuality, as it is an innate and indivisible part of who we are (Saral, 2003). The very foundation of transpersonal psychology supports the reality that the human is already whole, and that the experiences one has with one's world transforms and builds upon this wholeness (Hartelius et al., 2013).

If the non-dual aspect of transpersonalism implies that equanimity exists with all experience because there is neither good nor bad, then it would make sense to include sexuality as non-binary as well, since it does not relate to, is not composed of, and does not involve two opposing extremes. Moving away from linear duality toward a multidimensional framework of sexuality involves the dynamic interaction among infinite and holistic components of sexuality, all of which are inclusively supported by a torus model.

A Torus Model of Transpersonal Sexuality

Perhaps static and finite qualities are only those that can exist as a dot on a line, which is outside the nature of energy, movement, and the constant transformation of life. And perhaps the ever-evolving, creative life force of sexuality in all of its constellations is already modeled by the infinite torus. As such, a proposed torus model of transpersonal sexuality would contain all of our introjects, barriers, traumas, and ways that we connect with the world as defined by our ideas about who we think we are. Within the torus would also exist our hopes for new possibilities that will flow from a present-centered connection.

Within the doughnut-shaped structure of a continually rotating torus pattern, the qualities of all spectra would have movement, could connect in a variety of pathways, and contain the opportunity for transpersonal transformation (Bermanseder, 2011). Some suggest that a torus reflects not only the shape of the universe but also everything in it—from reality to consciousness—with room for all as we really are (Bentov, 2000; Wilber, 1993). Constructs within a torus model may create more of a soup-like structure as ingredients meld and transform through interaction rather than maintaining singular, differentiated, and unaffected characteristics. In an ineffable soup of transpersonal sexuality, entangled elements relate or communicate with one another in ways that are unifying and transformational, changing the textures and flavors of the ingredients as well as the soup as a whole. While we seek to incorporate an inclusive view of transpersonal sexuality that contains quantifiable and measurable ideologies (i.e., biological, psychological, and social elements), the challenge is to then take these distinct parts and meld them with ineffable and infinite components of spirituality since "You can't study one ingredient in the soup, and understand the whole soup. It's the same with the Soul: Nothing stands alone, in this puzzle of multi-dimensional attributes" (Carroll as cited in Muranyi, 2015, para. 7).

As pioneering cosmologist Arthur M. Young states, "The self in a toroidal Universe can be both separate and connected with everything else" (Cosmometry Project, 2014, para. 5). When there is connection with anything, information is exchanged. If our energetic connection to another happens within the perspective of the torus, then all who are within this field speak to all those who incorporate the field of the other (Bermanseder, 2011; Cosmometry Project, 2014). Perhaps the torus is the flow of all things, the expansive field of consciousness containing all that is, of which a transpersonal sexuality is an integral part.

Conclusion and Considerations Moving Forwar

In our discovery of a paradigm of transpersonal sexuality that moves beyond the normative, we are left with far more questions to consider than when we began. So far, we have attempted to lay the groundwork for investigating the topic of human sexuality and transpersonal psychology that is timely in its relevance to research exploration and cultural transformation. We have seen that even with the more comprehensive biopsychosocial model, we currently lack a holistic construct that combines all aspects of human sexuality together with the transpersonal, especially since the multidimensional realm of sexuality is not easily definable or quantifiable. Looking to ancient and indigenous cultures offers us a perspective on integration of the spiritual and sexual, but our more recent historical religious and scientific past has altered the landscape of human holism through separation of the spirit and body. As we navigate our way back to creating a new cultural narrative that is supportive of nurturing congruent individual experiences and expressions, we may find better representations outside of binary spectra and within a living energetic model of development that the torus conceptually offers. We are multidimensional beings with limitless potential to become more ourselves beyond the constraints of cultural normativity, and it is time for a new paradigm that supports cultivation of our magnificent sexual complexity.

References

Bermanseder, T. (2011). Physical consciousness in a self-conscious quantum universe. *Journal of Consciousness Exploration & Research, 2*(2), 162–179.

Bentov, I. (2000). *A brief tour of higher consciousness: A cosmic book on the mechanics of creation.* (Rev. ed.). Rochester, VT: Destiny Books.

Bloch, R. H. (1992). *Medieval misogyny and the invention of western romantic love.* Chicago, IL: University of Chicago Press.

Brown, B. (2004). *Women & shame: Reaching out, speaking truth and building connection.* Austin, TX: 3C Press.

Cosmometry Project (2014). *The torus – dynamic flow process.* Retrieved January 16, 2016, from http://www.cosmometry.net/the-torus-dynamic-flow-process

Davis, J. L., Zimman, L., & Raclaw, J. (2014). Opposites attract: Retheorizing binaries in language, gender, and sexuality. In L. Zimman, J. L. Davis & J. Raclaw (Eds.), *Queer excursions: Retheorizing binaries in language, gender, and sexuality* (pp. 1–12). New York, NY: Oxford University Press.

Diamond, L. (2008). *Sexual fluidity: Understanding women's love and desire.* Cambridge, MA: Harvard University Press.

Eisler, R. (1996). *Sacred pleasure: Sex, myth, and the politics of the body—New paths to power and love.* New York, NY: HarperCollins.

Ellis, H. (1937). *Studies in the Psychology of Sex* (Vol. II). Kingsport, TN: Kingsport Press. (Original work published 1906)

Fessler, D. M. T. (2007). From appeasement to conformity: Evolutionary and cultural perspectives on shame, competition, and cooperation. In J. L. Tracy, R.W. Robins, & J. P. Tangney (Eds.), *The self-conscious emotions: Theory and research* (pp. 174–193). New York, NY: The Guilford Press.

Hartelius, G., Rothe, G., & Roy, P. J. (2013). A brand from the burning: Defining transpersonal psychology. In H. L. Friedman & G. Hartelius (Eds.), *The Wiley-Blackwell handbook of transpersonal psychology* (pp. 3–22). West Sussex, UK: John Wiley & Sons.

Health and Human Services Dept. (2001). Foreword. In D. Satcher, *Healthy people 2010,* (Vols. 1-2). *With understanding and improving health and objectives for improving health.* McLean, VA: International Medical Publishing.

Kaplan, H.S., (1974). *The new sex therapy*. New York, NY: Brunner-Routledge.

Kelly, G. F. (1995). *Sexuality today: The human perspective* (5th ed.). Guilford, CT: Dushkin/McGraw-Hill.

Kinsey, A. C., Pomeroy, W. B., & Martin, C. E. (1948). *Sexual behavior in the human male.* Philadelphia, PA: W.B. Saunders Company.

Lindau, S.T., Laumann, E.O., Levinson, W., & Waite, L.J. (2003). Synthesis of scientific disciplines in pursuit of health: The interactive biopsychosocial model. *Perspectives in Biology and Medicine, 46.* DOI 10.1353/pbm.2003.0069

Louvish, S. (2007). *Mae West: It ain't no sin.* New York, NY: Macmillan.

Masters, W.H. & Johnson, V.E. (1966). *Human sexual response.* Boston, MA: Little, Brown and Co.

Masters, W.H., Johnson, V. E., & Kolodny, R. C. (1988). *Masters and Johnson on sex and human loving* (Rev. ed.). New York, NY: Little, Brown and Company.

Muranyi, M. (2015). *The human soul revealed.* Montreal, Canada: Ariane Editions Publishing. Retrieved January 14, 2016 from http://monikamuranyi.com/books/human-soul-revealed/

Nagoski, E. (2015). *Come as you are: The surprising new science that will transform your sex life.* New York, NY: Simon & Schuster Paperbacks.

Ogden, G., (2002). *Sexuality and spirituality in women's relationships: Preliminary results of an exploratory survey*. Wellesley Center for Women, paper number 405, Wellesley, MA.

Saral, T. B. (2003). Mental imagery in sex therapy. In A. A. Sheikh (Ed.), *Healing imagery: The role of imagination in healing* (pp. 254–274). Amityville, NY: Baywood Publishing Company.

Tart, C. (1987). *Waking up: Overcoming the obstacles to human potential.* Boston, MA: Shambhala Publications.

Whipple, B., Ladas, A.K., & Perry, J.D. (1982). *The g spot: And other recent discoveries in human sexuality*. New York, NY: Holt, Reinhart and Winston.

Wilber, K. (1993). *The spectrum of consciousness.* Wheaton, IL: Quest Books.

World Health Organization. (2006). *Defining sexual health*. Retrieved May 31, 2016 from http://www.who.int/reproductivehealth/topics/sexual_health/sh_definitions/en.

Zilbergeld, B. (1978). *Male sexuality.* New York, NY: Bantam Books.

Chapter 12
A Thousand Invisible Threads: A Pedagogical Tool Weaving Together Transpersonal Psychology, Sustainability, and Ecopsychology

Deb Piranian

Humankind has not woven the web of life. We are but one thread within it. Whatever we do to the web, we do to ourselves. All things are bound together. All things connect.
(Chief Seattle as cited in Stibbe, 2015, p. 72)

Here again we are reminded that in nature nothing exists alone.
(Carson, 2002, p. 51)

When we try to pick out anything by itself we find that it is bound fast by a thousand invisible cords that cannot be broken, to everything in the universe.
(Muir, 1911, p. 211)

Across time and place, across spiritual traditions, and in scientific communities, there is a shared understanding of how inexplicitly everything is connected. Nothing stands alone. Yet we in the United States are surrounded by the mainstream myth that time and again tells us we are independent individuals who can "pull yourself up by your bootstraps," as though our lives did not depend on others and without asking the question of where the bootstraps came from or who made them. How do we learn to listen past the cultural myth to a deeper understanding of our interconnection? How do we learn to see and really know the intricate and extensive web of life?

In this chapter, I first review the intersections of transpersonal psychology, sustainability, and ecopsychology, and then offer one pedagogical tool—the Interconnectedness Maps Activity (IMA)—that can deepen our understanding of our interconnectedness. For many years, I have utilized the IMA in a graduate transpersonal counseling program to help students explore the *web of life*. This experiential activity explores and integrates important concepts from transpersonal psychology, ecopsychology, and sustainability.

Although these fields share some of the concepts that arise in the IMA, they often use different terminology, understand the concepts slightly differently, or emphasize different aspects. While transpersonal psychology focuses on spirituality and optimal health, and sustainability focuses on the long-term health of the whole earth, ecopsychology's primary interest is the human–nature relationship. I will discuss some of these overlapping concepts from the three fields that surface in the IMA, as well as some relevant research. After describing the IMA, I will discuss how students have been impacted by the activity in relation to the concepts and in their everyday lives. Also, two possible modifications to the IMA will be offered.

Without going into depth, I want to note that behind phrases like "nature," "the natural world," and "humans, in contrast to nature" there is a rich, ongoing conversation The ideas embedded in such phrases are complex and culturally informed. For example, in the dominant U.S. culture, there is a tendency to create a binary of "human" and "nature"—a binary that often "deurbanizes" nature (Peña, 2005). How we think about nature and race is historically intertwined (Outka, 2008). The notion of "wilderness," much cherished by environmental groups such as the Sierra Club and by John Muir, is not without cultural biases (Cronon, 1996). In ecopsychology literature, the phrase "rest of nature" or "non-human nature" is often used to acknowledge that humans are part of nature, while still being able to talk about a "human–nature relationship." For simplicity's sake, I shall use "nature" and "human" here.

Transpersonal Psychology

Transpersonal psychology has helped expand mainstream psychology beyond its traditional cognitive, behavioral, and affective domains; transpersonal psychology has highlighted the importance of spirituality as a critical aspect of the human experience. Although there is no single definition of transpersonal psychology, there are common core areas of study across the various definitions, including self-transcendence, service to others, individual and collective, transformative experiences, unitive experiences, states of consciousness, non-duality, and optimal health (Friedman & Hartelius, 2013). In the context of discussing the Interconnectedness Maps Activity, I will focus primarily on the following: healthy spiritual development as essential to optimal health, self-transcendence (moving beyond the individual, egoic self), and non-duality.

Spirituality deals with the meaning of life and an understanding of who we are at our essence beyond our ego identification. It fosters awareness of the sacredness of life, a sense of unity and being part of a greater whole, self-transcendence, awareness of a universal life force (sometimes called the Divine or God), and cultivation of compassion toward self and others (Standard, Sandhu, & Painter, 2000). Healthy spiritual development engages multiple ways of knowing, not just the cognitive or logical approaches commonly prioritized in modern Western society. As we engage with spirituality, we may develop what Vaughan (2002) calls our spiritual intelligence. It is important to note that this intelligence, rather than implying an escape from the physical world, calls us into deeper engagement with the everyday world and people around us, but from a different perspective.

Spiritual intelligence is concerned with the inner life of mind and spirit and *its relationship to being in the world*. Spiritual intelligence implies a capacity for a deep understanding of existential questions and insight into multiple levels of consciousness. Spiritual intelligence emerges as consciousness evolves into an ever-deepening awareness of matter, life, body, mind, soul, and spirit.

> Spiritual intelligence, then, is more than individual mental ability. It appears to connect the personal to the transpersonal and the self to spirit. Spiritual intelligence goes beyond conventional psychological development. In addition to self-awareness, *it implies awareness of our relationship to the transcendent, to each other, to the earth and all beings.* (Vaughan, 2002, p. 18, emphasis added)

One can see this engagement with the greater world take a newer form in recent decades, extending beyond social concerns to concern for the whole earth. An increasing number of spiritual leaders from many traditions speak out about environmental crises, and spiritual organizations, often ecumenical, focus on action for sustainability.

Two interrelated transpersonal concepts relevant to the Interconnectedness Maps Activity are self-transcendence and non-duality. Self-transcendence can be understood as the process of moving beyond a narrow sense of identity tied to the individual egoic self to an identity that includes others or a greater whole. This should not be confused with a denial of self out of self-hatred or poor ego development. Rather, it is an awareness of the transitory nature of the egoic self and of our being part of an ever-changing, bigger whole. Self-transcendence requires holding the seeming paradox that we are each an individual "self" that is, for example, fulfilling everyday tasks, and that this "individual self" is an illusion.

> But one has to be somebody before one can be nobody. The issue in personal development is not self *or* no-self. Both a sense of self and insight into the ultimate illusoriness of its apparent continuity and substantiality are necessary achievements. Sanity and complete psychological well-being include both, but in a

phase-appropriate developmental sequence. (Engler, 1993, p. 52, italics in the original)

Non-duality points to the concept of not being separate, of interrelatedness, of being part of a greater whole, and of both rather than either–or. Davis (2011) describes non-duality as encompassing self-transcendence, a deeper sense of self, and unitive states, resulting in a more vivid engagement in the world.

> In transcending a sense of separate self, one realizes a nondual relationship with Being. It is not awareness or consciousness which is transcended, only the sense of a self which is grounded in separation, narcissism, and defenses (the so-called ego in many spiritual traditions)… The world does not melt away, perception gains greater clarity and richness, and actions flow more harmoniously. At the same time, the self is no longer experienced as separate or ultimately autonomous. Instead, an expanded, more open, and more inclusive view of the world becomes foreground. (p. 140)

Non-duality should not be confused with lack of differentiation. There are individual parts with their individual expression and worth, and there is a greater whole. As Mathew Fox writes, "The realization that we and all other entities are aspects of a single unfolding reality—that 'life is fundamentally one'—does not mean that all multiplicity and diversity is reduced to homogeneous mush" (as cited in Davis, 2011, p. 140). In fact, the experience of non-duality can lead to a deep awareness of *and* appreciation for all the parts.

> Indeed, all spiritual traditions that have described nonduality have pointed out that the world becomes more real, beautiful, alive, and whole when one steps outside the confinement of duality. When the separate identity, with its filters and expectations based on personal needs, history, cognitive schemata, and the like, is not reified or identified with, the world

appears to us as *more* vivid and vital. (Davis, 2011, pp. 140–141)

One expression or outcome of the development of self-transcendence and of non-duality awareness is service to others. This development supports the ability to take a broader perspective, to not be self-focused, and to have concern for a larger whole. This development is also part of optimal health. From the lens of ecopsychology, it is important that the "greater whole" means going beyond the human sphere. In other words, optimal health includes moving beyond self- and human-centric perspectives to an earth-centric one and developing awareness of the non-duality of *all*, not just all humans.

Ecopsychology

Although ecopsychology draws from indigenous wisdom and builds on the ideas of various Western thinkers of the 1990s, it arose as a formal field of study in the 1990s. The first peer-reviewed journal, *Ecopsychology*, came out in 1999. The *European Journal of Ecopsychology*'s first volume was in 2010. The object of its study is the human–nature relationship, examining the different types of human–nature relationship, the consequences for both humans and the natural world that arise from the quality of that relationship, and practices for enhancing the relationship—optimizing its healthiness. A core premise is that the human psyche is deeply bonded with the earth and that humans' physical, psychological, and spiritual health is dependent on the quality of that bond. As Roszak (1995), who is credited with creating the term ecopsychology, writes:

> Ecopsychology suggests that we can read our transactions with the natural environment – the way we use or abuse the planet – as projections of unconscious needs and desires, in much the same way we can read dreams and hallucinations to learn about our deep motivations, fears, hatreds. In fact, our wishful, willful imprint upon the natural environment may reveal our collective

state of soul more tellingly than the dreams we wake from and shake off, knowing them to be unreal. (p. 5)

From the perspective of ecopsychology, attending to our deepest or fullest health requires us to expand beyond intrapsychic, interpersonal, or familial content (the traditional foci of mainstream psychotherapy) in our therapeutic work. Archetypal psychologist James Hillman was an early ecopsychology voice advocating for turning our attention both inward and outward in our search for our "deep self." This search "requires not merely a journey to the interior but a harmonizing with the environmental world... If we listen to Roszak, and to Freud and Jung, the most profoundly collective and unconscious self is the natural material world" (Hillman, 1995, p. xix). His call to turn outward as well as inward aligns with the discussion above about spirituality helping us to engage *with* the world, not turn away from it.

As previously mentioned, ecopsychology is the study of the human–nature relationship, but its focus on the fundamental interconnectedness of humans and the natural world distinguishes it from other fields of study on the human–nature relationship, such as environmental psychology, environmental justice, and conservation psychology (Davis & Canty, 2013). Two important concepts of the nature–human interconnectedness are the *ecological self* (the part of self-identity related to nature and the nature world) and the *ecological unconscious* (a parallel to Jung's *collective unconscious*). Ecopsychology is also distinguished by the importance it places on "phenomenological and sensorial connections with the natural world, and the integration of practices based on the healing potential of direct contact with the natural world (i.e., ecotherapy), *with practices oriented to environmental action and ecological, personal, and community sustainability*" (Davis & Canty, 2013, p. 597, italics added).

Ecopsychology emphasizes the importance of the human–nature relationship to the development of optimal health—not just human health but also the health of the planet. Non-duality, a notion of deep interconnectedness, underlies this link between humans and earth. As discussed further below, awareness of the non-duality, a felt experience of our interconnectedness, is linked with pro-environmental behavior and, thus, with sustainability. In this way, ecopsychology is one bridge between transpersonal psychology and sustainability. As Davis (2011) notes, "Ecopsychology is based on the recognition of a fundamental non-duality between humans and nature and on the insight that the failure to experience, value, and act from this non-duality creates suffering for both humans and the environment" (p. 140).

There are a number of terms used in ecopsychology that correlate with the transpersonal notion of self-transcendence. These terms capture the idea of an identity that extends beyond the individualistic self and specifically include the non-human, natural world: *ecological identity* (Thomashow, 1995), *environmental identity* (Clayton, 2003), *ecopsychological self* (St. John & MacDonald, 2007), and Deep Ecology's *ecological self*. Without minimizing any important distinctions between these terms, in the context of discussing the Interconnectedness Maps Activity, I want to focus on their shared emphasis: a self-concept that includes connection with the natural world. This identity is:

> one part of the way in which people form their self-concept: a sense of connection to some part of the nonhuman natural environment, based on history, emotional attachment, and/or similarity, that affects the ways in which we perceive and act towards the world; a belief that the environment is important to us and *an important part of who we are*. An environmental identity can be similar to another collective identity (such as a national or ethnic identity) in providing us with *a sense of connection, of being part of a larger whole*, and with a recognition of similarity between ourselves and others. (Clayton, 2003, pp. 45–46, emphasis added)

Davis (2011) delineates three ways, one might even say levels, of experiencing the human–nature relationship: nature as home and family (e.g. Mother Earth, Sister Fox), nature as self (e.g., ecological identity), and *both* nature and self as expressions of the "ground of Being." In distinguishing the second and third ways, he writes,

> Conceiving of nature as an expanded and more-inclusive self may be a necessary step in developing a more transpersonal view of the human–nature relationship. However, this broader self is not a final understanding. What is needed is an articulation of a transpersonal view that goes beyond the nature-as-self view without invalidating it. Such a transpersonal view recognizes that both human and nature are expressions of the same ground of Being. An understanding of unitive, nondual states, and practices for developing this understanding is the foundation for an effective integration of transpersonal. (p. 139)

Much of what I discuss below relates to Davis' (2011) first two ways of viewing nature, either as home/family or as self. The impact of the IMA does seem to help some students move toward the "nature as self" view. Because developing an embodied understanding of both nature and self as expressions of the ground of Being typically happens from extended practice, it is not surprising that this level of human–nature relationship does not arise in the IMA, which is a small, time-limited activity. However, if one views Davis' three ways as being on a spectrum, then any progression along the spectrum toward the transpersonal way would be useful for promoting optimal health.

The terms *interconnectedness* and *connected* are prevalent in the research literature on the human–nature relation. In some cases, authors have delineated different types of interconnection that bear similarity to Davis' distinctions. For example, Hoot and Friedman (2011) discuss nature as "intimately relevant to oneself" (similar to Davis' home or family), "part of oneself" (similar to Davis' nature as self), and "a sense of oneness with the universe across space and time" (similar to Davis' unitive, non-dual state; p. 90). While there are numerous psychometric scales related to the human–nature relationship—including the Inclusion of Nature in Self Scale (Schulz, 2001), the New Ecological Paradigm Scale (Dunlap, Van Liere, Mertig, &

Jones, 2000), and the Nature Inclusiveness Measure (St. John & MacDonald, 2007)—Mayer and Frantz's (2004) The Connectedness to Nature Scale (CNS) contains questions that seem to address Davis' (2011) different types; for example "I think of the natural world as a community to which I belong" (like Davis' home/family) and "I feel that all inhabitants of Earth, human, and non-human, share a common 'life force'" (like Davis' ground of Being).

Before turning attention to sustainability, I would like to note some of the threads weaving together ecopsychology and transpersonal psychology. The two fields are certainly good friends, if not siblings. The concepts of non-duality, self-transcendence, interconnectedness, and ecological identity are all based on the understanding that we are not separate, individual beings.

While some take a non-transpersonal approach to ecopsychology (Kahn & Hasbach 2012), Davis (2011) has been one of the strong transpersonal voices in ecopsychology, as can be seen from the discussion on non-duality and types of human–nature relationships, In the decades spanning the beginning of the 21st century, numerous authors planted more squarely in transpersonal psychology have been writing about the critical need for psychology to expand its attention to include the natural world and the importance such expansion can play in addressing the environmental crisis and sustainability. There has been recognition that transpersonal development has the potential to increase human concern for the natural world.

Grof and Grof (1993) point to aggression and "insatiable acquisitiveness" as roots of modern global problems and as obstacles to "a more appropriate division of resources among individuals, classes, and nations, as well as a reorientation toward ecological priorities essential for the continuation of life on this planet" (p. 250). Noting the role of spiritual development in issues of environmental crises and social justice, they observe that people going through spiritual emergence "tend to develop a new appreciation and reverence for all forms of life and a new understanding of the unity of all things, which often results in strong ecological concerns and greater tolerance toward other human beings" (p. 251).

Fox (1993, 1995) explicitly bridges the two fields of transpersonal psychology and ecopsychology in his writing about *transpersonal ecology*. Emphasizing the intrinsic value of the natural world, he writes, "The nonhuman world is...valuable *in and of itself* and not simply because of its obvious use-value to humans" (1993, p. 240). Recognizing this intrinsic value and being able to identify beyond the egoic self (self-transcendence) are integral to transpersonal development.

> We are all capable of identifying far more widely and deeply with the world around us than is commonly recognized, and that this form of self-development, self-unfolding, or "Self-realization," as Naess would say, leads us spontaneously to appreciate and defend the integrity of the world around us. I refer to this...as "transpersonal ecology" because it clearly points to the realization of a sense of self that extends beyond (or that is *trans*) any narrowly delimited biographical or egoic self of self. (pp. 240–241)

While recognizing transpersonal psychologies that have spoken out for the natural world, I would still say that one of ecopsychology's gifts to the field of transpersonal psychology is its loud and clear *explicit* inclusion of the non-human world in the goal of going beyond the personal. One could perhaps call this an explicitly trans-human approach. As deep ecologists Devall and Sessions (1993) maintain, spiritual growth may begin with expanding our identity beyond our "isolated and narrow competing egos" but state that we need to go beyond humans, that our "sense of self requires a further maturity and growth, an identification which goes beyond humanity to include the non-human world" (p. 243).

Sustainability

I am using the term sustainability to describe a way of living that meets present needs without compromising the needs of future generations, respects the integrity of the ecosystem, factors in the interconnections between economy, society, and the environment, and promotes equitable distribution.

Since the early part of this century, as climate change became more widely accepted and experienced as a reality, there has been a louder call for sustainability to be included in educational curricula across all disciplines, not just in disciplines that can provide technological solutions (see Bartels & Parker, 2011; Johnston, 2013; Jones, Selby, & Sterling, 2010; Petersen-Boring & Forbes, 2014; Schmuck & Schultz, 2002). In order to effectively implement a more sustainable culture, we must look not only to technology but also to psychology and spirituality; we must address the psychological and spiritual factors that hinder us from creating sustainability and that help motivate people to make necessary changes.

Ecologist Orr (1992), an early voice advocating for bringing the topic of sustainability into educational institutions, explicitly addressed the need for a spiritual component. "Is cleverness [technology, rational approaches] enough, or will we have to be good in both the moral and ecological sense of the word?" (p. 17). He answers the question of what goodness means with the often-quoted Land Ethic of Aldo Leopold, which states that a right land ethic considers what is good for the biotic whole (think earth-centric, as discussed above). In his call for a "theological perspective," Orr emphasizes the need for humans to acknowledge all the suffering in the world and see "that in the act of consumption and fantasy fulfillment we are scratching in the wrong place" (p. 18).

In discussing sustainability in education, Howard (2011) emphasizes the need to cultivate a relationship with nature in order to increase an attitude of care. Students must gain scientific knowledge *and* an emotional connection with the environment. As contemporary philosopher and activist Wendell Berry notes, "We know enough of our own history by now to be aware that people exploit what they have merely concluded to be of value, but they defend what they love" (as cited in Howard, 2011, p. 154). In other words, having a relationship that is based on knowing details about "the other" increases the likelihood that we will love and, consequently, defend the "other."

Increasingly, mainstream psychologists and counselors are speaking about the need to bridge issues of climate change (and sustainability) and their work, which traditionally has not focused on the human–nature relationship. There is an invitation not only to allow, but to even invite climate change and sustainability as appropriate topics in psychotherapy (see, for example, American Psychological Association, 2009; Cooper, 2011; Pipher, 2013). As researchers Mayer and Frantz (2004) note, "Because issues of environmental sustainability are in large part about human choices and actions, psychologists have much to contribute to understanding and formulating how such change might occur" (p. 503).

In 2009, the American Psychological Association released a 108-page report from its Task Force on the Interface Between Psychology and Global Climate Change, the goal of which was to study the psychological aspects of climate change and determine ways that psychologists can contribute to addressing the issues. Of the six questions addressed by the Task Force, three are about the psychological factors that help or hinder people to address climate change:

1. Section 1, *How do people understand the risks imposed by climate change?*, examines psychological and social factors that prohibit people from taking a more realistic view of climate change.
2. Section 2, *What are the human behavioral contributions to climate change and the psychological and contextual drivers of these contributions?*, focuses primarily on factors that drive consumerism. This is, interestingly, a mainstream version of issues raised by early ecopsychology authors such as Glendinning (1995), Durning (1995), and Kanner and Gomes

(1995).

3. Section 5 of the APA report, *Which psychological barriers limit climate change action?*, also parallels the work of early ecopsychologists. Answers to the question in Section 5 have been a significant part of the work of scholar and environmental activist Joanna Macy.

Based on research into psychological factors that contribute to environmental despair and grief, she has worked with others to develop methods to help people reduce their grief and despair and to increase their motivation and capacity for effective action (Macy, 1995, Macy & Brown, 1998; Macy & Johnstone, 2012).

Over the past 15–20 years, there has been a surge in research on the human–nature relationship, especially in the areas of psychological and health benefits for humans from having direct nature contact (see Chalquist, 2009; Davis, 2004; Frumkin, 2012; Selhub & Logan, 2012) and of the link between pro-environmental behavior and feeling connected with nature. I will discuss some of the second area as it relates to the Interconnectedness Maps Activity.

Koger and Winter (2010) describe three types of values, only two of which predict environmentally friendly behaviors on a broad scale. Not surprisingly, "Egoistic Values," which are driven by personal interest (e.g., "How does this impact me?"), was the value that did not correlate with pro-environmental behaviors. The other two values, "Altruistic Values" (e.g., "How will this impact other humans, current or future?") and "Biospheric Values" (e.g., "How will this impact the biosphere, including non-human beings, ecosystems, etc.?"), are based on interests beyond the personal. Although such values are not indicative of self-transcendence, they are relevant because they imply a perspective beyond the egoic self. Based on research done in North America, Latin America, Europe, India, and New Zealand, Koger and Winter (2010) note a cross-cultural consistency: "across cultures, biospheric concerns directly correlate with proenvironmental behavior; egoistic concerns correlate negatively" (p. 110).

12. A Thousand Invisible Threads

Building on social psychologists' work showing that feelings of relational closeness with another human lead to increased empathy and greater altruism or willingness to help that person, Mayer and Frantz (2004) studied the same phenomenon, replacing "another human" with "nature." Their Connectedness to Nature Scale (CNS) measures an individual's *affective and experiential connection* with nature. Based on results from five studies using the CNS, they found a connection between affective connection with nature and an orientation towards sustainability. Their results highlight issues related to connectedness, consumerism, and identity—a perspective beyond the personal and health.

> They [the results] support [Aldo] Leopold's contention that connectedness to nature leads to concern for nature, as the CNS has also been shown to relate to a biospheric value orientation, ecological behavior, anticonsumerism, perspective taking and identity as an environmentalist. Lastly, they suggest that personal well-being is linked to a sense of feeling connected to nature. (p. 512)

Noting that their findings are correlational, not causal, Mayer and Frantz (2004) posit the possibility of a bidirectional causality: The more connected we feel, the more we choose eco-friendly behavior, and the more we choose eco-friendly behaviors, the more connected we feel. Intuitively this makes sense, but more research is needed.

In research on interconnectedness and pro-environmental behavior, Hoot and Friedman (2011) looked specifically at self-expansiveness, described as "how individuals construct their self-concept through identifying with varying aspects of reality" (p. 90). Self-expansiveness becomes relevant to the issue of sustainability because "the process of identification relates to activating personal involvement by seeing some aspect of reality as intimately relevant to oneself and even a part of oneself, thus presumably worth protecting" (p. 90). Note the intersection with the concept of self-transcendence.

Hoot and Friedman (2011) examined three levels of interconnectedness: a broader or "generalized" transpersonal sense of connection, a sense of connection specifically with nature, and a connection with the future. The transpersonal level is "the broadest type of identification: an interconnectedness that radically transcends the conventional sense of the isolated individual—namely, a sense of oneness with the universe across space and time" (p. 90). This bears similarity to Davis' (2011) categories of human–nature relationships, although it is not clear to me whether their description would match more closely with his "self as nature" or "self and nature as expressions of the ground of Being." Interestingly, in their results, pro-environmental behaviors did not correlate with the transpersonal sense of interconnectedness but did with the other two types: a sense of interconnectedness with nature and a sense of interconnectedness with the future. Although their results were based on only 195 people, the results seem in line with the work of Schulz and Zelezny (1998). Using a measure of "self-transcendence," they found the strongest correlation to pro-environmental behavior to be with items measuring environment-oriented self-transcendence. These results were true in only four of the five countries studied: Mexico, Nicaragua, Spain, and the United States (almost 800 subjects combined), but not in Peru (160 subjects).

If these studies capture the relationship between types of interconnectedness (or self-transcendence) and we determine a causal relation, it would point to the usefulness of tools to increase people's sense of interconnection with nature. These findings seem compatible with biospheric values (Koger & Winter, 2010) and affective and experiential connection with nature (Mayer & Frantz, 2004).

Although transpersonal psychology has not traditionally focused on the human–nature relationship, it has an important contribution to make to sustainability. It offers understanding of and tools for developing aspects of spirituality that play a role in people making choices that support sustainability. It offers tools for increasing awareness of interconnection and non-duality, for fostering healthy self-transcendence. Part of healthy spiritual development includes cultivating gratitude and deep life satisfaction, both integral to skillful choices in consumption.

The Interconnectedness Maps Activity

In the discussion of Interconnectedness Maps Activity (IMA) and its relevance to transpersonal psychology, ecopsychology, and sustainability, it is helpful to consider the context of self-transcendence, non-duality, interconnectedness, and ecological identity. First, I will describe the activity and its impact for students in a master's-level counseling program. I will draw heavily from student papers because I believe students' own words provide the best sense of their experience. I will close with a few ideas for modifications to the IMA.

    The original intention in using the IMA was to help students deepen their felt sense of how their existence is intertwined with the greater world across both space and time. The activity is a modification of one described by Thomashow (1995) in which students work in groups to "pool their knowledge and use a magic marker to draw a diagram that traces various resource transformation steps" (p. 183). There are two steps to the activity as I use it. In the first step, much like Thomashow, I have students work in small groups in class to discuss and draw a "map" of an object's life. I entitle it "Exploring the Web of a Life Cycle," which primes students for the notion of interconnection. In order to have the object be of personal relevance to the students, I have had students in class map an object that they personally use on a regular basis. The instructions for the wilderness therapy students are: "Map out the life span of one of your jackets or backpacks. Include resources, places, people and other intertwined aspects of the web. On your map make a distinction between what you know and what is speculation/assumption." When I have used the exercise with other students I used different prompts, such as having art therapy students map items they use in art-making, such as paint or clay. For the exercise I supply student groups with drawing supplies and flip chart-zied paper. Because of the word "map," the diagrams are always very visual and creative, and the number of words on the maps is very limited. The activity has a sense of playfulness and allows students to take in the experience very differently than if they made predominantly word-based diagrams.

The second step of the activity is homework. The syllabus states that the assignment is to explore their "perspective on interrelatedness geographically and temporally." They are instructed to map the life cycle of three items from their daily life, with the maps showing "the full life of this item, including elements (people or things) that have contributed to it coming into existence and its projected future." Two of the items must be human-manipulated (e.g., jacket, car); one item should have minimal human manipulation (e.g., a plant in their yard, an animal). Students are encouraged to do research on some of their speculations and assumptions to gain more accurate information. The final part of the homework is writing a short paper discussing how their experience with maps impacted their perception of the world around them. Because they hand in the three maps with the paper, I also get the pleasure of seeing their creativity.

Thomashow (1995) states that our possessions can be tied to our identity, and can be symbols or "artifacts" of our self-concept. Having students select items from their daily life hopefully leads to them mapping items that have meaning for them. Usually at least one of the items they choose to map for the homework holds the kind of significance of an "artifact." The personal and emotional connection students have with their items helps deepen the activity, making it not just a cognitive activity but also affective.

The exercise combines cognitive and experiential learning. The students gain knowledge by their research into some of the assumptions in their maps and also are exposed to topics and the process of research that are often outside of traditional psychotherapy training. They are also involved in the hands-on process of making the maps. Use of art materials and engaging in visual creation increases the likelihood of students shifting their perspective not just cognitively, but also in an affective or felt sense. The maps are made up mostly of images with only a few words here and there. In addition, the activity happens in the context of contemplative education, so students are predisposed toward deeper self-reflection.

Based on student papers and classroom discussions, I have noticed the following categories of impact from the IMA: sense of being overwhelmed, sense of interconnection, increased knowledge, increased intimacy, an expanded identity, increased motivation, greater gratitude, and an increased sense of inner peace. Many of these categories relate directly to the themes discussed above on transpersonal psychology, ecopsychology, and sustainability education.

The majority of students comment on not having been aware of the extent to which any given object is dependent on people, resources, and processes across time and space before doing the IMA. Obviously, developing this kind of awareness is an important step in addressing sustainability; without this knowledge, one could easily see one's own choices as disconnected from, or even irrelevant to, sustainability. As students realized the extent of interconnectedness, it was not uncommon for them to initially experience negative emotions. One student wrote, "This exercise brought up some hopelessness in me, thinking about the consumer society we live in and how much we buy and simply 'trash it' when it is no longer of use to us." Another described the effect of seeing the amount of interconnection, commenting that the activity opened his eyes "to a world that is significantly affected and impacted by what I eat, what I drink, what I wear and how I navigate. And to be honest, the activity brought up a little strain, or stress, for me."

As noted above in discussing the American Psychology Association's Task Force (2009) report and the work of Joanna Macy, addressing difficult emotions in relation to environmental change (e.g. feeling overwhelmed, denial, grief, anger) is critical to helping people engage with building sustainability (Macy, 1995; Macy & Brown, 1998; Macy & Johnstone, 2012). Conscious and unconscious avoidance of these challenging emotions leads people to turn away from engaging with the tough environmental issues or, if they do get involved, experiencing burn-out. Because the IMA makes conscious the level of interconnection, it can evoke some of these difficult emotions. Thus, it is important to provide some context for processing these emotions, such as additional time and encouragement for writing or classroom discussion.

Some students expressed amazement, rather than feeling overwhelmed, at the extent of interconnection between their mapped objects and the rest of the world, even the whole universe. Regardless of what emotions arose, it was clear that for many students this was not just an intellectual exercise but also an activity that penetrated to more of a felt sense, a kind of "experiential connection" (Mayer & Frantz, 2004).

> The majority of the products I use every day come (at least partially) from some sort of petroleum derivative. Almost anything that is plastic comes from oil! As well as most synthetic clothing. This may have been obvious to the majority of people my age, but it was not to me….I am wearing oil products, eating and drinking out of oil products, typing up my papers for school on laptops made of oil products, calling people on a phone encased with oil products. A conservative estimate would be that at least half the things I own contain oil products…It was staggering to think about and I quickly ran out of space on my piece of paper to continue to draw in all of the branching products, people and processes that would have been necessary to make it a faithful diagram…I knew that when I bought products they had to come from somewhere, and that someone had to make them, and so on and so forth. However, I had never really sat and pondered how my living and purchasing habits affected the lives of so many other people, animals and environments.

This type of response was not limited to the human-made objects mapped by the students, even though the maps of human-made objects as a rule were more complex. One student focused on the amount of energy required for him to have a feather. This object carried significant emotional and spiritual value for this student because of his spiritual practices. Choosing objects that have significant personal meaning may increase the affective and felt-sense impact of the activity. The student described how in order for his raptor feather to make it all the way from a bird near the Northwest coast to Boulder, it took multitudes of people and resources. There was road building, which required digging, drilling, and exchange of money. All the people involved needed food and shelter, which meant farms, ranches, grocery stores, and other supplies. And these all involved sunlight, water, and trucks for transportation. The student's writing captured the seemingly endless cycles of people, work, and fossil fuels needed for us to exist as we do today, even for something as simple as having a feather.

Connectedness is not limited to the "whole earth," but can extend to the "whole universe." On a few occasions, students have reported finding themselves back at the Big Bang as they mapped natural objects. Their discussion of the experiences in class made it clear that this was not an intellectual experience but rather a felt sense about connection with the beginning of the universe.

Asking students to research some aspects of their maps where they were making assumptions added cognitive learning. They come away with more knowledge about the processes involved in their objects. This knowledge, combined with the experiential sense of connectedness, increases the likelihood that they will make more sustainable choices. Obviously creating sustainability is more complex than individuals changing their daily consumer habits. However, changing small habits can be a step toward larger action. Koger and Winter (2010) cite a number of studies indicating that people are more likely to increase their pro-environmental behaviors once they make a small change in that direction. One student described how mapping all three items helped her see her own impact on the earth more clearly. Researching a tea company connected to the tea mug she mapped gave her a deeper understanding of the role of both businesses and individuals in creating sustainability. Her research (cognitive learning) served as a spark to examining her own habits of consumption.

In some cases, the intimacy with the world that developed through the mapping resulted in less objectification of the world, not seeing the world so much as an "it" revolving around the "I."

> I have never thought much about the things around me: where they come from, what goes into them, where they will end up. For the most part I take them for granted and barely notice them unless they don't work. It is a very objective view of the world, meaning I treat things as objects for my use, completely separate from me. Tracing the map of where four things come from (including the jacket from class) and where they are going across time has given me a completely different connection to things and people in my world…
>
> This [not having much detailed understanding of the elements of an object] generality is a result and a cause of my taking things for granted…I realized during this project that through a great knowing, a greater sense of interrelatedness can emerge…
>
> So the plastic in my refrigerator, and all the other things I use that contain plastic, directly connects me with the matter from millions of years ago. The process of turning the crude oil into plastic also has a number of steps in the process, each of which have humans involved. So the plastic connects me to hundreds of people who have worked to create it. (student paper)

The IMA increased students' awareness of the future. A common response in discussions after the first in-class mapping has been that students had never really thought much about where their jacket or backpack would go once they were done with it. This new future awareness is important in light of the correlation found by Hoot and Friedman's (2011) connection between the future and pro-environmental behavior. It also brings to mind the Seventh Generation Principle, originally from Iroquois philosophy as expressed in "The Great Law of Iroquois Confederacy" and frequently quoted in environmental materials. This principle states that "decisions we make today should result in a sustainable world seven generations into the future" (Joseph, 2012). For students, this future focus was not limited to the future of the object being mapped. In the words of one student whose paper described mapping her dog, "Because she was a living being like I am, doing her map helped me to see my connections and interrelatedness to my ancestors, to the earth that helps to feed me, *to the next generations that come from me*" (emphasis added).

Reading student papers over the years, I have been struck by the spiritual themes that emerge. In some cases, these themes are expressed more in *how* students write about their experiences. In the excerpt of a paper below, a student has come to see a pen as connected to the same universe as a walnut, perhaps similar to the students' experience with the Big Bang discussed above. This shift is especially significant because, like many students in the wilderness therapy concentration, this student tended to elevate natural objects above human-made ones, attributing greater inherent worth to them.

> The first thing that jumps out at me after diagramming the systems surrounding the creation and lifespans of two manmade and one natural objects is the stupefying interconnectedness of each object to endless other objects and events—past, present, and future. For one thing to exist, a perhaps infinite number of other things has to exist to bring it into being. *Something as simple a ballpoint pen, for example, is just as dependent upon the lives of stars as is a walnut.* (emphasis added)

Other spiritual themes were more explicit. In the excerpt of a paper below, the student draws on the Buddhist notions of impermanence and interdependent co-arising (i.e., nothing exists independent of other things).

> I live between a world of concepts and a world of sensations. This exercise helps to combine both in a fashion that brings me

into a more intimate communion with the ecosystem of which all things are a part. All things are interdependent and have a beginning and an end.

Another spiritual theme is the mystery of life, along with the recognition that we as humans cannot fully grasp all of reality. We see the world through our cultural and personal lenses, leading us to not appreciate the inherent worth and depth of each and every entity, whether animate or inanimate. Again, keep in mind that wilderness therapy students tend to place greater value on "natural" objects.

> As I was able to contemplate this activity over the last few days, I appreciate both the stories we create in order to find meaning as well as the hidden factors that are beyond my human mind. Knowing that so much time and energy throughout the world has gone into making things helps me connect with items that sometimes do not resemble the natural world at all — they hold a long trail of people, places, and the cultural narratives that follow. Whether it is a rune, a spoon, or an apple tree, all hold the mystery about the origin of their life, as everything is derived from the Earth. (student paper)

The Interconnectedness Map Activity has the potential to help people expand their sense of identity beyond the personal. The grounding of the transpersonal and ecopsychological concepts of interconnectedness, self-transcendence, ecological identity, and non-duality in immediate experience, linked with tangible objects from everyday life, may be a step in facilitating such integration.

> This project had a big impact on me. I remember when we did a transpersonal assessment in class last year where we were asked our level of agreement with a number of statements about how we defined who we are. I tended to agree with statements about me being an individual who was defined mostly by my current behavior, beliefs and relationships. I identified least with

being defined by past or future relationships or with things outside myself. This exercise really shifted my perspective on this. I feel much more that "I" am defined and a part of so much more than just me, not just in the present, but in the past and the future as well. (student paper)

Part of spiritual and psychological maturity is the ability to hold complexity and even paradoxes. Can we move beyond an "either/or" perspective to see the "both/and"? Transpersonal psychology is explicit about the need to go beyond dividing the world into "good" and "bad," beyond our personal likes and dislikes, in order to experience inner peace (Maslow, 1969; Vaughan, 2002; Daniels, 2005). The 13th century Sufi mystic Rumi captures it succinctly in his poem:

Out beyond ideas of wrongdoing and rightdoing,
there is a field. I'll meet you there.
When the soul lies down in that grass,
the world is too full to talk about.
 Ideas, language, even the phrase *each other*
doesn't make any sense.
         (translation by Moyne & Barks, 1999, p. 8)

In questioning her perception of "good and bad," one student was able to experience more gratitude for the simple things in life. Her non-judgmental perspective and gratitude became intertwined with motivation for pro-environmental behavior.

Holding the rune in my hand again in this moment, I perceive that it is smooth, oval, cream-colored, and comforting to touch. Somehow it has been assigned sacred/spiritual meaning in my life, while another item might never be noticed, or even considered "bad," even though both items come from materials from the Earth. Logically, I cannot proclaim that anything is "better-than," simply because everything is interconnected …

However, I realize something within myself— the more I become aware of the interconnectedness of all things throughout place and time, the less I want to engage in conspicuous consumption within myself, because I can fully appreciate all that went into the simplest item in my life, and perhaps that is true for others. This felt-sense of gratitude for the mundane helps me see beyond right versus wrong. (student paper)

Using the IMA as described above has the potential to help people understand more fully how much the world is interconnected, across time and place, and to help them expand their sense of themselves, their identity. In addition, they can develop more intimacy with the world around them both through cognitive learning and experiential engagement. They may challenge some of their dualistic thinking and deepen their capacity for appreciation and gratitude. All of these can contribute to motivation for making choices in support of sustainability.

Extending the IMA
Before ending, I would like to propose two ways to enhance the effectiveness of the Interconnectedness Maps Activity (IMA). The first is related to humans involved in the mapping and the other to "sustainable happiness" (O'Brien, 2011). Over the many years of using the IMA, I have noticed that, in general, the maps do not include as many images of the humans involved as of the non-human elements such as buildings, vehicles, boats, and dinosaurs. (Most human-manipulated items depicted contain plastic, which comes from petroleum, which relates to the time of the dinosaurs.) It is not until writing the papers that students seem to focus much on people involved in the life cycle. This may be a reflection of the level of emotional connection they initially feel with the object being mapped. The one striking exception to the tendency to have fewer or more stylized people in the map was when the object being mapped was a jacket made in the factory owned by the student's father. For her, the factory and the people involved were not an abstraction. This seems

similar to Thomashow's (1995) experience with the activity: "Typically the groups prepare idealized and symbolic charts…in a way they are mini-creation myths, imaginative stories based on limited information…They can fill in broad outlines as well, but the information is nonspecific" (p. 183). I suspect that the student working on an item from her father's factory felt more connected to the jacket because of her emotional ties to specific humans, and that this led her to imagine more real-life humans in mapping.

Ozawa-de Silva (2010), using a similar type of interconnectedness activity in his teaching of Cognitive-Based Compassion Training with school children, describes the children focusing quite a bit on people. He wore a sweater he had inherited from his father and shared with the children the emotional connection between his father and the sweater. In being asked to name what was linked to the sweater, the children noted not only Ozawa-de Silva's father, but also the person who knitted the sweater, the person who sheared the sheep for the wool, the person who cooked meals for the farmer who raised the sheep, etc. The children's connections were not symbolical or idealized, but populated by people with real lives.

It may be that children, compared to adults, focus more on other humans than on machines and processes. Or it may be that Ozawa-de Silva's (2010) presentation prompted the children to focus on people. Keeping in mind the findings of Hoot and Friedman (2011) that a sense of interconnectedness with "the specific" showed greater correlation with pro-environmental behavior than generalized interconnectedness, and Howard's (2011) focus on intimacy and care (affective components), it might be beneficial to bring in more of the human element to the life-cycle maps. In order to help flesh out the people in the maps, one might include a contemplation on individuals in the maps—even if the people contemplated are not directly known to the students. For example, one might do a guided visualization asking students to imagine some people from their map going through their daily lives, growing up from infancy, having disappointments and hopes for themselves and their families, etc., just as the students themselves experience. The point would not be to minimize differences between themselves and, say, a factory worker in Southeast Asia, but to help build more affective connection through seeing the shared humanity.

As people begin to grasp the extent of interconnectedness, they can think that they must choose between meeting their needs and happiness, on the one hand, and sustainability, on the other. Given that advertising often makes a false link between material possessions and happiness, helping people discover what brings them genuine, lasting happiness can be a piece of the sustainability puzzle. It would, perhaps, be useful to couple the IMA with some activities from O'Brien's (2012) work on sustainable happiness. "Happiness that contributes to individual, community and/or global wellbeing and does not exploit other people, the environment, or future generations" (para. 1). In her teacher education courses, students explore their personal psychology in relation to sustainability and personal satisfaction. O'Brien (2011) links sustainable happiness and sustainable behavior:

> Our natural desire for happiness can become the entry point for discovering that our well-being is inextricably linked to the well-being of others and the natural environment. It can also dispel a common misconception that living sustainably will lower our quality of life. (p. 44)

Although the link between individual satisfaction (happiness) and awareness of interconnection showed up in some student papers in my courses, providing a structure for students to explore their personal sustainable happiness within the IMA might help more students make these links.

Conclusion

As we have seen through the words of the students, the Interconnectedness Maps Activity (IMA) has the potential to serve students in many ways. The experiential and reflective nature of the activity touches students on cognitive, affective, and spiritual levels. The IMA nudges them toward acknowledging and processing some of the difficult emotions that inhibit actions in support of sustainability. Through the activity, students develop a felt sense of the ways they are infinitely connected to the rest of the world across time and place. Knowing this interconnectedness, both cognitively and experientially, helps them grasp some concepts central to transpersonal psychology and ecopsychology: ecological identity, self-transcendence, non-duality, and interconnectedness. The IMA also can support sustainability education by helping students make stronger links between their choices and the rest of the world and increasing their sense of connection with the natural world, which research suggests is correlated with pro-environmental behaviors.

Obviously the IMA is only a small step in a much larger process. But it can be one small thread linking ecopsychology, sustainability, and transpersonal psychology and joins others in weaving a larger fabric of spirituality and sustainability. As exemplified by the experience of one student who tracked the past and future of the moon, doing the IMA highlighted the impermanence of life and the fact that it has taken many disasters on earth in order for humans to exist. The realization of impermanence initially triggered fear of annihilation, but then evolved into resignation, gratitude, and even peace. The student was left with an appreciation of life's preciousness and beauty and a sense of the importance of preserving and enjoying it as long as possible.

References

American Psychological Association (2009). *Psychology & global climate change: Addressing a multifaceted phenomenon and set of challenges.* A report of the American Psychological Association Task Force on the interface between psychology and global climate change. Retrieved from http://www.apa.org/science/about/publications/climate-change-booklet.pdf

Bartels, K. A., & Parker, K. A. (Eds.). (2011). *Teaching sustainability/teaching sustainably*. Sterling, VA: Stylus Publishing.

Caplan, M., Hartelius, G., & Rardin, M. A. (2003). Contemporary viewpoints on transpersonal psychology. *The Journal of Transpersonal Psychology, 35*(2), 143–162.

Carson, R. (2002). *Silent Spring*. New York, NY: Houghton Mifflin Harcourt.

Chalquist, C. (2009). Ecotherapy research and a psychology of homecoming. In L. Buzzell & C. Chalquist (Eds.), *Ecotherapy: Healing with nature in mind* (pp. 69–82). Berkeley, CA: Counterpoint Press.

Clayton, S. (2003). Environmental identity. In S. Clayton and S. Opotow (Eds.), *Identity and the natural environment: The psychological significance of nature* (pp.45–65). Cambridge, MA: The MIT Press.

Cooper, G. (2011). Therapists and climate change. *Clinician's Digest.* Retrieved from https://www.psychotherapynetworker.org/magazine/recentissues/2011-septoct/item/1368-clinicians-digest?tmpl=component&print=1

Cronon, W. (1996). The trouble with wilderness; Or, getting back to the wrong nature. In W. Cronon (Ed.), *Uncommon ground: Rethinking the human place in nature* (pp. 69–90). New York, NY: W.W. Norton & Company.

Daniels, M. (2005). *Shadow, self, spirit: Essays in transpersonal psychology.* Exeter: Imprint Academic.

Davis, J. V. (2004). Psychological benefits of nature experiences: An outline of research and theory with special reference to transpersonal psychology. Retrieved from http://ival.nl/wordpress/wp-content/uploads/PsychBenefitsofNature.pdf

Davis, J. V. (2011). Ecopsychology, transpersonal psychology, and nonduality. *International Journal of Transpersonal Studies, 30*(1–2), 137–147.

Davis, J. V., & Canty, J. M. (2013). Ecopsychology and transpersonal psychology. In L. Harris & G. Hartelius (Eds.), *The Wiley-Blackwell handbook of transpersonal psychology* (pp. 597–611). West Sussex, UK: John Wiley & Sons.

Devall, B., & Sessions, G. (1993). Deep ecology: Living as if nature mattered. In R. Walsh & F. Vaughan (Eds.), *Paths beyond ego: The transpersonal vision* (pp. 242–245). Los Angeles, CA: Jeremy P. Tarcher, Inc.

Dunlap, R. E., Van Liere, K. D., Mertig, A. G., & Jones, R. E. (2000). Measuring endorsement of the New Ecological Paradigm: A revised NEP scale. *Journal of Social Issues, 56*, 425–442.

Durning, A. T. (1995). Are we happy yet? In T. Roszak, M. Gomes, & A. Kanner (Eds.), *Ecopsychology: Restoring the earth, healing the mind* (pp. 68–76). San Francisco, CA: Sierra Club Books.

Engler, J. H. (1993). Becoming somebody and nobody: Psychoanalysis and Buddhism. In R. Walsh and F. Vaughan (Eds.), *Paths beyond ego: The transpersonal vision* (pp. 118–121). Los Angeles, CA: Jeremy P. Tarcher.

Fox, W. (1993). Transpersonal ecology. In R. Walsh & F. Vaughan (Eds.), *Paths beyond ego: The transpersonal vision* (pp. 240–241). Los Angeles, CA: Jeremy P. Tarcher.

Fox, W. (1995). *Toward a transpersonal ecology: Developing new foundations for environmentalism.* Albany, NY: State University of New York Press.

Friedman, H., & Hartelius, G. (Eds.). (2013). *The Wiley-Blackwell Handbook of Transpersonal Psychology.* West Sussex, UK: John Wiley & Sons.

Frumkin, H. (2012). Building the science base: Ecopsychology meets clinical epidemiology. In P. H. Kahn & P. H. Hasbach (Eds.), *Ecopsychology: Science, totems, and the technological species* (pp. 1142–172). Cambridge, MA: MIT Press.

Glendinning, C. (1995). Technology, trauma, and the wild. In T. Roszak, M. Gomes, & A. Kanner (Eds.), *Ecopsychology: Restoring the earth, healing the mind* (pp. 41–54). San Francisco, CA: Sierra Club Books.

Grof, S., & Grof, C. (1993*). Transpersonal experience and the global crisis.* In R. Walsh & F. Vaughan (Eds.), *Paths beyond ego: The transpersonal vision* (pp. 251–252). Los Angeles, CA: Jeremy P. Tarcher.

Hastings, A. (1999). Transpersonal psychology: The fourth force. In D. Moss (Ed.), *Humanistic and transpersonal psychology: A historical and biographical sourcebook* (pp. 192–208). Westport, CT: Greenwood Press/Greenwood Publishing Group.

Hillman, J. (1995). A psyche the size of the earth: A psychological foreword. In T. Roszak, M. Gomes, & A. Kanner (Eds.), *Ecopsychology: Restoring the earth, healing the mind* (pp. xvii–xxiii). San Francisco, CA: Sierra Club Books.

Hoot, R. E., & Friedman, H. (2011). Connectedness and environmental behavior: Sense of interconnectedness and pro-environmental behavior. *International Journal of Transpersonal Studies 30*(1–2), 89–10.

Howard, P. (2011). Who will teach the teachers? Reorienting teacher education for the values of sustainability. In K. A. Bartels and K. A. Parker, (Eds.). *Teaching sustainability/teaching sustainably* (pp. 149–157). Sterling, VA: Stylus Publishing.

Johnston, L. F. (Ed.) (2013). *Higher education for sustainability: Cases, challenges, and opportunities from across the curriculum*. New York, NY: Routledge.

Jones, P., Selby, D., & Sterling, S. (Eds.) (2010). *Sustainability education: Perspectives and practice across higher education*. New York, NY: Earthscan.

Joseph, B. (2012, May 29). What is the seventh generation principle? [Web log post]. Retrieved from http://www.ictinc.ca/blog/seventh-generation-principle.

Kahn, P. H., & Hasbach, P. H. (2012). Introduction to ecopsychology: Science, totems, and the technological species. In P. H. Kahn & P. H. Hasbach (Eds.), *Ecopsychology: Science, totems, and the technological species* (pp. 1–21). Cambridge, MA: MIT Press.

Kanner, A. D., & Gomes, M. E. (1995). The all-consuming self. In T. Roszak, M. Gomes, & A. Kanner (Eds.), *Ecopsychology: Restoring the earth, healing the mind* (pp. 77–91). San Francisco, CA: Sierra Club Books.

Koger, S., & Winter, D. (2010). *The psychology of environmental problems* (3rd ed). New York, NY: Psychology Press.

Macy, J. (1995). Working through environmental despair. In T. Roszak, M. Gomes, & A. Kanner (Eds.). *Ecopsychology: Restoring the earth, healing the mind* (pp. 240–259). San Francisco, CA: Sierra Club Books.

Macy, J., & Brown, M. Y. (1998). *Coming back to life: Practices to reconnect our lives, our world*. Gabriola Island, BC: New Society Publishers.

Macy, J., & Johnstone, C. (2012). *Active hope: How to face the mess we're in without going crazy*. Novato, CA: New World Library.

Maslow, A. H. (1969). The various meanings of transcendence. *Journal of Transpersonal Psychology, 1*, 56–66.

Mayer, S., & Frantz, C. M. (2004). The connectedness to nature scale: A measure of individuals' feeling in community with nature. *Journal of Environmental Psychology 24*, 503–515.

Moyne, J., & Barks, C. (Trans.). (1999). *Open secret: Versions of Rumi*. Boston, MA: Shambhala Publications.

Muir, J. (1911). *My first summer in the Sierra*. Boston, MA: Houghton, Mifflin.

O'Brien, C. (2011). Sustainable happiness and education: Educating teachers and students in the 21st century. In K. A. Bartels & K. A. Parker, (Eds.), *Teaching sustainability/teaching sustainably* (pp. 41–52). Sterling, VA: Stylus Publishing.

O'Brien, C. (2012). Sustainable happiness. Retrieved from http://sustainablehappiness.ca

Orr, D. W. (1992). *Ecological literacy: Education and the transition to a postmodern world*. Albany, NY: State University of New York Press.

Outka, P. (2008). *Race and nature from transcendentalism to the Harlem renaissance*. New York, NY: Palgrave Macmillan.

Ozawa-de Silva, B. (2010). Educating the heart and mind: Teaching cognitive-based compassion training to children. Presented at Emory University, The Visit of His Holiness the XIV Dalai Lama. Retrieved from https://www.youtube.com/watch?v=tVes5vao2a8

Peña, D. G. (2005). *Mexican Americans and the environment: Tierra y vida*. Tucson, AZ: University of Arizona Press.

Petersen-Boring, W., & Forbes, W. (Eds.), (2014). *Teaching sustainability: Perspectives from the humanities and social sciences*. Nacogdoches, TX: Stephen F. Austin University Press.

Pipher, M. (2013). *The Green Boat: Reviving ourselves in our capsized culture*. New York, NY: Riverhead Books.

Roszak, T. (1992). *The voice of the earth*. New York, NY: Simon & Schuster.

Roszak, T. (1995). Where psyche meets Gaia. In T. Roszak, M. Gomes, & A. Kanner (Eds.). *Ecopsychology: Restoring the earth, healing the mind* (pp. 1–20). San Francisco, CA: Sierra Club Books.

Roszak, T., Gomes, M., & Kanner, A. (Eds.). (1995). *Ecopsychology: Restoring the earth, healing the mind*. San Francisco, CA: Sierra Club Books.

Schmuck, P., & Schultz, W. P. (Eds.). (2002). *Psychology of sustainable development*. New York, NY: Springer.

Schultz, P. W. (2001). Assessing the structure of environmental concern: Concern for self, other people, and the biosphere. *Journal of Environmental Psychology, 21*, 327–339.

Schultz, P. W., & Zelezny, L. C. (1998). Values and proenvironmental behavior: A five-country survey. *Journal of Cross-Cultural Psychology, 29*(4), 540–558.

Selhub, E. M., & Logan, A. C. (2012). *Your brain on nature: The science of nature's influence on your health, happiness, and vitality*. Mississauga, Ontario, Canada: John Wiley & Sons Canada.

St. John, D., & MacDonald, D. A. (2007). Development and initial validation of a measure of ecopsychological self. *The Journal of Transpersonal Psychology, 39*, 48–67.

Standard, R. P., Sandhu, D. S., & Painter, L. C. (2000). Assessment of spirituality in counseling. *Journal of Counseling & Development, 78*, 204–209.

Stibbe, A. (2015). *Ecolinguistics: Language, ecology and the stories we live by*. New York, NY: Routledge.

Thomashow, M. (1995). *Ecological identity: Becoming a reflective environmentalist*. Cambridge, MA: The MIT Press.

Vaughan, F. (2002). What is spiritual intelligence? *Journal of Humanistic Psychology, 42*, 16–33.

Chapter 13
Awaking to Presence: The Potential of Ritual in Transpersonal Education

John Davis

It is time for class to begin. This is a graduate psychology course I teach at Naropa University, but it could be a course at any college or university level. I straighten a bit in my chair and wait for students to come to a quiet place. We may sit like this for just a few seconds or for a few minutes. In time, someone—not always me—starts a simple bow, and everyone follows suit. Some simply nod their heads, while others bow deeply in their seats. As we return upright, a collective exhale signals a more settled feeling for having come together in this way for a moment of quiet presence.

Brought to Naropa University by its founder, Chogyam Trungpa Rinpoche, the practice of a bow has become infused into Naropa's educational culture. It is used in meditation practice classes, process classes in psychology, studio classes in the arts, and theory classes like research methods. One-on-one meetings, committee meetings, and even large gatherings like convocations and graduation ceremonies generally start and end with a bow. These bows are non-religious, simple, and human ways of gathering the group and coming into a more mindful and present-centered state. They reinforce a tone of mutual respect and openness and evoke a deeper foundation for our work together.

In my classes, I describe the bow at the start of the semester and invite the class to begin and end our meetings this way. This practice is presented as essentially pan-cultural, rather than belonging to any particular religious or cultural tradition. Most of my recent classes are online, and it seems especially important that we create such a ritual, simple as it is, to bring a more embodied and heartful presence to complement the tendencies of the online medium to isolate the intellect. I emphasize that this is an invitation, not a requirement, and that if students feel uncomfortable with this practice, they are welcome not to do it. Based on Trungpa Rinpoche's instructions for this practice, I describe the bow at the beginning and end of our classes in three stages:

> The first stage is coming present in the moment. Whether you are sitting or standing, come a bit straighter in your posture—not hard or stiff—a strong back and a soft front, simply a bit more dignified and present. Notice your breath and your senses for just a moment, not to analyze your experience but simply to let yourself be here as you are in this moment.
>
> The second stage invites your heart to soften. Notice what you feel and sense. It may be fear, sadness, excitement, kindness, delight, contentment, confusion, or something else entirely. You don't need words for your feelings here, simply a willingness to contact your own heart. Allow a gentleness into your awareness.
>
> The third stage is the bow itself. Let this be a gesture of respect. I bow to recognize and honor your wisdom, your challenges, and your ways of learning and growing. I also bow to my own ways of learning and growing. The bow is a gesture of generosity and humility in the highest sense. After bowing, come back upright, facing forward and willing to be present to the next moment. Though we can never know what it will bring, we remind ourselves that we can approach the next moment with integrity, trust, courage, and openness. Sit upright again for a moment, ready and willing to be alive to this moment.
>
> Find your own bow each time; it will never be the same twice. Experiment with this as a practice in other areas of your life. If you are working online, bow as you sit down in front of

your computer. Find a place where you can both respect this practice and play with it; find the heart of the bow for yourself.

This practice of bowing is one example of a simple, non-religious ritual that can both exemplify and support transpersonal education. In this chapter, I present a view of ritual appropriate to a variety of higher education settings and discuss four functions of ritual relevant to transpersonal education. Finally, I offer three other examples of simple rituals I have used in my undergraduate and graduate transpersonal psychology courses.

A View of Ritual

For people in many cultures, ritual is a central means of discovering and developing intrapersonal, interpersonal, and transpersonal connections (Eulert, 2013). It provides a means of communicating with one's unconscious, each other, and the deepest dimensions of meaning and totality. Ritual is inclusive, integrating mind and body, individual and collective, and personal and transpersonal (LaChapelle, 1978). Because of its potential to evoke spiritual experiences, ritual is often associated with religious practices, but it need not be. Particularly in secular educational settings, it is important to honor the potential of ritual without connecting it to specific belief systems or religious frameworks.

Ritual has the power to open us to deeper psychological and spiritual dimensions and the realms of archetypes and the transpersonal. Students may connect their ritual experiences with their own meaning systems, but this is not necessary. Most students find relief in connecting with deep, even profound, experiences without having to fit them into a particular belief framework. Presenting simple rituals in a transpersonal context makes them more accessible to students regardless of their religious or spiritual orientations. Undoubtedly, a simple, private bow to a sunrise or a simple, shared bow or handshake between people predated any particular religious or spiritual belief system, yet these meaning-laden acts contain the essence of the transpersonal. Transpersonal psychology invites this approach in the classroom.

Occasionally, a student will associate some aspect of a ritual with particular religious or spiritual traditions. For example, in the United States, the use of objects from nature, such as feathers, may be associated with Native American Indian ritual practices. I welcome such discussions of cultural appropriation when they arise, even though they are often difficult, even painful (Grimes, 2000). Multiculturalism, including its shadow of cultural appropriation, is highly relevant to transpersonal psychology, and so these questions provide important teaching opportunities (Davis, 2003). I feel it is important to respect others' traditions, and so I avoid symbols that might raise associations with specific traditions. On the other hand, ritual is embedded deeply in us, and as humans we have a right, even an obligation, to practice ritual. This is an important and complex question, and although it is beyond the scope of this chapter, I encourage thoughtful, open consideration of it.

Rituals in the classroom can support the goals of transpersonal psychology: full and optimal development of the learner, quieting the automaticity of the mind created by habit and conditioning, livelier and more curious perception, willingness to encounter oneself and the world with openness, and encouragement of surprise, delight, transcendence, transformation, and authentic encounter with others and the world (Friedman & Hartelius, 2013). Ritual can draw learners out of old ways of being into greater wakefulness, compassion, self-inquiry, embodiment, and motivation for service. Both ritual and transpersonal education also value deep listening and support for non-reactive presence. Both call for students to tolerate their own reactions and to inquire into the nature and sources of those reactions without either acting them out or suppressing them. Both invite students to listen both to their own responses and to each other without judgment. In these ways, transpersonal education and ritual cultivate an openness to learning without becoming either defensive or acquiescent. As with transpersonal education in general, ritual encourages students to go beyond their familiar conceptual categories, habitual responses, and rigid representations of self, others, and the world, giving it the potential to change them in fundamental and profound ways.

13. Awakening to Presence

I admit I am of two minds about ritual. In many ways, we are a culture cut off from ritual. Many of the rituals that supported and guided our ancestors and gave focus, rhythm, and meaning to the lives of individuals, families, and communities have lost their meaning; we go through the motions of what were once potent sources of inspiration and support. Meaningful ritual has been replaced by social obligation and empty gesture—ritualistic behaviors, we might say. At the same time, we live in a sea of ritual, often without recognizing it. From the small, almost invisible rituals of daily life to the once-in-a-lifetime complex ceremonies around birth and death, seasonal rituals, rituals of healing, and more, ritual is a powerful element in our lives (Krippner, 2013). Birthday celebrations, family holiday gatherings, sports events, rock concerts, regular walks home, sitting on the porch after dinner, Saturday morning pancakes with bluegrass music playing on the radio (one of my personal favorites)—all take on a significance that indicates the potential of ritual. These rituals all have the potential of revealing the bonds between the mundane and the sacred, the ordinary and the extraordinary, the personal and the transpersonal.

It is more accurate to say that we are cut off from the depth and potential of ritual. Most of our rituals have become mindlessly automatic. While the automaticity of rituals reduces anxiety and information overload and gives us an illusion of control and the safety of the familiar, we are left spiritually hungry. Conscious ritual, as with other transpersonal practices, does just the opposite. Rather than putting us to sleep, it wakes us up. Instead of a numbing familiarity, authentic ritual takes us into unknown territory. Ritual has the potential to deaden or enliven. Rather than a defensive dullness, intentional ritual can provide the safety to step out of defensive structures and into a spontaneous, unrehearsed relationship with the present moment. In a word, the key to whether ritual is authentic or not is whether it opens us to the present moment or closes us down.

Functions of Ritual in the Classroom

Rituals have four functions, each of which is relevant to transpersonal education: They are signs, they reinforce social reality, they provide safety, and they create (or reveal) significance. As signs, rituals identify a setting or context and give direction. A ritual of lighting a candle and sitting down on a meditation cushion signifies the time for mindfulness rather than problem solving or planning. The bows at the beginning and end of a class are markers, and between those markers is a specific time with its own intention and depth, a liminal time outside of normal routines and preoccupations.

Rituals can reinforce shared realities. A bow at the beginning of class reminds us that we have agreed to certain ground rules of shared inquiry such as openness to new ways of seeing things and a willingness to listen to one another, and they bring us together with a common purpose. With longer and more complex rituals, this shared reality can deepen into a sense of nonduality with others. Of course, such a connection can extend to the natural world as well as the human world (Davis, 2011, 2013). A collection of individuals becomes a group organism, and we realize our oneness with all of creation. At the same time, we recognize the power of ritual to reinforce *any* social reality, including those that are harmful. History continues to provide us with examples of rituals used in the service of social manipulation and cults.

Ritual also creates a safe space or sanctuary in which to test new ideas and explore difficult emotions. For example, rituals for grieving are common in many cultures. One of the functions of these rituals is providing permission and support for expressing emotions that are typically not expressed so fully in everyday life. In a classroom, a ritual atmosphere helps those who are reluctant to share their feelings and insights to speak up, while those who chatter in order to maintain an image or distract themselves are more willing to honor openness and receptivity. Equally important for transpersonal education are the ways in which ritual cultivates a sanctuary in which new ideas and roles can be tested. Transpersonal education seeks to challenge our old ideas and ways of thinking about ourselves, others, and the world. A "beginner's mind" (Suzuki, 1970/2011) is essential to transpersonal education. This opens the possibilities for transformation in conceptual frameworks and for creativity. This is not to say that ritual takes the risk out of the classroom. Rather, the safety created by ritual allows us to tolerate the risk and move forward in learning and transforming in spite of the risks.

Finally, rituals give deeper significance to our actions. When I light a candle in a ritualistic way, I am not only lighting a candle. On a deeper level, I am also committing myself to acting respectfully toward another, affirming a wish or prayer, or acknowledging gratitude to someone or something greater than myself—that is, to the transpersonal. Objects used in ritual do not merely represent their inner nature: they *reveal* that nature. The ritual context of such an act or symbol calls our attention to its deeper meaning and inner nature. We open from the surface into the depths of consciousness, and our actions or words thus carry more meaning. The question of the significance of an action can eventually lead to a sense of ultimate significance, opening to a dimension that is transpersonal and full of meaning by its nature. While the classroom setting does not often invite such ultimate significance, the simple ritual of an opening bow, as with other ritual acts, does bring a sense that this time is about more than ordinary information or a grade at the end of the semester. The potency of a transpersonal approach to education is recognized implicitly. This may be a lot to ask of a simple bow at the beginning of a class, but this act evokes the profound potentials of ritual.

Other Classroom Rituals

I have found a number of simple rituals that can be easily and fruitfully integrated into my graduate and undergraduate psychology courses. While students at Naropa University have come to expect a bow and other rituals in their classes, these practices have had similar influences on my students at a large public undergraduate college where I taught for many years and in professional trainings I have conducted. Although teachers must always stay attuned to the needs and sensibilities of their students, my experience has shown me that a wide variety of higher education students take quite well to rituals in classrooms when invited and given a non-religious context for them. I will briefly outline three rituals in addition to the bow I have described, that I have used in a variety of undergraduate and graduate courses and other settings.

Nature as Mirror
While its applicability is wide, this practice is especially useful with people not used to talking about themselves in personal ways and with new groups. I often use it early in a semester, and I have used it with groups of teens on summer wilderness programs, adults on wilderness vision fasts, first-year college students, graduate students nearing the end of their training, and professionals in in-service trainings. I learned this practice from Steven Foster and Meredith Little, founders of the School of Lost Borders, a training facility for wilderness rites of passage guides and field-based ecopsychology (1988, Personal Communication). Generally, I bring a variety of small natural objects, such as stones of various shapes and textures or a collection of small sticks, stones, feathers, and other natural objects. I have found that the objects don't need to be special or striking; any objects will do, though it helps to have a variety. I start by placing the stones on a small cloth or a table, attracting students' curiosity. Then, I pose a question or focus and ask each student to pick an object that relates to that question for them. For example, at the end of a semester, I may ask them to pick an object that reflects a quality they feel they have developed through their work in the course. After choosing our objects, we go around the group, and students respond to the question by describing their object. Typically, some students have a lot to say about their object and its relationship to their lives, while others are spare with their self-disclosures. However, having permission to simply describe the object helps to open quieter students. This practice provides encouragement and a safe setting within which students can talk about their inner lives, listen to others, and explore their experiences.

Using these natural objects as mirrors for one's inner life brings a number of ritual and transpersonal elements into the classroom. The unusual nature of this exercise is a sign that this will not be a typical class period. Students' curiosity is engaged as I bring out various objects. The ritual elements signal a safety to these disclosures that tends to be much more personal and revealing than those in an ordinary class discussion. In this practice, simple objects take on deep, even profound, significance as they come to embody and reflect important aspects of students' inner lives. A smooth rock that fits my hand not only represents some aspects of my inner life; it reveals its nature as not separate from my wisdom, evolution, or support. A broken rock is an opportunity to talk about a wound. Some students will pick an object and barely pay attention to it as they talk fluently about their inner experience prompted by this object; others simply describe the object—even as they are describing themselves. Potential adaptations of this practice abound, and I invite you to experiment.

Council Practice

I often use council practice in my classes, and I have seen its usefulness in many kinds of groups, including those composed of adolescents, couples and families, and seasoned professionals. With ancient and widespread roots, this practice has recently been developed and taught by the Center for Council and described by Zimmerman and Coyle in *The Way of Council* (2009). At its core, council practice invites authentic sharing and deep listening. Sitting in a circle, a "talking piece" or object is typically passed from one participant to another. A specific question may be posed, or the topic of the council may be open-ended. While there is usually an experienced facilitator, council practice is essentially non-hierarchical. Participants take turns speaking to the topic, while others listen with attentiveness and openness. Participants are encouraged to avoid rehearsing (both to allow full attention on the speaker and to promote more spontaneous, authentic sharing). There are many variations on this form, including having an inner circle that speaks and an outer circle of silent witnesses. Councils can be used for conflict resolution, personal growth and exploration, group development, and spiritual practice.

While such sharing creates vulnerability and though at times conflicts surface, the ritual elements of council provide a greater degree of safety. Generally, students move quickly to a deeper level of listening and sharing. A liminal, transpersonal space often arises. In many ways, a council is, itself, a transpersonal practice grounded in present-centeredness, mindfulness, deep listening, and present-centered spontaneity. It relies on each individual to be authentically present while it creates a unity of all involved. This dynamic interplay of personal and transpersonal expresses some of the core themes of transpersonal psychology (Davis, 2003). Even when there is a specific goal, council practice is essentially open-ended. It cultivates an appreciation for not-knowing and for working with thoughts, projections, and reactions as they arise. In council practice, the group awakens to the story that is developing. Council cultivates non-judgmental attentiveness, respect, and interest in others' offerings without settling for a habitual dullness or premature resolution of differences. Differences are valued in council, and these differences are the foundation for new possibilities for relating, creative insights, and new ways of being. In a kind of dialectic process, differences are held together so that a new higher order synthesis arises. In this sense, council can be a transformative practice. While there are many formats for class discussions, the ritual elements of council give it special safety, significance, and depth.

Creating a Centerpiece
A third example of ritual with application in university classes is the creation of a centerpiece by a class or group. While this can be called an "altar," I prefer the less religious connotations of a "centerpiece." I use this most often in intensive courses where we will be together for a block of time without having to deconstruct it between class sessions. I may invite students ahead of time to bring an object that is meaningful or special to them. Alternatively, such objects can be produced spontaneously, or I may give students time to gather objects outside the classroom. With mindfulness and attentiveness, we arrange these objects in the center of the classroom, and they provide a focal point for our work together. As students add their objects—some with a descriptive story, some simply naming the object, and some in silence—an artistic and symbol-rich living expression of the class-as-community and even

the class-as-organism arises. Over the time we are together, the centerpiece continues to grow and evolve. The centerpiece becomes a physical and artistic display of the learning community. At the end of the course, we take it apart ceremonially, another opportunity for mindfulness and appreciation of the poignancy and inevitability of endings.

Building a centerpiece in this way brings the group together quickly, and its presence throughout the class is a steady, if sometimes unconscious, reminder of the deeper significance of our purposes together. There is room for those who appreciate more drama around this practice and those who take it more casually. Yet, students come to respect the meaning it has for the whole class, and the felt sense of ritual it provides.

Other Ritual Practices

There are, of course, many other ritual practices that can be adopted or adapted for use in classrooms. I have not discussed two obvious and common types of rituals: those intended to induce non-ordinary states of consciousness such as shamanic or trance states (Krippner, 2002) and rites of passage (Brenner, 2007; Foster & Little, 1989). Both are valid uses of ritual in the context of transpersonal education and transpersonal psychology, but they are beyond the scope of this chapter.

> Checking the clock, I realize that our class is about to end. I point this out to the class, but rather than a hurried gathering of papers and books, there is a palpable quieting. The students come to a relaxed attention in their seats. Those who had been slumping sit up, and those who had been on the edge of their chairs settle. I also come to a relaxed, upright posture with my hands resting on my thighs. With a breath, we soften into the moment, and shortly one of the students initiates a bow. The rest of us join, bowing into the center of the group. Returning upright, we move on, more open to whatever comes next.

References

Brenner, A. (2007). *Women's rites of passage: How to embrace change and celebrate life.* Lanham, MD: Rowman Littlefield.

Davis, J. (2003). An overview of transpersonal psychology. *The Humanistic Psychologist, 31*(2–3), 6–21.

Davis, J. (2011). Ecopsychology, transpersonal psychology, and nonduality. *International Journal of Transpersonal Studies, 30*, 89–100.

Davis, J. (2013). Ecopsychology's niche: Why the transpersonal matters to ecopsychology. *Ecopsychology, 4*(5), 215–216.

Eulert, D. (2013). *Ritual healing: Stories of ordinary and extraordinary transformation.* Henderson, NV: Motivational Press.

Grimes, R. (2000). *Deeply into the bone: Re-inventing rites of passage.* Berkeley, CA: University of California Press.

Foster, S., & Little, M. (1989). *The book of the vision quest: Personal transformation in the wilderness.* New York, NY: Touchstone.

Friedman, H., & Hartelius, G. (Eds.). (2013). *The Wiley-Blackwell handbook of transpersonal psychology.*, West Sussex, UK: John Wiley & Sons.

Krippner, S. (2002). Conflicting perspectives on shamans and shamanism: Points and counterpoints. *American Psychologist, 57*, 962–977.

Krippner, S. (2013). Foreword: We still need rituals in the twenty-first century. In D. Eulert (Ed.), *Ritual healing: Stories of ordinary and extraordinary transformation* (pp. 13–17). Henderson, NV: Motivational Press.

LaChapelle, D. (1978). *Earth wisdom.* Silverton, CO: Finn Hill Arts/Guild of Tutors Press.

Suzuki, S. (2011). *Zen mind, beginner's mind.* Boston, MA: Shambhala Publications. (Original work published 1970)

Zimmerman, J., & Coyle, V. (2009). *The way of council.* Wilton Manors, FL: Bramble Books.

Chapter 14
Know Thyself: A Most Appropriate and Yet Most Resisted Ancient Directive for the 21st Century Human

Sandy Sela-Smith

Nearly every human holds multiple life-stories that when woven together form an extremely intricate, evolving set of complex patterns that direct how life is experienced and what responses to life one makes. These programmed patterns are what Feinstein and Krippner (1988/2009, 1997) referred to as personal mythologies, which often diminish spontaneity and authentic choice while creating automatic thoughts, programmed behavior-patterns, and pre-set interpretations of one's self and the world that often do not fit as they once might have fit. Many of these stories are deeply embedded in the psyche and remain unknown, forming one's personality, influencing psychological and physical health, and directing one's life path.

A child who experienced being accidentally or intentionally abandoned by a parent could hold on to a story that he or she is unwanted or unworthy of love and might spend an entire life feeling lost and alone, whether or not there are loving and accepting people in that person's life. A child born into a family system that focused on fear of financial ruin as a result of past generational suffering from the Great Depression might become a successful entrepreneur and accumulate significant wealth but never feel financially secure with that wealth, even if he or she becomes a part of the commonly referenced 1% of the population. A child born into a society that holds racial prejudice against persons from a minority group could learn of the injustice of such prejudice and consciously transform thinking patterns, considering themselves to have evolved into a racially inclusive being, but when considering a mate or an employee, would rule out someone from the race rejected by that society without awareness of having done so.

Of course, these examples are one-dimensionally simple in the context of an extremely complex internal system of human responses that weave together to create experience, meaning, decisions and behavior. However, until a person decides to know themselves, the person will likely not be able to discern what thoughts, life choices and behaviors are authentically and spontaneously arising from the true-self—what Jung (1938/1966, 1957/1990) identified as unknowable essence of the Self that can be accessed only through experience. Without self-knowledge or self-understanding, a person would not be able to discern if what is emerging is from what Winnicott (1974) identified as the false-self and what Jung (1928) referred to as the persona, which he explained as being:

> a complicated system of relations between individual consciousness and society, fittingly enough a kind of mask, designed on the one hand to make a definite impression upon others, and, on the other, to conceal the true nature of the individual. (p. 305)

The false-self/persona is what I have suggested is the mask most humans wear to prevent not only others but, more important, the self from knowing what would seem too overwhelming to acknowledge as present within (Sela-Smith, 2007, 2008, 2011).

The Power of Reconnecting with Infinite Connections

Reconnecting to Feelings: A Doorway to Know Thy Self

A woman, who had been my client for several months, felt an obligation to return to her family home after the death of her father. She wanted to find a way she might be able to tolerate the hostile relationship she had with her mother as far back as she could remember. She hoped to attend the funeral without an emotional explosion between them, as had happened in nearly every past encounter. She began the session telling me about the coldness and judgment she had nearly always experienced in her mother's presence no matter what this client did to try to improve these very uncomfortable interactions. The client asked to take an inner journey, as she had in many past sessions, by connecting with what she had experienced as her spiritual guide to see if she could find the source of the conflict.

I invited her to lean back in a recliner chair, close her eyes, and become aware of her breathing. When she was in a state of deep relaxation, I asked if she would be willing to have her guide take her back to whatever it was that caused the rift between her mother and herself. In a moment, the client experienced herself in a large room that, upon investigation, appeared to be an operating room in a hospital. She saw people dressed in white coats looking as if they were doing something to a woman on a surgical table. She sensed frantic energy, but she herself felt alone, cold, and extremely upset. I suggested she could pull back from the scene just enough to avoid getting lost in the frantic energies and notice the surroundings to see what was happening.

In her internal vision, she reported being in a room with very large windows; sunlight was pouring into the space, making everything appear to be somewhat hazy. I asked if she could see a calendar or a clock anywhere. She saw a large wall clock, which indicated it was 12:50. She experienced her body as being quite small and naked. She sensed she was a newborn and her mother was not there for her. She watched her infant-self cry out with rage for having been abandoned. With her eyes closed, in a deep-trance state, sitting in the chair in my office, she began to cry with the pain and rage, sounding like an infant rather than an adult. She struggled in the chair as her adult arms and legs appeared to try to lift her body from the coldness she said her infant self was experiencing. I asked my client if she, in her current adult form, would go over to the crying infant, pick her up from the cold table, and hold her in her arms to reassure the newborn that she was safe and loved. The woman's face softened as she experienced embracing the child, and then, I asked her if she would be willing to allow herself to see what was happening to her mother. She shifted her attention from the child to the surgical table and saw that the sheets around her mother were covered with blood.

I asked the client to move forward in time to see what was happening to mother and child after they arrived home. She found herself as the infant crying a great amount of time and seemed inconsolable as her mother felt more and more disconnected from her baby. By the time the client was walking, she and her mother had constant battles, with the toddler throwing tantrums, and mother becoming increasingly hostile to the child she now believed was a curse, probably punishing mother for some unknown sin she had committed. The two never resolved the conflict, and my client left home before graduating from high school, returning only occasionally for what ended up being miserable holiday visits. Finally, she stopped making any contact until she got the notice of her father's death.

During the deep work, the client told me she could feel the terror in the baby's body, afraid that she had been left to die; she sensed that her infant self had concluded her mother must not have loved her to place her in such a frightening situation. But her adult self could see that mother did not abandon her newborn baby. The complicated delivery had resulted in excessive bleeding and her mother had nearly died. Without knowing the truth, her infant self had created a story, without words, just minutes following her birth, and she spent her childhood and adult life believing that her mother did not love her. As she moved through her growing-up years, she could see that the child's inconsolable distress caused her mother to feel distraught and experience self-judgment around her failure to bond with her child. Mother preferred others to care for her daughter and eventually had little to do with her child, which further separated the two.

After consoling her newborn infant-self and letting the child from the past know she was safe and loved in the arms of her future-self, my client was capable of seeing the struggle her mother experienced and felt compassion for a woman who did not want to die. She could see how hard her mother tried but failed to create a bond with her infant, and she understood how painful it must have been to have a child who constantly reminded her of her failure. My client shared the new information with her child-self and forgave the infant for the misinterpretation that created a pain-filled story. Her decision to know herself led her to forgive her mother for not being there for her following her birth and then for withdrawing from her when she had become an older, cantankerous child. For the first time in her entire life, my client felt compassion and love for the woman who had given her birth. This woman left my office feeling confident that she could attend the funeral without getting into an explosive fight with her mother.

Following the session, my client called to tell me her mother had phoned her after years of no contact saying she realized they had a strained relationship and wondered if it might be possible for them to talk. My client and her mother arranged for a meeting, and they began a process of healing a badly damaged relationship. I have found that in this kind of work it is not uncommon for other people not in therapy to shift when therapy clients heal the patterns that greatly influenced their relationship with them, an occurrence that fits what Jung (1998) identified as synchronicity. At the funeral, my client asked her mother if she could see her birth certificate and found that her birth had occurred at 12:50 p.m.

Reconnecting to Body Consciousness to Know the Soul-Self

Based on my psychotherapy work with many clients who have been willing to go even deeper into self-knowledge, it seems that what some interpret as past-life experiences (Linn, 2008; Jue, 1996; Weiss, 1988) also carry stories that become triggered by events in this life. Bringing insight and healing into those events, whether historical or metaphoric, causes the client to expand their understanding and increase consciousness in the parallel concerns in this life. In my own work to heal from an extremely damaging childhood, I was willing to go anywhere within me to find the stories I held that made me feel so unworthy that no matter how many successes I had I felt like a failure. I was compelled to change those unhealthy mythologies.

Long before I had begun psychotherapy in my adult life, I longed to be a mother, and yet I dreaded being a mother at the same time. I had five miscarriages in the first few years of my marriage, for which I had both mourned and felt relieved, something I did not express to anyone. I both wanted children and did not want them, but I did not know why. More truthfully, it did not occur to me to ask myself why I was so conflicted.

Much later in therapy, while struggling with menopause, which made it clear I would never have children, I did deep work with my body and accessed cell-level consciousness (Rossi, 2005; Salk, 1983). I communicated with the cells in my arms that ached because they did not get to experience the joy of holding a child, with the cells in my heart that were in agony for not being able to feel the love a child might have returned to me, and the cells in my uterus that believed they had failed by not creating a child.

I asked my inner guide, the aspect of me I came to call my *Spark of God* and what Jung (1938/1966) identified as the *God within* or the essence, to take me back to the pattern that created such a life path for myself. I saw what I interpreted as flash images of events from multiple lifetimes, many of which were very short and painful. One image that seemed to draw me into it was a lifetime when I was a young woman who died shortly after giving birth to a son. My village was being invaded by a group of sword-wielding warriors on horseback. When an invader came into my tent, my newborn son was ripped from my arms, and his tiny body was pierced with a sword. Still in shock from what I had just experienced, I was raped and then murdered. At the moment of my death, mournful sadness overwhelmed me for not having been able to suckle or even name my infant before he was taken from me, and my dying thought was that having a child was too painful because children could not be kept safe. Repetition compulsion (Diamond, 2008), recreated many lives that ended painfully before I had grown to adulthood and that were replicated in my childhood in this life, which was as exceedingly traumatic as those previous lives, although obviously I lived beyond childhood.

Once I was able to see the roots of the story line I carried about children in the world, I was able to feel compassion for those parts of me still caught in the energy fields of past lives. I could hold the woman who had lost her son even before she had a chance to name him, and I worked with her on what I experience as higher planes of my consciousness, where she was able to have a conversation with the soul of the infant who had been murdered. I was able to bring higher truth to the children from the intervening past lives and offered support to the aspects of myself that I sensed still identified with those tragic past-life experiences. I felt compassion for those who were so compelled to repeat the stories about the world they held as true. The healing message I offered was to release the belief that children could not be protected, and introduce a new personal myth that if negative experiences occur it is possible to overcome those experiences with love; after all, I lived past my childhood, which was evidence that I had been protected. I had come to accept another belief—that even if I were to die, who I am still exists and, therefore, I am eternally safe.

This transpersonal awareness moved my understanding of who I am beyond the limitations of the story I had told myself about who I was based the many past lives and on the first 40 years of my life. My search to know myself allowed me to embrace the idea that I am an eternal being who has incarnated into many lifetimes, each one leading to this lifetime—and will continue beyond this life into an ongoing future in which I create the universe I contain within myself based on the organizing principles of my beliefs (Lipton, 2008). I have come to understand the concept that my internal universe is connected to the universes others carry within themselves and the Universe with which we are all infinitely connected through what Buddhism identifies as *unitive consciousness* (Scotton, 1996). Access to past-life experiences, whether or not such experiences can be verified—and even if they are lives from others who lived in the past that I access by way of the ocean of the collective unconscious (Jung, 1959/1980)—open the pathway to stories that wrote those lives and have written the one I live now. And, for the first time, in this life, I learned that I have the ability to consciously release the unacceptable stories and create new ones that fit who I am choosing to become.

**Reconnecting to the Stories
That Write Our Lives to Discover Ourselves**
Many of the stories individuals live could break a heart, elicit feelings of shame or guilt, cause a person to fight known and unknown enemies, run away from life in defeat, escape from life itself, or cause one to wonder if she or he has value. Stories could provide some with the strength and determination to make it through any challenge that might cause most others to withdraw in defeat, collapse in fear, or push so hard against all odds to prove the story wrong. Stories can cause individuals to seek the life paths that are not connected to their authentic selves, living life without spontaneity or authenticity, losing the greatest gifts of living the experiences in the moment.

Whether stories provide what one might consider to be dark and unacceptable about one's identity or are interpreted as positive and acceptable, giving strength to carry on in difficult situations, they have the potential to propel one's life in ways that separate persons from their authentic selves. But until one searches deeply enough to find the stories that propel their life, motivations for behavior will remain elusive, and it is possible to live life without being connected to the authentic self within.

Hidden stories with generational patterns. A 72-year-old woman, whom I will call Merriam, came to my office under advisement from her oncologist. She agreed to begin therapy because she wanted to understand what was happening to her on the deeper emotional and spiritual levels, and perhaps to find her way to experience peace despite whatever the outcome might be for her stage 4 lung cancer. At times, discovery of their hidden stories allow patients not only to find peace and understanding, but in some cases to experience remission of the cancer, especially when they are willing to make significant changes in life patterns that create stress, often caused by the stories that direct their lives. This stress results in cancer cells overpowering the immune system, and removal of stress empowers the immune system (Wolford, et al., 2013).

14. Know Thyself

Merriam's family was planning a reunion, which shifted the focus of our work from her cancer to the upcoming gathering. In the process of sharing with me stories about her children, she realized that although she expressed love for her all children, she could not recall having loving moments with her second-born child, and, to her surprise, had almost no memory of the early years of that second child. She expressed shame for the lack of love for that child, which left her feeling empty. When I asked her where she felt the emptiness, she discovered she felt the emptiness in her chest. When I asked her if she was willing to go into the place of emptiness, she agreed. But instead of seeing her second child as she thought she would, she found herself as a toddler sitting all by herself on her aunt's front porch, fighting for breath as she sobbed alone and unheard. She had not thought of that experience for seven decades, and when the memory returned, she found the emptiness and loneliness opened into a deeper place of pain and rage that she had never known was there.

When she was two years old, my client's mother gave birth to a second child, and rejected her eldest daughter, my client. The mother apparently had told her husband she could not take care of two children, so her parents gave Merriam to the mother's spinster sister who was not fond of children while her mother kept the new baby boy. Mother seldom visited her abandoned child, and her first-born grew up feeling lonely, rejected, and abandoned.

As she searched the long-hidden story, Merriam began to understand why she could not connect with her own second child. She realized she did everything she could to protect her own first child from ever experiencing the pain her two-year-old self had felt; her solution was to ignore her second child as a way to keep her first child from being abandoned and hurt as she had been. Without ever intending to do so, she had become a replica of her mother.

Further investigation indicated that my client's mother had a similar experience when she was a little girl. She, too, was sent off to live with her relatives shortly after she was born because having two children was too much for her mother to handle. My client's mother was the second-born child, who was rejected by her mother, who rejected her own first-born child, my client. Unexpressed pain keeps repeating itself, either by people doing to another what was done to them or trying to do the opposite of what was done to them, both of which create another generation of pain. It was not a surprise to discover that my client's adult children had done the same thing in their families. Second- born children who were rejected, turned their backs on first-born children, and first-born children who were rejected turned their backs on second-born children. When my client saw this pattern that was embedded in her family system, she was able to forgive herself and release the conclusion her child-self had made about how to heal the pain. For the first time in her life, her heart felt love for her second child and for her own child-self. As of this writing, the pattern seems to be unraveling in the younger generations despite the fact that they are not involved in psychotherapy.

Merriam found the process of going inside to connect with her essence, which she came to call the spark of god inside her, to be a healing, peaceful experience. Not only did she bring healing and love to her two-year-old self, she also worked with many other unacknowledged pain-filled areas of her life that had been hidden deep within her body/mind, creating stress she did not know existed. She brought love to and forgiveness for herself for decisions she had made when she was a young woman, and she gained understanding of what those who had hurt her had experienced that caused them to fall into patterns that caused her pain. During the process of her work, her fourth-stage lung cancer went into remission, and treatment for the metastasized cancer was successful. It has been four years since Merriam has been cancer free. She believes she was able to overcome her lung cancer because of the inner work she did that led her to the spark of god inside her that continues to bring her peace.

Masked stories as a cover for facing hidden stories. Compared to extreme physical abuse, sexual abuse, or wickedly damaging neglect, something as common as parental preference might be considered a minor wound. However, any wound can deeply distort people's ability to be who they are in the world. Instead, the answer they often find even before they learn to speak is to put on a mask that covers who they are and shows to the outer world who they think the world wants them to be—and they do this without knowing that is what they have done. In time, they come to believe they are the mask and are unaware it is not who they are (Sela-Smith 2007, 2008, 2011). They continue to believe they are the masks until something happens that causes them to discover the emptiness they have spent most of their lives trying to fill with something external to feel safe, loved, or worthy. It is in the process of the inner search that they discover the mask. Of course, it is not pleasant for them to find that what they thought was the true self was, in reality, a mask to cover the pain, the guilt, or the dark self-defining beliefs they held, perhaps from infancy. People often become terrified of doing inner work because they are afraid the empty place on the inside is *actually* empty, or they believe that without the mask they are nothing.

It is terrifying to face the potential that emptiness is real; to let go of the mask and stop living from the false self can be too frightening to consider. Letting the masked-self go feels like death to the part of self that attached its identity to the mask. To remove the mask would mean experiencing what would feel like an earthquake-like shattering of everything that was built to adjust to the world and experience the pain that was too overwhelming to feel at the time the mask was first constructed.

Unless their adjusted lives become overwhelming, many people would rather live with what is false than experience the shattering that would come from knowing the truth. However, truth has a way of pushing itself into human consciousness in order for it to heal. Resisting the truth can create life patterns and behaviors that stress the body and challenge the immune system in the individual, leading to ill health. The same dynamics can be said for the collective of humans as a species, which can become ill, as well.

Crossroads

Recently, Hawking (as cited in Breyer, 2013) acknowledged in an interview that the human species' only possible hope for the future would be space colonies. Hawking pointed out:

> Our population and our use of the finite resources of planet Earth are growing exponentially, along with our technical ability to change the environment for good or ill. But our genetic code still carries the selfish and aggressive instincts that were of survival advantage in the past. It will be difficult enough to avoid disaster in the next hundred years, let alone the next thousand or million. (para, 5)

The world in the 21st century seems to have created an explosion of metaphoric and actual earthquakes in the collective of our species as we interact with one another and with the world. Just as my client's family system experienced generational shockwaves of rejection and abandonment that influenced the lives of all its members, the human species is experiencing millennia-old shockwaves, with aftershocks being played out in the world arena today in the form of terrorist acts, long-time tribal and religious wars, racial injustice, sexual discrimination, and political and national wars. With technological advancement, they have the potential to destroy mankind and the planet, not unlike a malignant cancer in the collective. At the core of so many of these species-wide conflicts are the feelings of guilt, shame, anger, hatred, and fear that grow from feeling survival is threatened. Struggles abound, but the root causes remain in the unconscious we all carry.

At these deep levels, hidden dynamics are seldom noticed in a worldview that has chosen to believe people are all fairly simple machines that can find solutions to human problems by reprogramming the mind, or providing the right chemical combinations to correct what has gone wrong, or using old programming that no longer works with the body-machine in our present state of evolution. A highly specialized group of theorists who are developing Artificial Intelligence (AI) theories related to consciousness and self-aware programming seem to base their assumptions on the belief that humans are already programmed biological, carbon-based mechanisms with flaws that might be fixable by external intervention to correct a mechanical or biological programming failure (Buchanan, 2013), making enhancement beneficial to human beings. Others believe humans will eventually evolve into silicone-based replacements of human beings in some future evolutionary leap (Ghose, 2013), which could create a species that does not struggle with complicated and often dangerous feelings, the shadow side, dark places within, or with pain and wounding that seeks healing.

If something goes wrong with the computer-based species, the new holder of consciousness would be developed to self-repair. Those in the AI field believe human beings are not far from creating computers and robotics capable of surpassing human intelligence, making the human species as obsolete as the dinosaurs. Commenting on this perspective in their book, *Beyond Humanity,* Paul and Cox (1996) suggested that humanity is currently in a waking dream, experiencing itself in biological form. But perhaps sooner than we think, humanity will transcend biology and assume what they see as a better form of existence that is computer and robotically based.

To those who remain afraid of knowing what is within, it is possible they might consider the acceptability of *crowding out* the flawed, biological human species and the creation of what they interpret as a more evolved and less complex species to hold consciousness. This could appear to be a potential solution to the human biological programming that seems dedicated to destruction of all threats in order to survive, until there is a last man—or woman—standing.

But based on 30 years of following the directive to *Know Thyself,* I have discovered that there is something within me that is not limited to the programming of my biology and the stories I carry that direct me toward survival. The will to survive did direct me to remove the mask and enter the emptiness, because something in me knew I would not survive had I not done so. Yet, the courage required to take the leap into the empty darkness and shatter the identity I had come to believe was me had come from another aspect of myself, not recognized by many and not acknowledged by most science. Although humans are individually unique and very complex physical beings composed of evolving biological programming learning to become conscious, there is a non-physical essence that is infinitely connected to Universal Essence that I believe flows in and through everything in the universe. My search to know myself led me to experience this non-physical essence. Its uniqueness allows me to discover life from the essence that has been flowing through me for all time, continues to exist within me in this moment; its connection to Universal essence provides my unique essence with an awareness of its connection to all that exists.

Even if people do not choose to look at what they hold deep within themselves, in both dark and light aspects of one's humanness, and if individuals do not choose to acknowledge that there is something far more profound entwined with the physical and mental beingness, that essence remains. Based on the experience of my unique essence connected to Universal essence, I speculate that even if the human species self-destructs before it discovers its essence, that essence will remain and, somehow, find its way to integrating with physical presence.

The Drive to Know and the Resistance to Knowing

For the past 30 years, I have been focused on a path of self-search to not only know but to understand my being as an authentic person, unique in so many ways and yet not unlike my fellow humans. The three decades of work have been personal in relation to my own being in mind/body/spirit: to bring healing to the wounded places and the stories entwined in the wounds, as well as to discover what I have come to identify as my Unique God Essence, the Spark of God that is in me that is inseparable from my authentic self, and ultimately inseparable from the essence of the Universe. I have also worked with individual clients who have expressed a willingness to go deep within themselves to heal what resisted healing for most of their lives, a psycho-spiritual process that supports them in finding what caused them to see who they thought they were from a place where they saw distortions instead of truth. In the past decade, I have supported students with more formal Heuristic Self-Search Inquiry (HSSI) in academic work, which many have used in their masters theses and dissertations to discover who they are. HSSI is a personal, subjective, and qualitative research method that supports self-discovery in relation to a concern that impels understanding of oneself and spurs transformation that forges connection to one's transpersonal consciousness.

Transformation occurs when the biological programming, which evolved from fear-based survival, opens its consciousness to incorporate the spiritual wisdom of love-based experience that melts fear and opens to infinite connection of the unique essence to Universal essence. This is the transpersonal that connects all that exists on all the levels of being. In these three arenas—personal, psychotherapeutic, and academic research—I have become aware of how strong resistance can to be to discovering the authentic, spiritually, and physically integrated self because of the attachment to the worldview constructed from fear in order to maneuver in what nearly all experience as a frightening world—a belief that seems to be programmed into our DNA.

The only way I know that people can work with resistance and experience who they truly are is to find a means to access the defensive patterns and behaviors that were first created to prevent them from feeling the pain they once believed would destroy themselves if they were to feel it. A two-year-old child who believed she would die if she felt the devastation of being rejected by a mother who preferred her second child built a lifetime of patterns that led to her own rejection of her second child. Life stress related to her buried story of rejection, and abandonment created habits that were destructive of her immune system and led to cancer. Like so many people who take up smoking, she used cigarettes to distract herself from a lifetime of pain. The gift of her patterns that led to cancer and her fear of dying from that horrible disease marked the path on which she discovered her authentic self and the peace that allowed her to know "all is right with the world" no matter what was happening in her world. Her cancer then went into remission.

Current science remains leery of considering the *experience* of emotion from the perspective of a personal, subjective *I who feels* (Sela-Smith, 2001, 2002), as something worthy of study. By its very nature, personal experience cannot be generalized to a population or used for prediction of future behavior, and replication of such a study is not a consideration. Observation and categorization of the phenomenon of experience is acceptable. However, uniquely personal and subjective research—which is so very human and likely the cause of much of how each human interprets and acts within their experientially constructed world—might be better understood if there could be access to individual human information in which the researcher is also the participant.

Being aware of the experience of one's own emotions is of paramount importance for humans if they are going to truly know their own humanity, understand where their pain and suffering originates, and identify the patterns and behaviors the pain and suffering produces. The 21st century seems to be set in a petri dish of individual and collective oppositional and life-threatening behaviors that demand attention if people are to survive the outcome of the stories they believe are true. Past methods of objectively, quantitatively, and experimentally researching human behavior do not seem to be adequate to address these behaviors because of the underlying stories that cannot be known without inner searches to *know thyself.*

Healing of the original pain has the potential to release the suffering and allow individuals to change the patterns that do not serve them in the present. My 72-year-old client eventually was able to bring love to her child-self, forgiveness to her own self for not loving her second child, and forgiveness to her mother for treating her as she, herself, had treated her own child. I invited this client to release the pattern of child-rejection that seemed to have been a part of the family pattern for generations. As she did this deep-level work, she saw images of her parents, grandparents, and great grandparents, and more people she did not recognize, which she had a strong feeling were relatives from many past generations. I believe she had demonstrated to all these people what it took to embrace the pain of her abandoned child-self and bring love to her, and forgive herself for what she had done. In that moment of self-forgiveness, she accessed forgiveness for her mother, and all of her pain and anger melted.

I suspect everyone carries the energy patterns of all past generations in *energy DNA* held in the nucleus of every cell, which might be parallel to the research done by Lipton (2008) that suggests our DNA can be reprogrammed. This might explain that when people bring truth and healing to their past, the beliefs or personal mythologies based on the pain of wounding heal their DNA programming that had been passed on for generations and lifetimes until the story becomes conscious.

Introducing love for the wounded self is experienced, and understanding of the pattern that held onto the wounding allows transformation of the energy patterns. Without this transformation these ongoing past wounds might have remained embedded in the family system, the human species, or in the consciousness of the universe for thousands, millions, or perhaps, billions of years.

If individuals are willing to venture even more deeply into knowing themselves, they might begin to understand others in their lives, the humanity of the species, and at least some of what lies beyond all people who are learning to co-exist in the amazing gift of experiencing life from a union of biology and spirit.

Oracle of Delphi: Know Thyself

Know Thyself, one of the three aphorisms carved thousands of years ago above the door to the Oracle of Delphi as spiritual guidance to ancient Greeks, is still a profound directive. While psychotherapy has been swimming in the subjective waters of self-discovery for decades, research psychology has generally avoided subjective, qualitative research that focuses on individual human experience, especially if it is provided by the researcher-as-participant. Though subjective psychotherapy has accepted experience as being important, there remains a resistance in mainstream psychology to access the subjective and, even more so, the transpersonal, or spiritual aspects of oneself. Many of the most common modalities of psychotherapy focus on the cognitive–behavioral medical model of reprogramming the mind to get it to respond in a more effective way, or perhaps on providing chemicals to create what might be considered a normal balance and stop unwanted expression of emotion and feelings.

However, emotions and feelings provide a personal doorway that allow an individual entry into the internal universe of the unique self. This doorway offers one of the most profound ways to discover who one truly is instead of knowing only what can be verifiable and replicable from an objective, surface perspective. By taking an inner journey, such as the one articulated in Heuristic Self-Search Inquiry (Sela-Smith 2001,

2002), each person has the opportunity to become aware not only of what exists within but also to discover the interconnection that exists among all humans, as well as the interconnection of our unique inner universe with the essence of the outer universe.

To *Know Thyself* holds the potential for one to come far closer to healing what has been hurt within and creating an opportunity to release the false-self and finally experience being authentic, Knowing the Self within holds the potential for both far greater personal awareness and a deeper understanding of the relationship one has to all of humanity and the transpersonal universe—far beyond what can be known about the self, other humans, and what is called the external world based on objective observation by the senses.

References

Breyer, M. (2013, Apr. 11). Stephen Hawking predicts the imminent end of humanity on Earth, *Mother Nature Network*. Retrieved from www.mnn.com/earth-matters/space/stories/stephen-hawking-predicts-the-imminent-end-of-humanity-on-earth

Buchanan, A. E. (2013). *Beyond humanity?* Oxford, UK: Oxford University Press.

Diamond, S. (2008, June, 14). Essential secrets of psychotherapy: Repetitive relationship patterns. *Psychology Today*. Retrieved from https://www.psychologytoday.com/blog/evil-deeds/200806/essential...

Feinstein, D., & Krippner, S. (1997). *The mythic path*. New York, NY: Jeremy P. Tarcher/Putnam.

Feinstein, D., & Krippner, S. (2009). *Personal mythology: Using ritual, dreams, and imagination to discover your inner story*. New York, NY: Putnam's Sons. (Original work published 1988)

Ghose, T. (2013, May 7). Intelligent robots will overtake humans by 2100, experts say. Retrieved from www.livescience.com/29379-intelligent-robots-will-overtake-humans.html

Jue, R. W. (1996) Past life therapy. In B. W. Scotton, A. B. Chinen, & J. R. Battista, (Eds.), *Textbook of transpersonal psychiatry and psychology* (pp. 377–387). New York, NY: Basic Books.

Jung, C. G. (1928). The Relations between the ego and the unconscious. In *CW 7: Two Essays on Analytical Psychology*. Princeton, NJ: Princeton University Press.

Jung, C. G. (1966). *Psychology & religion*. Birmingham, NY: Vail-Ballou Press. (Original work published 1938)

Jung, C. G. (1980). *The archetypes and the collective unconscious*. (R. F. C. Hull,

Trans.). Bollingen Series XX. Princeton, NJ: Princeton University Press. (Original work published 1959)

Jung, C. G. (1990). *The undiscovered self.* (R. F. C. Hull, Trans.). Princeton, NJ: Princeton University Press. (Original work published 1957)

Jung, C. G. (1998). *Jung on synchronicity and the paranormal: Key readings selected and introduced by Roderick Main.* Princeton, NJ: Princeton University Press.

Linn, D. (2008). *Past lives, present miracles: The most empowering book on reincarnation you'll ever read…in this lifetime.* Carlsbad, CA: Hay House.

Lipton, B. H. (2008). *The biology of belief.* Carlsbad, CA: Hay House.

Paul, G. S., & Cox, E. (1996). *Beyond humanity: Cyber evolution and future minds.* Clifton Park, NY: Delmar Thompson Learning.

Rossi, E. L. (2005). *A discourse with our genes: The psychosocial and cultural genomics of therapeutic hypnosis and psychotherapy.* Benevento, Italy: Editris SAS Press.

Salk, J. (1983). *Anatomy of reality: Merging of intuition and reason (convergence).* New York, NY: Columbia University Press.

Scotton, B. W. (1996). The contribution of Buddhism to transpersonal psychiatry. In B. W. Scotton, A. B, Chinen, & J. R. Battista (Eds.), *Textbook of transpersonal psychiatry and psychology* (pp. 114–122). New York, NY: Basic Books.

Sela-Smith, S. (2001). *Heuristic self-search inquiry: Clarification of Moustakas' heuristic research.* (Unpublished doctoral dissertation). Saybrook Graduate School and Research Center. San Francisco, CA. Available through UMI # 223575231

Sela-Smith, S. (2002). Heuristic research: Review and critique of the Moustakas method. *Journal of Humanistic Psychology, 42*(3), 53–88.

Sela-Smith, S. (2007). *The meaning of three: The mask.* Bloomington IN: Authorhouse

Sela-Smith, S. (2008). *The meaning of three: Behind the mask.* Bloomington IN: Authorhouse.

Sela-Smith, S. (2011). *The meaning of three: Under the mask.* Bloomington IN: Authorhouse.

Weiss, B. L. (1988). *Many lives, many masters: The true story of a prominent psychiatrist, his young patient, and the past-life therapy that changed both their lives.* New York, NY: Simon & Schuster.

Winnicott, D. W. (1974). *The maturational process and the facilitating environment: Studies in the theory of emotional development* (3rd ed.). New York: International Universities Press.

Wolford, C. C., McConoughey, S. J., Jalgaonkar, S. P., Leon, M., Merchant, A. S., Dominick, J. L., Yin, X., Chang, Y., Zmuda, E. J., O'Toole, S. A., Millar, E. K. A., Roller, S. L., Shapiro, C. L., Ostrowski, M., Sutherland, R. L., & Hai, T. (2013). Transcription factor ATF3 links host adaptive response to breast cancer metastasis. *Journal of Clinical Investigation, 123*(7),

2893–2906. doi: 10.1172/JCI64410.

Index

Acceptance and Commitment Therapy, 53,
Active Imagination, 47, 58
Activism, 25,
Addiction, 60, 64 78, 140 221, 222, 229
Advocacy, 41
Aikido, 200
Altered states (see consciousness)
Alternative health, 9
Altruism, 74, 77, 263
American Counseling Association (ACA), 18
American Psychological Association (APA), 18, 37-38, 75, 91, 198, 261, 262
Analytic psychology, 35, 53, 73, 223
Anger, 140, 143, 229
Anxiety, 58-59, 229, 287
Anthroposophy, 34
Archetypes, 13, 46, 73, 116, 156,157
Aristotle, 47
Armstrong, K. 108,
Art, 1, 102-112, 115-117, 129
   Art therapy, 13, 53, 110-111, 116, 265
Artificial Intelligence, 306-307
Ascending
Assagioli, R., 14, 46, 47, 50, 58, 60, 63, 185, 197
Assessment, 35, 75, 81, 84-85, 123-145, 199, 229, 272
Assimilation, 9, 35
Attunement, 80, 90, 176
Authentic, 17, 78, 182, 186, 188-189, 192, 220, 286, 287, 291, 292, 295-296, 302, 308-309, 312
Awareness, 18, 21, 35, 54, 73-74, 77-78, 80, 82-83, 91, 102, 105-108, 111-118, 140, 159, 165, 174-177, 182-184, 188-192, 200, 203, 210, 214, 217, 219, 222, 237, 241, 251-254, 264, 267, 270, 276, 284, 301, 308, 312
Awe, 2, 3, 6, 187
Ayahuasca, 214, 218, 220

Bad trip, 224
Bhagavad Gita, 3
Bible, 153, 155
Binary, 239- 240, 244, 246, 250
Biofeedback, 124, 138, 139, 143
Biopsychosocial, 234, 236, 239
Bodhichitta, (Bodhicitta), 123, 153,
Body armor, 60
Book of Morman, 155
Brown University, 18
Buddha, 152, 155-156,
Buddhism, 2, 13,19, 24, 32, 134, 175, 301
   Theravada, 174
   Tibetan, 125, 127, 156,
Bugenthal, J. F. T., 16

California Institute for Integral Studies, 18
Canty, J., 2
Castonguay, L., 85, 91
Chaco Canyon, 4
Chief Seattle, 249
Christianity, 11, 86-88, 108, 131, 152, 154, 155, 156, 175, 217, 235, 241
Clements, C., 4-6
Cognicentric, 19
Cognitive–Behavioral, 53, 73, 87, 90
Collective unconscious, 14, 46, 55, 151, 255, 301
Colorado Rocky Mountains, 3
Common Factors, 89, 90
Compassion, 39, 124, 125, 129-131,

141, 145, 174, 177, 187, 199-203, 251, 275, 286
   self-compassion, 176
Conflict Resolution, 177
Consciousness, 11, 15, 22, 23, 24, 46, 50, 63, 77, 114 177, 183, 184, 190-193, 216
   altered states, 20, 73, 188, 251, 289, 311
   non-ordinary states, 12
   states of, 1, 22, 74
   subliminal, 12
Consensus trance, 241
Constructivist therapy, 79, 85
Contemplative practice, 104, 110, 124-126, 129-130, 132, 135-143, 174-175
Countertransference, 187
Core energy, 53
Cortright, B., 75, 125, 126
Creativity, 114, 289
Cross cultural, 32, 74, 115, 160, 167, 235, 262
Crusades, 40
Culture, 24, 25, 32-38, 73, 75, 76, 79, 83, 181, 192, 200, 214, 220, 227, 235, 238, 240, 242, 245, 262, 285, 288
Curiosity, 2, 176, 179, 213, 290, 291
Cynicism, 25

Dalai Lama, 115
Daniels, M., 7, 23, 76
Darkness, 4-7, 101, 107, 108, 118, 307
Davis, J., 2, 22
Death, 3, 4, 14, 103, 155, 157, 165-166, 206, 222, 227, 287, 297, 298, 300, 305
Deep ecology, 256
Depression, 82, 221- 222, 229, 295
Dharma, 183
Dharmapala, Anagarika, 11
Diagnostic and Statistical Manual (DSM), 82-83
Dialectical Behavior Therapy (DBT), 18, 53
Diamond Approach, 175
Divine Consciousness, 48
Dimethyltyptamine (DMT), 214
Double-blind studies, 24, 80-81
Dreams, 13, 23, 53, 114, 151-167
   lucid, 127, 139, 158, 197
Drumming, 140, 156,
Dualism, 10

Ecological Identity, 272
Ecological self, 255-256
Ecological unconscious, 255
Ecopsychology, 22, 250, 254-265, 290
Ecosystems, 112, 218, 229, 260, 262, 272
Ego, 23, 45, 61-62, 253
Egocentric (egoic), 200, 203, 222, 251, 252, 259, 262,
Elkins, D., 83, 90
Embody, 2, 3, 6, 114, 176, 182, 183, 192, 257, 284, 286, 291
Emotion, 113-114, 140, 142, 161-163, 165
   Emotional Intelligence, 112-112
Empathy, 77, 89, 111, 137, 141, 205, 210
Emptiness, 303, 305, 307
Enculturation, 35, 39
Energy psychology, 53
Epstein, M., 12
Eros, 33
Ethnicity, 19
Ethnocentric, 19, 37,
Evidence Based Practice, 75-76, 87, 91
Evil, 17, 34
Exceptional Human Experiences (EHEs), 197
Existential psychology, 6, 53, 73,
   Existential-humanistic, 17, 80
Exposure techniques, 90
Extra-therapeutic factors, 89

Faith, 130, 186, 187

Index

Feminine, 33, 205,
　Divine feminine, 209
Flashbacks, see Hallucinogen Persisting Perception Disorder (HPPD)
fMRI studies, 114
Focusing, 53, 58
Fox, M., 253, 259
Francis of Assisi, 154
Freud, S., 12, 13, 14, 15, 45, 46-47, 57-58, 60, 63, 64, 78, 196, 197, 234
Freidman, H., 32, 75, 257, 263-264, 270, 275,
Forgiveness, 177

Gardner, H., 112-113, 115
Gender Identity, 237-239
Gestalt, 47, 58, 60-61, 63, 64, 65
Gnostic gospels, 5
God(s), 47, 49, 86, 103, 108, 112, 152, 162, 165-166, 218, 251, 300
Goldman, D., 113, 115
Great Chain of Being, 47
Great Nest of Being, 45-48
Greening, T., 16-17
Grief, 79-80, 131
Grof, S., 18, 75, 151, 214, 217, 258
Group Psychotherapy, 65
Guided Imagery, 139

Happiness, 274, 276
Hartelius, G., 21, 24, 25, 39, 197, 242
Heuristic self-search inquiry, 308, 311, 312.
Higher Self, 50
Hillman, J., 255
Hinduism, 156
Hocoy, D., 5-6, 74
Hoffman, L., 6-7, 58, 74, 76, 80, 90, 91
Holism, 15, 22, 24
Holocaust, 79,
Holon, 46-48, 50-66
Homeostasis, 184
Human potential, 17, 22, 80, 102, 173
Humanistic psychology, 16, 53, 80, 128-129

Humility, 284
Hypnosis, 134-135, 139, 141
　self-hypnosis, 124, 130, 145
Hypnotic ability, 133-135, 139-141

Id, 23
Identity, 61, 80, 88,
Indigenous, 11, 101, 214, 225, 227, 235, 245, 254
Institute of Transpersonal Psychology (see Sofia University)
Integral, 201, 214
Interconnectedness, 250, 257, 264-277
Interconnectedness Maps Activity, 250-252, 257, 265-277
Interdependence, 39-40, 272
Internal Family Systems (IFS), 53, 58, 60, 63, 65
Intrapsychic, 255
Intuition, 74, 115, 197, 205, 209
Islam, 154, 156
Islamic state (ISIS), 31, 39

James, W., 1, 11-12, 19, 46, 71, 151, 196
Jesus, 3, 152, 154, 156, 208
John F. Kennedy University, 18
Judaisim, 153
Jung, C., 13, 14, 33-34, 46, 47, 50, 55, 57-58, 60, 63, 103, 110, 151, 156, 197, 296, 299, 300

Kaklauskas, F. J., 3-4
Keen, S., 15
Kinesthetic, 59
Kinsey, A., 236
Krishna (Lord), 156
Koran, 154
Krippner, S., 2, 214, 293, 295

Lakota Sioux, 156
Lambert, M., 85
Lief, J., 2
Love, 17, 63, 140, 155, 178, 210, 220, 295, 298-305, 309-311

LSD, 214-215, 217, 226

Macy, J., 262
Marginalization, 38, 93, 117
Manta, 104, 189
Marijuana, 9
Masculine, 33, 205, 209,
Maslow, A., 14, 16, 17, 18, 73, 75, 93, 151, 216
Materialism, 11
May, R., 16
McWilliams, N., 82
MDMA, 213
Meaning, 74, 84, 91, 101, 156, 269, 287
Meditation, 9, 115-117, 124-125, 126, 131, 137-141, 158, 173-193,
    resistance to, 184-185
Mental illness, 36, 225 (see also anxiety, depression, obsessive compulsive disorder)
Mescaline, 215
Meta-analysis, 91
Metaphor, 118, 166
Metaphysical, 55
Micmac Tribe, 36
Mind-body assessment 126-132, 145.
Mindfulness, 2, 18, 53, 65, 74, 101-102, 115, 117, 126, 129-131, 137-139, 144-145, 173, 187, 200, 202-203
    Mindfulness-Based Stress Reduction (MSBR), 18
Monoculture, 36-37
Multicultural, 20, 31, 32, 35, 37-41, 74-75, 79, 88, 142, 286
Multidisciplinary Association for Psychedelic Research (MAPS), 20
Mystic, 39, 108
Myth, 1, 73, 103, 156
Mystical Experience, 13
Mysticism, 217, 225, 235,
Mitakuye Oyasin, 24
Muhammeed, 154, 156
Muir, J. 249-250
Murphy, G, 151

Muslim, 40
Naropa University, 2, 18, 21, 71-72, 117, 174, 283, 289-290
Narrative Psychology, 53
Nihilism, 25
Nondual (non-dual), 24, 102, 189, 214, 243-244, 253, 255, 257
Norcross, J., 89
Numinous, 108, 112, 114, 152

Obsessive-Compulsive Disorder, 86-88, 90
Old Saybrook Conference, 16
Oppression, 79, 80, 82, 87
Outcome Measures, 88

Parapsychology, 22
Patriarchy, 33
Peak experience, 216
Pedagogy, 176-181, 188, 191, 193, 201, 209, 250
Perls, F. 47
Hallucinogen Persisting Perception Disorder (HPPD), 224
Peyote, 214-215, 219
Phenomenology, 125, 126, 132, 185
Plato, 3, 47
Placebo effect, 89
Pluralism, 85
Poetry, 106-107
Pope Innocent, 154
Positivism, 11, 85
Postmodernism, 33
Posttraumatic stress disorder (PTSD), 20, 36, 56, 140, 213, 229
Practice-based Research, 84
Prayer, 88, 115, 116, 124, 129, 140,
Presence, 17, 55, 76, 77, 90, 176, 184, 203, 283-284.
Privilege, 82
Progressive Muscle Relaxation, 138
Psilocybin mushrooms, 214, 219, 222-223,
Psychedelics, 12, 20, 213-229
Psychic, 11

Psychic functioning, 197
Psychoanalysis, 53, 74, 80,
Psychosynthesis, 14, 15, 47, 50, 53, 58
Psychotropic Medication, 87

Qualitative Research, 85, 91, 126, 128, 175,
Quantitative Research, 85, 91, 126, 128, 142, 199-200

Race, 37, 87, 296
Racism, 34, 80, 296,
Randomized Control Trials, 80-82, 91-92
   limitations of, 81-84, 91
Reich, W., 14, 59-60
Reincarnation, 34
Relational Therapies, 80, 81
Religion, 10, 22, 130, 159, 197, 217
   Religious experience, 11
   Inter-religion, 31
Rites of passage. 290, 293
Ritual, 215, 226, 285-290
Rogers, C., 16
Rothberg, R., 210
Roszak, T. 254-255
Rumi, 273

Sabina, M. 219
Sacred, 104, 105, 108, 112, 114, 151, 152, 159, 160, 162, 165, 219, 235, 251, 273, 287
Saybrook University, 2, 18
Siegel, D. 63, 187
Self, 14, 15, 24, 46, 47, 49- 67, 78, 82, 111, 112, 113, 156, 159, 173, 180, 181, 184, 189, 201, 214, 218, 234, 238, 242, 245, 286, 295, 305, 308, 311
   self-actualization, 17
   limitless self, 23
   self-transcendence, 21, 73, 102, 103, 173, 200, 251-259, 262-265, 272, 277
   self-refection, 77

Sexual orientation, 37-38, 237-238
Sexuality, 14, 37, 38, 82, 83, 181
Shadow(s), 105, 110-111
Shamanism, 11
   shaman, 20
   shamanic drumming, 140
Shedler, J., 91,
Skinner, B. F., 16,
Smith, Hudson, 47
Social action, 41
Social justice, 38-39, 87, 89, 296
Sofia University, 18, 195-202, 204-210
Somatic therapies, 60
Soul-spirit, 52, 55-57, 62
Spectrum of consciousness, 46, 49, 127
Spiritual direction, 194-195
Spiritual Intelligence, 114-115, 251-252,
Spirituality, 9-10, 15, 19, 22, 31, 45, 48, 73, 83, 86-88, 109, 114-115, 130, 152, 154-155, 158-167, 183, 184, 195, 200, 207, 217, 218, 229, 235, 250, 251, 273, 285,
Spirit-Soul, 54-57, 62
Springsteen, B., 6-7
Steiner, R., 34
Sue, D. W., 37, 38
Sufism, 217
Sullivan, 79
Superego, 23, 45, 46
Sustainability, 250, 252, 255-256, 258, 260-265, 267. 269, 271, 274, 276-277
Sutich, A., 17, 18, 151
Suzuki, D.T., 11
Swami Vivekananda, 11
Synchronicity, 197, 206, 209, 299
Systems theory, 73

Tagore, R., 3
Talmud, 153
Taoism, 156, 174, 217
Tarot Cards, 73
Tart, C., 2

Taylor, E., 1, 11
Therapeutic Alliance, 77, 80, 85, 88, 89
Thorndike, E., 16
Traditional medicine, 9
Transcend and include
Transcendence, 15
    Self-transcendence, 251-254, 256, 258-259, 262-265, 272, 277
Transference, 187
Transformation, 1, 10, 11, 21, 22, 25, 38-39, 41, 80, 110, 152-157, 162-167, 173-175, 182, 197, 199-201, 210, 213, 229, 235, 242, 251, 265, 286, 289, 292, 308-309
Transpersonal will, 15
Trauma, 79, 140, 229 (see also Post traumatic stress disorder)
Trungpa, C., 2, 110, 115, 283, 284

University of California at Los Angeles, 18
Unconscious, 34, 55, 184

Vaughan, F., 71, 75, 77-78, 90
Vegetotherapy, 14

Walsh, R., 2, 75
Wampold, B., 89
Watson, J. B., 16
Western Association of Schools and Colleges (WASC), 198
Wheaton College, 40
Wilber, K., 19, 22, 45-50, 73, 75, 124,
Wilderness, 6, 250
Wilderness therapies, 2, 53, 73, 265, 271, 290
williams, a. K., 2, 80
Winnicott, D., 296
Witchcraft, 155
World Health Organization (WHO), 237, 240
Wundt, W., 11

Virgin Mary, 154-155

Xenophilia, 32

Yalom, I., 76,
Yin/Yang, 5
Yoga, 9, 53, 124, 129, 217

Notes on Editors

Carla Clements, PhD, LPC, BCPC has been chair of the Transpersonal Counseling Psychology Department at Naropa University for 8 of the last 13 years, where she has mentored professors in transpersonal pedagogy and personally taught hundreds of this generation's transpersonal psychotherapists. She has served as a transpersonal psychotherapist for 30 years in Denver and Boulder, CO, specializing in post-traumatic stress disorders in women and has published several articles on transpersonal psychology and empathy. Her training was in Gestalt and Reichian therapies. In addition, she is currently the independent rater for the MAPS-supported study of MDMA-assisted psychotherapy for chronic, treatment-resistant PTSD. She is a long-time yogini, musician, and naturist who published a CD in 1999 entitled, *Creationship*. Her daughter, Cate, is the delight of her life.

Dan Hocoy, PhD, is Chief Strategy Officer (and Past President) of Antioch University in Seattle and also serves as Associate Vice Chancellor of Advancement for the Antioch University System. Dan failed in his efforts to become a Catholic priest and settled for being a licensed clinical psychologist instead, so that he could at least serve souls in psychiatric hospitals and private practice. He has authored numerous publications that intersect culture, social change, and psychology. Dan is particularly obsessed with the transformative power of art as well as the notion of synchronicity and spends an inordinate amount of time trying to get the universe to conform to his personal interests.

Louis Hoffman, PhD, is a faculty member at Saybrook University and director of the Existential, Humanistic, and Transpersonal Psychology Specialization. He is a fellow of the American Psychological Association (APA) as well as three APA divisions (10, 32, & 52). An avid writer, Dr. Hoffman has eight books to his credit, including *Existential Psychology East–West*, *Brilliant Sanity*, and *Journey of the Wounded Soul: Poetic Companions for Spiritual Struggles*. He serves on the editorial boards of the *Journal of Humanistic Psychology*, *The Humanistic Psychologist*, *PsycCRITIQUES: APA Review of Books*, and *Janus Head*. Dr. Hoffman is also a licensed psychologist in private practice. He lives with his wife and three sons along with their dog in beautiful Colorado Springs, Colorado.

Francis J. Kaklauskas, PsyD, facilitates the Group Psychotherapy Training Program at the University of Colorado, Boulder, and is core faculty at Naropa University Graduate School of Counseling and Psychology. He is a fellow and past board member of the American Group Psychotherapy Association. Dr. Kaklauskas' other publications include being the primary psychological consultant and on-screen presenter for the three part video series, *Hooked: The Addiction Trap*, and co-authoring the Group Psychotherapy chapter in *The Handbook of Clinical Psychology*. He has co-edited three previous volumes: *Brilliant Sanity: Buddhist Approaches to Psychotherapy, Existential Psychology East–West*, and *The Buddha, The Bike, the Couch, and the Circle*. He is passionate about music and feels fortunate to have studied under Milt Hinton, Chuck Rainey, Bill Douglas, and Mark Miller and often tries to enlist his wife, Elizabeth, and son, Levi, to be his rhythm section partners.

Notes on Contributors

Charles W. Angelo, MA, holds a Masters in Transpersonal Ecopsychology from Naropa University. He is an author, a songwriter, and a massage therapist. He is passionate about holistic wellness, healing, the evolution of human consciousness, and the ways that natural medicines, including psychedelics, can contribute to these areas.

Debra L. Azorsky, MA, received her Masters in Transpersonal Counseling Psychology at Naropa University and currently works in private practice and teaches the graduate courses in Human Sexuality. She as a Licensed Professional Counselor and a Certified Sex Therapist through the American Association for Sexuality Educators, Counselors and Therapists (AASECT).

John Davis, PhD, is the former chair of the Transpersonal Psychology and Transpersonal Psychology–Ecopsychology departments at Naropa University. He is the author of *The Diamond Approach: An Introduction to the Teaching of A.H. Almaas*, and entries on Transpersonal Psychology and Wilderness Rites of Passage in the Encyclopedia *of Religion and Nature*. Other publications include a number of articles and book chapters on transpersonal psychology, ecopsychology, wilderness rites of passage, and research methods. His primary interest is full human development and self-realization, with a special focus on the intersection of spirituality, psychology, and the natural world. John is an ordained teacher of the Diamond Approach of A. H. Almaas and a staff member of the School of Lost Borders, where he trains wilderness rites of passage guides and leads wilderness retreats.

Daphne M. Fatter, PhD, is a licensed psychologist specializing in mindfulness and trauma. She earned a Masters in Transpersonal Counseling Psychology from Naropa University, and received her PhD in Counseling Psychology from the Pennsylvania State University. Her dissertation examined the relationship between meditation practice, mindfulness, differentiation of self, and countertransference management among psychotherapists who practice meditation. She has studied and practiced in both Buddhist and Taoist meditation traditions, and has taught meditation at the Dallas Yoga Center, Southern Methodist University, the University of Colorado at Boulder, the Pennsylvania State University, and the University of Tennessee Knoxville. She currently has a private practice in McKinney, TX, and is a mother of triplets.

Michael A. Franklin, PhD, ATR-BC, chair of the Naropa University graduate art therapy program, has practiced and taught in various academic and clinical settings since 1981. The author of numerous articles, he is an international lecturer and founder of the Naropa Community Art Studio in 2001, a project dedicated to researching service as a spiritual practice, training socially engaged artists, and serving marginalized community members through the studio-arts. His research focuses on integrating visual art with meditation, Hindu-yoga traditions, and imaginal psychology.

Peter G. Grossenbacher, PhD, teaches and conducts research as Professor in Contemplative Psychology and Contemplative Education at Naropa University. His doctoral work in experimental psychology at the University of Oregon focused on electrophysiology and attention to vision and touch. After researching multisensory attention and synesthesia at the University of Cambridge and the National Institute of Mental Health, he joined the Naropa faculty in 2000. His book, *Finding Consciousness in the Brain: A Neurocognitive Approach*, offers insights into the brain's involvement in conscious experience. His scholarship and research focus on the instruction of contemplative practice, transformation of personal worldview, and development of compassion.

A meditator since 1980, he teaches meditation and trains teachers in a variety of settings.

Stanley Krippner, PhD, is Alan Watts Professor of Psychology at Saybrook University. He has received Lifetime Career Awards for his research in dream studies, humanistic psychology, and parapsychology. He has authored or co-authored over 1,000 books, monographs, and articles on such topics as anomalous dreams, post-traumatic stress disorder, shamanism, hypnosis, creativity, and psychedelics. He is the recipient of the American Psychological Association's Award for Distinguished Contributions to the International *Advancement of Psychology.* He is the co-author of the award-winning book, *Personal Mythology* and the co-editor of another award-winning book, *Varieties of Anomalous Experience: Examining the Scientific Evidence.*

Pat Luce, MA, and **Robert Schmitt, PhD,** are a married couple who were co-presidents of the Institute of Transpersonal Psychology (now Sofia University) from 2000 to 2005. Their work, writings, and presentations emphasize the balancing of feminine and masculine energies and integrating spiritual practices. Pat has a Masters Degree in Counseling and a global range of experience as a director of organizational development, management and training in industry. She also has years of experience as a faculty member of a university graduate school and as a spiritual director. Bob has a PhD in Spirituality and graduate degrees in Counseling, Philosophy and Theology. Besides his years of faculty and spiritual direction experience, Bob has been a president at three colleges, dean at two graduate schools, Jesuit master of novices, and is now on the faculty at Saybrook University.

Satori S. Madrone, MA, received her Masters in Transpersonal Counseling Psychology at Naropa University and has been in private practice for over 20 years, incorporating a wide variety of mind- and energy-based modalities. Currently, she specializes in sex therapy for individuals and couples, including LGBTQ+ and non-traditional relationship communities, and is a doctoral student in the Human Sexuality at California Institute of Integral Studies. She is a member of the American Association of Sexuality Educators, Counselors and Therapists.

Deb Piranian, PhD, is associate professor and chair of the Transpersonal Wilderness Therapy Concentration in Naropa University's Graduate School of Counseling and Psychology. Her clinical work settings have included private practice, a psychiatric hospital, and wilderness therapy. She has worked with groups in outdoor settings since 1984, including three summers leading a multinational mountaineering program in the former Soviet Union. Her publications and presentations include an article on climbing and meditation, as well as workshops on contemplative training for therapists and on diversity issues within the field of wilderness therapy. She has been an avid climber for 40 years.

Lindsey Randol, PsychD, is core faculty in the mindfulness-based transpersonal counseling program at Naropa University. Previously, she worked in the UK as a counseling psychologist in various capacities, including university counseling, addictions counseling, and facilitating mindfulness groups. Her work brings together relational and postmodern theories with contemplative approaches. She is also in private practice.

Laurie Rugenstein, EdD, MT-BC, is a professor in the Transpersonal Counseling and Psychology Program at Naropa University. She founded the Music Therapy Concentration in this program and directed it for 13 years. She then served as Coordinator of the Mindfulness-based Transpersonal Counseling Concentration for 9 years. In addition to her work at Naropa, Laurie served as a music therapist with hospice for 22 years. Laurie has a long interest in music and voice and has studied voice work with members of the Roy Hart Theatre for many years. She is a primary trainer in the Bonny Method of Guided Imagery and Music and uses this transpersonal approach in her private practice. Laurie is a mindfulness instructor at Naropa University, and her current spiritual practice is caring for her husband, who has advanced Parkinson's disease.

Sandy Sela-Smith, PhD, has been an adjunct faculty member of Saybrook University since 2001 teaching Transpersonal Psychology and Psychotherapy as well as Academic Writing. Her work focuses on Heuristic Self-Search Inquiry, which clarifies and expands the groundbreaking Heuristic Research method as articulated by Clark Moustakas. She is an author, having written *E Pluribus Unum: Out of*

Many, One, and a trilogy, *The Meaning of Three: The Mask; Behind the Mask; and Under the Mask.* She is also a mental health counselor, licensed in Colorado, Florida, and Washington State and works with clients throughout the country and internationally from a depth-psychology, transpersonal, mind/body/spirit perspective. Her work focuses on bringing healing to the internal blocks that separate her clients from experiencing integration of heart and mind, body and spirit. She currently resides in Colorado and travels throughout the country presenting on inner communication and integration of the whole self.

Uri Talmor, MA, graduated from Naropa University's Transpersonal Counseling Psychology program in 2004 with a masters in counseling. He has since worked in private practice and in six treatment centers focusing on conduct disorders, sexually abusive youth, and eating disorders. He currently is in full-time private practice in Boulder and Denver, Colorado while teaching at Naropa University as an adjunct professor. His greatest joy is raising his daughter.

Todd Thillman, MDiv, is currently enrolled in the Mindfulness Based Transpersonal Psychology Graduate degree program at Naropa University. In 2004 he received his Master of Divinity degree from Naropa University. He spent the next 11 years working as a chaplain for a local non-profit Hospice program. He has been involved in mindfulness based meditation practices since 2001. In addition to his work with others, his main passions are his beautiful wife Karlene, his 12-year-old son Gavin, and his brand new son Declan.

Ian E. Wickramasekera, PsyD, teaches transpersonal counseling and psychology at Naropa University in Boulder, CO. He is the President-Elect of the Rocky Mountain Humanistic Counseling and Psychological Association and serves on the Executive Council for the American Psychological Association's (APA) Society for Humanistic Psychology (Division 32). Ian is also a Past-President of the APA's Society of Psychological Hypnosis (Division 30). He has had a lifelong fascination with topics such as Affective Neuroscience, Bon-Buddhism, Empathy, Hypnosis, Integrative Medicine, Transpersonal Psychology, and Lucid Dreaming. His research in these areas has won him a number of awards including the Milton H. Erickson Award for Scientific Excellence from the American Society of Clinical Hypnosis and the American Psychological Association's Early Career Contributions Award to Hypnosis. Ian enjoys hiking, live music, meditating, and running when he isn't at work or reading an obscure tome of ancient lore.

Xiaodan Zhuang, MA, MBA, is a registered clinical psychologist in China, specializing in Mindfulness-based intervention, Gestalt therapy and Equine-assisted psychotherapy. She earned her Masters in Transpersonal Counseling Psychology from Naropa University, has studied and practiced in various contemplative traditions, and has collaborated in meditation research at Naropa University and the University of Colorado at Boulder. She has been teaching mindfulness to therapists and the general public and is currently in private practice in Beijing. She also authored the book *Healing Paths Toward Flourishing* (2015).

CPSIA information can be obtained
at www.ICGtesting.com
Printed in the USA
BVHW011646030222
627985BV00012B/370